Reform, Identity and Narratives of Belonging

Reform, Identity and Narratives of Belonging

The Heraka Movement of Northeast India

Arkotong Longkumer

BLOOMSBURY
NEW DELHI • LONDON • OXFORD • NEW YORK • SYDNEY

BLOOMSBURY INDIA
Bloomsbury Publishing India Pvt. Ltd
Second Floor, Building No. 4
DDA Complex LSC, Pocket C – 6 & 7
Vasant Kunj, New Delhi 110070
www.bloomsbury.com

BLOOMSBURY, Bloomsbury Academic India and the Diana
logo are trademarks of Bloomsbury Publishing Plc

First published in India 2020
First published 2010 by Continuum

British Library Cataloguing-in-Publication Data
A catalogue record for this book is available from the British Library.

Library of Congress Cataloging-in-Publication Data
A catalog record for this book is available from the Library of Congress

ISBN: 978-93-89391-53-4

For sale in the Indian subcontinent only

Typeset by Newgen Imaging Systems Pvt Ltd, Chennai, India
Printed at Manipal Technologies Limited, Manipal

Temeim Oja aser Oba atema

Contents

List of Illustrations

Maps

Figures

Photographs

Acknowledgements

My first foray into the 'Heraka world' came through a series of coincidences, least of which was a book on the Nagas by Miladi Ganguli. These wonderful coincidences have continued over the length of my work on the Heraka. My initiation into the Heraka began in Kohima with my conversations with the President of the Zeliangrong Heraka Association of North East India N. C. Zeliang, who sadly passed away when I was undertaking my fieldwork in 2005. The invaluable discussions I had with him, especially about Heraka history, as well as sharing his small collection of pamphlets and books have been a valuable source of information for this book. In Haflong I was fortunate enough to meet many Zeme people who willingly accepted me into their fold and encouraged my research. Mr Ramkhui Newme, the current President of the Zeliangrong Heraka Association of North East India provided me with helpful resources, clarified aspects of Heraka practice and patiently answered many of my questions. My conversations with I. Zeme over the course of my stay in North Cachar Hills illuminated much of my ignorance and provided a sanctuary for knowledge through his breadth and insight of the history of the Zeme people. I am ever grateful to K. Kuame for sharing with me his unfinished manuscript on 'ancient Zeme history'. I am also thankful to Josias and Allan Jeme and their families for their hospitality and helping me on several occasions. My thanks are also due to Abuan Kamei, the former personal secretary to Rani Gaidinliu, for providing me much needed information, and to Catriona Betts who provided me with important Zeme resources from her mother's (Ursula Graham Bower) library.

Travelling around North Cachar Hills and staying in different villages has been of great importance to my own understanding of the dynamics of Heraka life. Everywhere, Heraka and Christian villages, I was welcomed as a brother passing through and their hospitality surpassed my expectations, especially in Herielo village where we were treated to a wonderful feast over Easter. For the people I encountered in this journey, I remain eternally grateful. In the village where I was based, I am thankful to the Baptist church for letting me stay on their land and to Amanda Bowden for enabling the construction of the hut. Similarly, the Heraka people took me in and did everything within their means to make me feel comfortable and welcome. They answered many questions and provided immense knowledge over endless cups of *zao.* My heartfelt gratitude to all of them. I especially remember with fondness my time in Hangrum, immortalized by the Hangrum war and the rich history interlaced with a vibrant sense of hope for the future. The place gave me the much needed creativity and realization that there is more than meets the eye. For this, the exceptional youths of the Hangrum parade are to be thanked for making their way to Hangrum especially to meet and share the 'sacred' parade with me. *Asu-ida!*

Tahulung has been my shadow ever since he agreed to be my co-worker. His breadth of knowledge, sense of belonging, conviction and the steadfastness in his Heraka beliefs, has made my time in North Cachar Hills rewarding and my research stronger and better. His patience over incessant questioning, hours upon hours of transcribing interviews, translating songs and managing at the same time to keep his commitments to his community has been inspiring for my own sense of duty and responsibility. I am indebted to him. I first met Adeule in September 2004 and since then she has always supported my research in the field and provided a safe and comfortable home in Haflong. Her inquisitiveness, her organization of interviews and persistence at searching for an explanation, provided endless insights into my own research and fieldwork methods. Takile and Ameile, women of storied courage, provided me with healthy doses of laughter and sanity. Nakaulang has provided much of the post-fieldwork analysis by filling the gaping holes in my field notes. To Atul Jog and Ehui Pame in the Kalyan Ashram office in Dimapur for providing materials for my research, and to Dr Rabi Pame for sharing his dissertation and answering many of my questions regarding Zeme Christian-Heraka relationship. To all of them, I remain indebted.

When I first initiated interest on the Heraka, it was my supervisor Dr Jeanne Openshaw who encouraged me over the viability of doing research which would eventually turn into a Ph.D. thesis and now this book. Our long conversations over the years have helped me appreciate the nuances of the complex relationship between religious practice and identity. The depth of knowledge she brought from her own work in Bengal has been invaluable to an understanding of my own work. For her unflinching support and patience over the years, I am most grateful. I would also like to thank Dr Elizabeth Koepping who not only acted as my second supervisor but also took over the helm when Dr Openshaw was away on sabbatical. Her insight into Christianity and 'traditional religion' in particular has greatly benefited the overall balance of the book. Thanks are also due to Professor Jim Cox who has provided continuous support for my work as Head of Department. Many people have contributed to reading materials from my research over the years from all over the world, and for their invaluable suggestions I would like to thank Dr Steve Sutcliffe, Dr Mark Turin, Dr B. G. Karlsson and Amanda Bowden. I am indebted to Dr Elspeth Graham who found the time to read the entire manuscript and offered constructive criticisms, especially those regarding fieldwork methodology from her own work as a human geographer, and to Jungtina Jamir who reproduced most of the illustrations for this book.

Many funding bodies have helped me over the years to undertake fieldwork, research trips to libraries in the United Kingdom, conferences and for general financial assistance. My thanks specially to the Spalding Trust, Sidney Perry Foundation and the Department of Art and Culture, Nagaland for providing me with financial support. I also express my gratitude to the people at the India Office Library, British Library, London; School of Oriental and African Studies Library, London; and the Pitt Rivers Museum Library, Oxford for the excellent services and professionalism.

Portions of Chapters 2 and 3 of this book have been published earlier in: 'Circling the Altar Stone: Bhuban Cave and the Symbolism of Religious Traditions', in Michael Oppitz, Thomas Kaiser, Alban von Stockhausen and Marion Wettstein (eds), 2008; 'Religious and Economic Reform: The Gaidinliu Movement and the Heraka in the North Cachar Hills', *Journal of South Asian Studies,* Vol. 30, No. 3 (December): 499–515, 2007. My thanks to these publishers for allowing me to reproduce them for this book.

My family have been my most ardent supporters. I am indebted to their warm and generous support. My father took an early interest in the Heraka and accompanied me to Haflong in the first leg of my trip. My parents lent me their car which made my trips a lot more efficient and quicker, raided bookstores for my research, and provided endless supply of food for my fieldwork. Their support over the years has been invaluable. My grandparents, in-laws and friends have also supported and encouraged me over the years. To my wife Lindsay, who championed my research since its inception, has been ever so patient, thoughtful and supportive of this endeavour. Her insightful reading of the material, and her meticulous editing and indexing has made this book many, many times better. To our daughter Ayimna who has brought us great joy over the last few months. I look forward to sharing this book and stories of the Nagas with her. To all, *kanga dang pelar!*

Chapter 1

Introduction

During the early twentieth century, the religious beliefs and practices of the Zeme people of southern Assam in the northeast corner of India evolved and changed in complex ways. Their roots are found in the encounter with the colonial power, Britain, the coming of Christianity and in the emergence of a political consciousness brought about by the changing scenario in the region. The movement known as Heraka embraced new rituals and new ideas of community, tradition and self, as identities and boundaries between people were (re)negotiated. This book examines the evolving project of reform and its intersection with narratives of identity. Before we enter into this discussion, an explanation into the historical backgrounds of the movement is needed.

Although the story of the Heraka has received some scholarly interest, it remains poorly understood. The following discussion seeks to provide new insights into the changing narratives of reform and identity that comprise the Heraka movement. This notion is developed by interrogating ideas of history, tradition and the evolving contextualization of these practices in the Zeme world. In light of this, the book will contribute to the growing literature on indigenous identity, ethnicity, nationalism and the importance of religious boundaries with regard to Northeast India and more broadly in the South Asian and Southeast Asian contexts.

Heraka

Heraka is a religious reform movement derived from the ancestral practice known as Paupaise.[1] It was taken up by the Zeme, among other Naga communities, during the period of British colonialism in Northeast India (see Map 1.1). From early descriptions of events in 1929 and over the next 45 years, Heraka has been known by various names, for example, Kacha Naga movement, Gaidinliu movement, *Periese* (old practice), *Kelumse* (prayer practice) and *Ranise* ('practice of the queen', a reference to Gaidinliu as people's queen), and sometimes pejoratively as *Khampai*,[2] all representing a different point in the development of the movement which finally came to be known as Heraka in 1974.[3] In this book, I have generally used 'Heraka' as shorthand to indicate all these stages. My analysis of the Heraka reform movement is primarily among the Zeme of North Cachar Hills, Assam.

Among the Heraka, there are two important figures who are seen as prophets, leaders and reformers. Jadonang (1905–31) and Gaidinliu (1915–93) are from the Tamenglong district of Manipur and are both Rongmei Nagas (see below). Due to their alleged threat to the British and their hatred of the Kukis, a neighbouring tribe in Manipur, Jadonang and Gaidinliu were accused of stirring up trouble. The British eventually hanged Jadonang in 1931 for alleged murder and human sacrifice, while Gaidinliu escaped to North Cachar Hills. Although Jadonang is often viewed as initiating the reform, for the Heraka it is Gaidinliu who is held in more esteem. The British captured Gaidinliu in 1932 after which she spent 18 years in prison. During this time Jawaharlal Nehru heard of her exploits and named her 'Ranee' (queen). Therefore, Gaidinliu is also known as Rani Gaidinliu, and Ranima (queen mother). Throughout the book, I use the names 'Ranima' and 'Gaidinliu' interchangeably; but the Zeme, above all, call her Ranima, as it indicates their more intimate connection with her.

The Zeme Nagas

The Zeme (also spelt Jeme, Nzemi, Zemi, Zemei) comes from the word *zemena* (human). To be human, they say, is to be Zeme. They are also known by their 'kin', that is the related communities, Rongmei (also spelt Rongme, Rongmai) and Liangmai (also spelt Liangme, Liangmei), as Zena or Nzie (frontier or periphery). The Zeme were supposedly the frontier people who moved on from their ancestral home Makuilongdi, in present-day Manipur (Kamei 2004: 36). During colonial times, they were also known as Kacha Nagas (along with the Liangmai and Rongmei), while in Manipur the Rongmei were known as Kabui Naga (Hutton 1969: 352).

It is said that before coming to Makuilongdi, the 'Nagas' gathered at a place called Makhel (a place believed to be near the Chindwin river in Myanmar). The people lived amicably and harmoniously with one another there. When they decided to disperse, they gathered around a wild apple tree at *Charaho* (miracle ridge) and took an oath, pledging that they would come together again and live as a kingdom. To keep this dream alive and the identity of the tribe intact, they proclaimed a *genna* (prohibition) to be observed every time a branch of the tree is broken. As recently as 1950, it is said, this tradition was maintained by the Angami, Sema, Rengma, Lotha, Zeme, Liangmai, Rongmei and Sepoumaramth people (Pamei 2001: 6). The Zeme, Liangmai and Rongmei people left the area and went in search of land until they came to Makuilongdi.

The population grew in Makuilongdi and the village expanded and grew to exactly 7,777 houses. They decided that in order to maintain a healthy habitat they needed to spread out and find fresh pastures. The 3 brothers, who represented the Zeme, Rongmei and Liangmai decided to split up. The oldest, Liangmai, decided to stay in the area. The Zeme spread out further west towards the Barak river (present-day North Cachar Hills and Peren district of Nagaland) while the Rongmei migrated far to the south (to present-day Manipur and Cachar) (Pamei 2001: 16–17). These narratives create strong bonds even today by helping people recreate strong unifying identities linking back to particular points in time. By establishing a collective memory they are able to envision a community built on shared history and culture. This brings us to the adoption of the term 'Zeliangrong' (see Map 1.1).[4]

Gangmumei Kabui (also Kamei), the famous Rongmei historian, mentions that the word Zeliangrong was coined in 1947, and that it is a combination of the three prefixes of these 'tribes': Zeme, Liangme and Rongme (Ze-liang-rong). Further, he says,

> Though chronologically the name was coined in 1947, a faint notion of their common ancestry was contained in their legends and the idea of inter-tribal solidarity and unity was implanted by Jadonang and Gaidinliu during their uprisings (1930–32). (1982: 53)

The purpose for such a union was to emphasize the need for a collective front with the objective of achieving the 'economic, social, educational and political advancement' of the Zeliangrong people (Kamei 2004: 176). Due to British classification and the imposition of separate administrative units in three regions, North Cachar Hills, Naga Hills and Manipur, the Zeliangrong people remained separated. It is said that the Jadonang and Gaidinliu movement attempted to unite the three groups into a common front to fight the British invaders by participating in a common tradition that unified their practices. The reform movement, Heraka, was the product and emblem of this unification. However, this has created certain problems

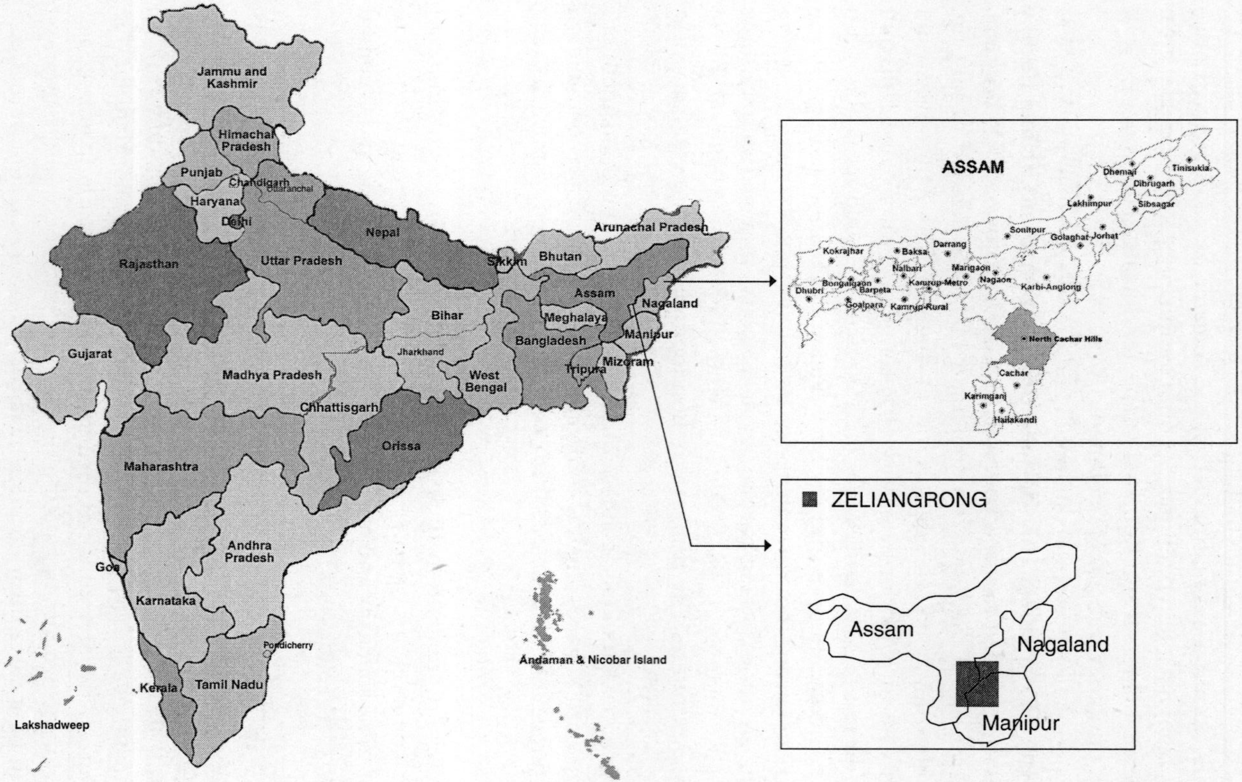

Map 1.1 India and Assam

as the term Zeliangrong is a continually (re)constructed and contested enterprise. Gangmumei Kabui emphasizes the problem. He says,

> A very interesting feature of the [Zeliangrong] movement, which is very flexible, is the absorption of small tribes into the fold of Zeliangrong. For example, one Chothe village of Bishenpur was declared to be absorbed into Zeliangrong. Wainem, originally consisting of immigrants from Tripura, is now converted into Zeliangrong. The inclusion of these tribes has raised the question whether such a composite name like Zeliangrong could cover all of them. For example, Puimei, a sub-tribe of the Rongmeis, have been demanding for some years that their name should be included in Zeliangrong nomenclature. (Kabui 1982: 62)

For this reason Rani Gaidinliu supposedly preferred the word 'Haomei', which means 'ourselves' to Zeliangrong.[5] A statement attributed to Rani Gaidinliu asserts,

> Rani Gaidinliu feels that it will be better to remove the name Zeliangrong and adopt the original name of 'Haomei' as the name and goal of the movement. She thinks that Haomei will cover all seven groups [Zeme, Liangmei, Rongmei and Maram, Mpumei, Kourang, Wainem and Toite], big and small, with similar traditions and will not encourage the separatist tendencies of the bigger sections of her people. (Mukherjee et al. 1982: 78)[6]

Rani Gaidinliu had already envisaged a mixed ethnic group signalled by the adoption of the word 'Haomai [or Haomei]'. This category can incorporate those on the fringes, and is necessitated by the common practice of intermarriage between various people. The marriages between these groups create a problem in the fluidity of categories because it means going outside the group, challenging the purity of the group. Indeed, 'ourselves' is a more inclusive concept, providing infinite probabilities in terms of people's belonging, rather than limiting the category as a term like Zeliangrong does; the former encompasses the fluidity of categories while the latter restricts them. However, 'Haomei' is not used now. It is tempting to speculate that Zeliangrong as a fixed identity is more prestigious due to its political profile, 'Haomei' seeming less prestigious. The ethnic construction of the word Zeliangrong is vital to their discourse (e.g. the recent book, *The Trail from Makuilongdi*), suggesting something unique and historical. These attempts to trace their origins have signalled a new revival within Zeliangrong society.

Nagas and the British

The Zeme are included in the category 'Naga'. Some say the word 'Naga' comes from the Bengali word Nangta, in Hindi 'Nanga' (naked). Others think that the Kachari word Naga (a young man) supplies the name, while others again derive it from 'Nag' (a snake). Colonel Woodthorpe, who worked in the Naga Hills in the late nineteenth century, notes that 'not one of these derivations is satisfactory, nor does it really concern us much to know more about it, seeing that the name is quite foreign to and unrecognized by the Nagas themselves' (1969: 47). This ambiguity remains unresolved at the descriptive level. On the level of representation, it is also still vague. There are now some 68 Naga tribes recorded both in India and Myanmar (Nuh 2006: 24–6), compared to only 9 recorded in the 1891 Assam Census. The word 'tribe', with its vague terrain of representation, is replete with conceptual problems. However, it is still a valid usage in India due to the protective discrimination accorded to those listed in the Schedule of Tribes (article 342 of the Indian constitution). The word 'tribe' is used here in conformity with the 'schedule list'. The word 'indigenous' is now being used in some Naga nationalist literature as part of the language of 'self-determination'. However, it is not used widely (see also Beteille 1998).

This large increase in the number of Naga tribes between 1891 and 2006 is due to expanding identities in the post-colonial situation: unlike earlier notions of fuzzy belongings, new identities now increasingly delineate 'those who belong from those who do not' (Karlsson 2000: 258). Identities in this sense are not invented randomly, implying a sort of 'constructionism'; they result from an ongoing process that occurs on many levels. Sometimes identities are labile to the extent that they are used for upward mobility; at other times identity projects commonality and purpose as a form of resistance against a dominant force; while sometimes its practicality is questioned. Jamie Saul, in his magnum opus *The Naga of Burma*, offers us his insights regarding some of the above points. He points to the fact that the term 'Naga', in use in the Assam region for some time, was simply adopted by the British based on loose linguistic and cultural associations, in order to separate the people into 'tribes' (Saul 2005: 17). This has created a 'political identity' for the Nagas in a two-way process: those who want in and those who want out. In the first case, some small groups like the 'Old Kuki' are absorbed into the Naga fold to increase their political profile. Others, like the Maring, though linguistically classified as Naga, are not sure if they want to be associated with the Nagas. They cite their cultural difference in terms of their social structure, architecture and personal appearances, which more closely resembles that of the Chin group of the south. Their absorption into the Naga fold, they say, would have 'little practical bearing' (2005: 17–19). In this way, 'Naga' identity is not a fixed entity that requires its members to stand by it unquestionably, but a shifting and, to some extent, voluntary concept.[7]

The same can be said of what 'Zeliangrong' means to those in it and those who want to be in it. The association of Heraka with the Zeliangrong identity is a contested matter. Most Heraka claim that Heraka and Zeliangrong are inextricably linked: to be Heraka is to be Zeliangrong. In other words, the Heraka was envisioned as uniting the Zeliangrong by giving the latter an aura of credibility and overall unity associated with the reform: the Heraka reform is for the Zeliangrong people. But due to the large presence of Christians among the Zeliangrong, the nature of Heraka as representing the larger sentiments of the people is contested. Moreover, the Heraka population is popular among the Zeme and Liangmai (together known as Zeliang in Nagaland) rather than Rongmei. Some Rongmei in recent years have also adopted reforms attributed to Jadonang, while the Heraka look up to Ranima as their preceptor. As will become clear in Chapter 2, these notions are pivotal in understanding the Zeliangrong as an evolving entity, as Gangmumei Kabui also mentioned earlier. In this book, I have maintained the word Zeliangrong as it appears in most primary texts and scholarly works. The Heraka also use the term Zeliangrong Heraka Association for the larger group from Assam, Nagaland and Manipur. My own usage is to distinguish 'Zeme Heraka' from the wider 'Zeliangrong Heraka' (this is not a distinction drawn by the Heraka themselves). Therefore, as the Zeme Heraka themselves do, I use Zeliangrong only when I mean Zeliangrong, referring to the group as a whole.

What is in a Name?

During my first week of fieldwork in North Cachar Hills district, I went around asking the Zeme people the question 'what is Heraka?' Many could not give me a straightforward answer; others would ponder and arrive at a conclusion. It was not because of their ignorance or for that matter their lack of interest that they failed to arrive at some answer, it was simply that they were not in a habit of explaining terminology that mattered to a researcher like me. 'Is there a right or wrong answer', they would often ask, or better still 'go ask the leaders, they are the ones you should be talking to'.

Even when I did manage to speak to the leaders, their response would often be the official – perhaps rehearsed – response, 'Heraka means "not impure"'. I soon realized that this definition is used in much of the wider Heraka literature to portray an image of the Heraka as practising the 'pure' indigenous tradition of the Zeme. In the introduction to the *Zeliangrong Heraka Preacher Handbook*, N. C. Zeliang, the past-President of the Zeliangrong Heraka Association, says, 'Heraka literally means, in Zemei "PURE". The Heraka religion is a pure or reformed religion of the Zeliangrong people comprising three kindred tribes, the Zemei, Liangmai and Rongmei' (1998: 3). What N. C. Zeliang refers to is attributed to the Heraka's adoption of one God, Tingwang, and the subsequent ban on animal sacrifices. Thus, the purity is a metaphor for no blood sacrifices and the adoption of a single God (this will be explored in Chapter 4).

For a while, I worked under the assumption that Heraka did mean 'not impure'. It was only later, when I visited the villages, that another explanation was offered to me for the origin of the word Heraka and its meaning. I was told that:

> *Ka* is to fence, to obstruct, to avoid, to give up – all these words can be used in different contexts. '*Hera*' means 'small gods'. So all these *neube* [prohibitions] and sacrifices associated with the smaller gods must be fenced out, avoided, and only Tingwang must be worshipped. This is the meaning of Heraka.

The two definitions provide us with the way Heraka reform is envisaged. The latter definition is more concerned with the actions that attempted to reform traditional practices of appeasing gods by sacrifices. By fencing themselves in, by their obeisance to one God, Tingwang, any threat is averted from the smaller gods. One must understand the intense anxiety associated with the smaller gods, which was deeply embedded in people's consciousness. On the other hand, the image of the fence that is protective retains much of traditional understanding of purity and danger associated with any period of ritual (this will be analysed in Chapter 4). In this way, by giving up these gods, and the associated blood sacrifices, the Heraka are able to envisage a pure state, protected by the fence.

Just what this means is explained by Pautanzan Newme, the General Secretary of the Heraka Association, in his article 'The Origin and Reformation of Heraka Religion' (2002),[8] published in the local Silver Jubilee Souvenir Magazine, a journal which often highlights Heraka operational achievements and ideological view points. It also acts as an official document that publicizes the Heraka agenda to the masses and measures their 'progress' as a movement. Pautanzan Newme says,

> The 1st phase of teaching: Ranima told them to offer sacrifices to one God, Tingwang. In this phase blood sacrifice was permitted.
>
> The 2nd phase of teaching: This was introduced after 15 years. Ranima advised them: while performing 'puja' to cut with a *dao* [hacking knife] if it was a big animal, and to use a piece of stick (*nkiadang*) with smaller animals (like hen or cockerel) while holding the legs and let blood shed. At this phase, the 'sacrificial ceremony was a bit diminished than the first phase'.
>
> The 3rd phase of teaching: In this stage, introduced after a further 10 years, Ranima instructed her followers that one should 'perform puja with the animal tied and its mouth stuffed with a rag and killed. But a chicken must be killed with the hand, by twisting the neck, without oozing any blood'. In this phase, the sacrifice of animals is further diminished.
>
> The 4th phase of teaching: After another 5 years the 4th phase was introduced. On the 11th of January 1990, at Kepelo village, North Cachar Hills, 'the preceptress (Ranima) vigorously declared and confessed before the general public that we have fully done the requirement of sacrificial oblation in puja. Now, influential sacrifices of animals in any puja are to be totally abolished. And we are free to perform puja with a clean mind and body at any specific time and day.' Ranima proclaimed to the people,
>
> while performing puja with a clean mind and body, recite the Holy psalms and sing the prayer songs; you would be blessed for sound health and to live a very happy life free from evil spirits. And if anything [is] wrong with you, you may throw it upon me – I can affirmably bear such things for your sake. (P. Newme 2002: 4)

The writer further declares 'as advised by our beloved mother, Gaidinliu, we the Heraka people followed her path and live happily free from trouble and worry' (P. Newme 2002: 4).

Abolishing of sacrifice brings about a strong sense of 'purity'. In freeing the people from sacrifices, Ranima alters the notion of sacrifice as gift. In other words, animal sacrifice constituted a gift to the gods, but now 'if anything [is] wrong with you, you may throw it upon me – I can affirmably bear such things for your sake' (P. Newme 2002: 4). As will be made clear in Chapter 6, this almost Christ-like figure represented by Ranima is crucial in the way she conceives herself as the 'daughter of God'. Hence, through her, the people are free from the 'old' way of appeasing gods. This gives way to the 'new' – simply singing the 'psalms' and praying with an empty hand. As the phases themselves suggest, the reform occurring over many years was connected to many factors, and it is helpful to understand more clearly what I mean by reform.

Reform and Identity

The Heraka themselves see the movement as a reform (*kantiabe*) based on retrospective reading of the past and not from 'suggestions made by the historical actors themselves' (Sen 2003: 7). Most of the literature by the Heraka and those writing on them refer to the Heraka as a reform movement. But I want to be more precise in this use. Therefore, I propose this following understanding. In everyday usage, reform denotes 'to improve', 'alter' and 'correct', or to bring about 'an improvement or change for the better' (*Collins English Dictionary* 2003: 1362). Its more varied connotations (which I adhere to) include an advancement, progress, a moving forward, but it can also revert to an older, more traditional way of acting that can be used for the supposed advancement of society and modernity (Blau 1987: 238–44). Embedded in the project of 'reform' is also the question of self-identity, or identity formation that is not only about altering beliefs and practices but also about questioning the 'self' in relation to the larger society.

In his edited volume *Social and Religious Reform*, Amiya P. Sen points out that, once the 'Hindus' were exposed to European civilization, the question 'What is Hindu' became inextricably linked to 'who is a Hindu?' or 'what does it mean to be a Hindu?' (2003: 3–4). These questions were tied in with a deep self-reflexive project about tradition, change and the response to this change. But it also meant that so-called Hindus began to conceive of themselves as a community with their own history, cultural forms and communal solidarity in a self-conscious act of negotiation (2003: 7). In this book I also attempt to address these questions.

It is clear in the way the reforms have been managed that they were far from homogenous – fissures are evident beneath the commonality. An important issue is 'who manages the reforms?' The growing educated elite with their exposure to the wider world largely attempts to project an image of Heraka as stable, cohesive and uniform. Yet their efforts to fashion the Heraka with its own history, beliefs, places of worship and rules are sabotaged by the fissures which persist as a strategy of resistance. The central tenet in the Heraka reform is the ban on sacrifices and the adoption of one God. However in the western Zeme regions, some villages still sacrifice and pray to two gods (Tingwang and Chuprai) known as *Periese* (old practice). Moreover, I was told that the Heraka practice in Nagaland is to sacrifice animals to Tingwang on the ground that 'Ranima never said that one should abandon sacrifices'. The inconsistency of the reform is also evident in the ideological disputes concerning the *heguangram* (free community) and the *heguang* (the agent of the free community). The rural population largely subscribe to these notions, with their millenarian implications, which are rejected by large sections of the urban population. The former believe that one day they will inherit this *heguangram* as a sign of their triumph, whereupon the Heraka will be free to do as they please. This is based on traditional notions of wealth, freedom and abundance connected to common folk heroes. The urban community see this as 'superstitious' and 'backward talk'. Could this be due to upward mobility and education that those in the town experience and those in the village lack?

In this sense, I view reform in the Heraka as having the following basic characteristics. First, the impetus for change was triggered by specific conditions surrounding immigration and near famines as will be discussed in Chapter 3. In this period, the millenarian components took centre stage. Second, this change is grounded on a 'retrospective' reading that saw tradition as a dynamic force which required reinterpretation if it was to legitimate the reforms based on an 'original' Zeme past. This is then employed to define the Heraka against the competitive other, the Christians, as 'authentic' and 'pure'. On the other hand, the 'prospective' that employs the past as 'the beginning of a future that is in the process of taking shape' (Lévi-Strauss and Moore 1974: 280–1) works itself into the reform as changing with the times. In this manner, both the tradition and change are juxtaposed effectively. Third, the reforms were connected with a certain amount of self-reflexivity that eventually highlighted the Heraka's sense of identity. In this emphasis on the self in relation to the 'other', a particular community is fashioned that is a self-conscious negotiation, constantly locating and relocating. But what do I mean by the 'other'? Or rather, who is the 'other'?

Attempts to define identity require an understanding of the 'other' in relation to the self. Writing about his own conscious adoption of 'black' identity in Britain, Stuart Hall makes the important point that old notions of identity found in the Cartesian subject as possessing the 'true' or 'real self' are outmoded. We must look, he says, at identity that constructs the 'other', a splitting 'between that which one is, and that which is the other'

(1997: 48; Karlsson 2000: 19). The idea is that identities are never fixed within themselves, nor do they emerge from nowhere; they are constructed primarily in and through relations, and are always involved in a process of translating (Karlsson 2000: 19; Hall and Maharaj 2001: 36). In this sense, identities are constructed in or through *différance* (Hall and du Gay 1996: 5). The notion of *différance* has been taken from Jacques Derrida, the French philosopher, from the French word *différer* which simultaneously means 'to defer' and 'to differ'. Words therefore cannot stand on their own to invoke meaning, but can only be defined through words from which they differ (1982: 7–8). We can find similarity of meaning concerning identity and the other through positional referents. In other words, identities are never fixed in one position but vary according to the situation. According to Stuart Hall, identities are therefore 'never unified [but are] increasingly fragmented and fractured; never singular but multiply constructed across different, often intersecting and antagonistic, discourses, practices and positions' (Hall and du Gay 1996: 4).

With regard to the Heraka, who is the 'other' and how are identities constructed? The 'other' in relation to the Heraka is not just one, but many. At any one time, one of the 'others' can take prominence creating different Heraka practices in the process. In the context of 'tradition' the immediate point of reference would be Paupaise; with respect to proselytization, the Christians will become the focus; if the Heraka are perceived to be 'Hindu' then both Christian and 'Hindu' groups will come to the forefront; the larger Christian Nagas and the 'neo-Hindu' organizations will figure prominently if the question of nationalism arises. The point I am trying to make is that Heraka identity is defined by difference in relation to the position of the other, akin to Derrida's notion of *différance*: words gaining meaning only through that from which they differ. *Différance* is a helpful way to envisage the construction of identity because it not only 'differs' but it also 'defers' and therefore makes identities a fluid process. Heraka identity, therefore, and indeed all identity, is an ongoing process of recognition and *différance*. And, with this I come to my main argument: reform and identity. The next point that needs to be addressed is the 'religious' aspect of the reform.

Religion and Religious

An important analysis of 'religion' is provided by the anthropologist Talal Asad. Asad argues against the universalist definition of 'religion' as an ahistorical or 'transhistorical essence', in this case, as expounded by Clifford Geertz (1973) (1993: 29; see also Chidester 1996; Fitzgerald 2000). This assumption, Asad argues, is centred primarily on a Western understanding of religion, closely related with the emergence of modernity in Europe. This understanding saw Natural Religion as a universal phenomenon with a common core of beliefs, worship and ethics (1993: 40–1). What happened was that 'religion' became common to all societies and also became deeply personal. In other words, 'religion' was shaped through a process of relations between 'different selves', 'different categories of knowledge' that it shaped and responded to, authorized and made accessible. Therefore, Asad argues, there cannot be a universal definition of 'religion' (1993: 29). Indeed, Asad's argument is a helpful point of departure for the Heraka with regard to 'religion'.

The Heraka do not have a word for 'religion', they prefer the word 'Hingde' which means 'rules governing everyday life'. Hingde is the divine rule that was given by Tingwang to Jadonang and Gaidinliu in Bhuban cave, an important pilgrimage site (see Chapter 2). Hingde is an attempt to define authority, which is divine and seen as 'orthopraxy'. In fact, to preserve the Heraka from any threat of outside influences, the leaders advocate total integration and uniformity of religious practice by eliciting 'orthodoxy', legitimized by reference to the Hingde Book (holy scripture). For example, they have introduced specific beliefs, worship and ethics within the Hingde Book as valid methods of expunging 'bad action' and correcting the individual and, eventually, society. This project of homogenization, unfortunately, has not had much success, as this itself has given rise to difference in practice between the rural and urban Heraka people, as will become clear in later chapters.

What I am interested to show throughout this book, however, is how, by the reform, what was once 'a matter of the group', became transformed in part into 'a matter of the individual' (Dumont 1971: 32; cited in Asad 1993: 28). This I suggest occurs by looking at the 'religious' as a subjective, personal experience that can both locate the individual in the communal, and vice versa, grounding it in the ability to choose. In other words, one chooses whether to be observant or not, to take part in a ritual or not and so on. Therefore, I suggest that 'religion' and 'religious' are not synonymous.

On the other hand, the 'religious' and the ascendance of religious features occurs, as the French sociologist Daniéle Hervieu-Léger says, when

> the group finds it needs to acquire a representation of itself that can incorporate the idea of its own continuity beyond the immediate context

> of its members' interrelating. This happens when the group takes on permanence and, seeking to legitimate its existence beyond the inevitable routinization of the emotional experiences that led to the sense of forming a single heart, needs to call upon a common spirit that transcends its individual members. (2000: 152)

Wider Literature on the Movement

The only comprehensive historical study on the Heraka has been done by Asoso Yonuo (1982) under the title *Nagas Struggle against the British Rule under Jadonang and Rani Gaidinliu 1925–1947.* His central argument is based on the idea that Jadonang and Gaidinliu aimed at creating some sort of 'religious nationalism' as the basis of the movement for the Zeliangrong people. His lengthy descriptions on the religious element of the movement are centred on what he defines as the reforming of 'animism'. He embellishes the religious element of the reform as a rational move to transform the local culture into one of moral purity and ethical aptitude. Indeed, he calls Heraka 'pure animism' (Yonuo 1982: 53–8). The strength of the book is with regard to nationalism. Yonuo treats the 'Jadonang movement' as a Naga renaissance 'in terms of awareness of their identity as a Naga people and also their distinct taste for political consciousness' (1982: 126). Yonuo goes on to say that this consciousness was brought about by Jadonang's involvement during the First World War serving with the labour corps in Mesopotamia and France that for the first time exposed him and other Nagas to their own tribal insularity (1982: 127; Mukherjee et al. 1982: 91; Regunathan 2000: 123).[9] However, it is difficult to find evidence to corroborate this claim, and it is discounted by other scholars such as Kamei (2002a: 17), who says that Jadonang was far too young to have enlisted or to have been involved in the labour corps. The second part of the book is a lengthy summation of the Naga nationalist movement and Gaidinliu's crusade, called Crusade of Animism (Yonuo 1982: 199–207) against Christianity and the tactics of proselytization. The book, though informative, is a sketchy historical summation of Jadonang and Gaidinliu's activities.

Another writer, Stephen Fuchs, looks at the 'Jadonang movement' from a messianic perspective in his work *Messianic Movements in Indian Religions* (1965). Fuchs' argument assumes that messianic movements are conditioned by particular situations (economic and social in this case) that require the arrival of some charismatic leader to deliver them (see also Lanternari 1963; Hobsbawm 1965).

Fuchs is persuasive on certain fronts but not so on others. One example of the latter, as Stephen Fuchs argues, is that the 'Jadonang movement' is a continuation of a previous claim by Sambhudan, a Kachari who came to prominence during the 1880s. He proclaimed himself as a *deo*, god, who initiated a form of resistance against the British in North Cachar Hills, Assam, but his movement quickly faded with the arrest of his key disciples and his eventual death (Fuchs 1965: 147–50; Mackenzie 1884: 147). Fuchs goes on to say that 'their [Kachari] desire for a revival of their original greatness was expressed by their belief in the return of a king who would drive out the foreign invaders and rule over "all who eat from the wooden platter", i.e. all Nagas' (Fuchs 1965: 147–8). The statement, 'all who eat from the wooden platter, i.e. all Nagas' was used initially by Hutton, a district administrator, while speaking of the Angami Nagas' prophecy that a king will arise from a cave in the Kacha Naga country, who will drive out the British. This king could be the Kachari King Bhim Raja, 'of whom such a story is told' (Hutton 1969: 252).

Certain facts must be clarified in this claim. First, the use of Hutton's account of the Angami to justify a link between Sambhudan and the promised messiah (king) is a little far fetched. This statement is further complicated by the argument that 'a Kachari Messiah appeared who promised to lead the Kacha Nagas to freedom and greatness' (Fuchs 1965: 148). Though possible, there is no link, nor any story told by the Zeme (present-day Kacha Nagas) of Sambhudan's messiahship over them. Indeed, I think Fuchs has confused the two ethnic groups: the Kachari and the Kacha Nagas. He states that 'a new Messiah arose among the Kachari. He promised to liberate the Nagas from the yoke of both Kukis and British. His name was Jadonang, and he was from the village Kambiron' (1965: 151). Both these facts disqualify him from being a Kachari; Kambiron is in Manipur and is a Rongmei Naga village. Therefore, I see no strong connection between Sambhudan's messiahship and the continuation of this prophecy through Jadonang, as claimed by Fuchs. These two events are highly unlikely to be significantly related.

Other studies done by historians such as Gangmumei Kabui (Kamei) (1982) and Mukherjee et al. in the book *Tribal Movements in India* (1982) base their argument on the centrality of ethnic unity as the underlying goal of the 'Jadonang movement'. This is a strong feature of the historical materials. In these works there is a predominant assumption that the 'Jadonang movement' is a precursor to the Heraka movement and that it was largely about Zeliangrong unity and identity, which, therefore, propagated a largely pan-ethnic agenda (Mahadevan 1974; Kabui (Kamei) 1982;

Mukherjee et al. 1982; Kamei 2004). The connection between the two mentioned movements is tenuous at best because the 'Jadonang movement' as we know it, exists largely in the pages of colonial reports, while the Heraka movement has dispersed into two geographical regions, reflecting different sets of conditions that have influenced and perpetuated its existence. Therefore, though it is sometimes assumed as 'knowledge' among historians of Northeast India that the Heraka and the 'Jadonang movement' are connected, forming a continuous chain of events since its inception in the late 1920s to its current form, I am not quite convinced that such is the case.

A similar study on the 'Zeliangrong movement' treated as synonymous with the Heraka, undertaken by Mukherjee et al. (1982: 67–95), expands on the above argument and reflects on the history of the movement while drawing attention to the ways it has coalesced and expanded to include various practices: 'in its political urge, its spirit of revivalism and search for customary laws and customs, in its use of Tantric-like cults, temples and hymns, the movement has led to a revitalization of the cultural processes both from within and from contacts with neighbouring people' (1982: 88). They argue that the movement is largely reformatory in nature, including key reforms in the social and political spheres. These reforms, they argue, were to remove 'undesirable' and 'meaningless rites and customs', 'laws of inheritance' and 'rules of marriage' (1982: 88). Although Mukherjee et al. provide a good description, most of what we learn of Heraka is boxed into the 'Jadonang' or 'Zeliangrong' movement. I think that this is a growing fallacy about the Heraka. Indeed, this study will remedy some of the shortcomings regarding the history of the Heraka movement, while also giving the first socio-anthropological analysis of the Heraka reform movement itself.

Undoubtedly, the Heraka count Jadonang as one of their reformers and in fact hold him in high regard. However, it is Rani Gaidinliu who has most prestige within the Heraka movement. The reason for this is quite simple. The Heraka movement is found largely among the Zeme in North Cachar Hills, Assam, among the Zeme and Liangmai in Nagaland, and among some Zeme in Manipur. While Jadonang succumbed to the British courts in 1931 and was hanged, Gaidinliu, then a young girl of 16, went to the Zeme region of North Cachar Hills where her popularity spread. It was Gaidinliu's activities in North Cachar Hills that gave rise to the present Heraka movement.

Aim of the Book

The aim of the book is to understand the predicament of a marginal religious reform movement known as the Heraka, among the Zeme of North

Cachar Hills. The focus is on reform and identity: How does the reform, by asking questions about self, tradition, community and change, form an identity that is self-reflexive as well as negotiated around difference? Identity is therefore formed by difference. Many definable actors help shape Heraka identity and also have a clear stake in it. The Heraka reaction is less overt, but it situates their struggles in everyday forms of resistance (see Scott 1985). If most studies on the Nagas start with the trinity – Christianity, ethnicity and nationalism – this book is an attempt to provide a different process by which this trinity is contested. I attempt to provide a clear analysis of these questions by grounding my research in the Heraka community.

Resources

Since this is an ethnohistorical book, most of my sources are either archival or fieldwork material. I was able to conduct archival research in the British Library, London, School of Oriental and African Studies (SOAS) library, and the Pitt Rivers Museum, Oxford. In the British library the sources are largely classified under the 'political section'; in SOAS I looked primarily at the 'Higgins Collection' and in Oxford a mixed collection of Hutton, J. P. Mills and Ursula Graham Bower who, except for Bower, were officially administrators/anthropologists working in the Naga Hills from roughly around 1910 to 1947. Some archive materials are also housed in the National Archives, New Delhi, which unfortunately, I was unable to visit. I have been able to assess some of these archival materials from a secondary source (Bhuyan 1978). The majority of the archive materials in London date from between 1920 and 1933 (which I consulted), while some from 1933 are in the Indian National Archives. I suspect that, since Gaidinliu was imprisoned in 1932 by the British, the movement would have remained relatively quiet after 1932 and not have merited much attention in the administrative reports. I have therefore paid less attention to these. However, I am confident that the materials I have gathered provide sufficient support for the arguments in this book.

Some of the archive materials were attained online (http://www.alanmacfarlane.com/bamboo_naga_front/front.htm), which can be assessed through the Alan Macfarlane site (www.alanmacfarlane.com). 'Bamboo Naga' is a valuable site that contains tour diaries, administrative reports, letters and also materials from private journals, from the early nineteenth century to the mid-twentieth century.

I conducted two pieces of fieldwork: the first one was during September 2004 for a period of one month and the second during January–June of

2005, for a period of six months. Most of the material gathered during this fieldwork has been transcribed by myself and Tahulung with the help of Adeule, who were both my co-workers in the field. The fieldwork materials and tapes are in my possession and can be made available at my discretion. During my fieldwork I spent time with, met and interviewed so many different people that sometimes those conversations may have gone into this text unnoticed. However, where possible I have quoted my source, although I have changed their names as some of what is said is controversial. I have also kept some of the places anonymous as I see no reason to intervene in the lives of villages by making their stories 'public'.

Fieldwork

My first encounter with the Zeme Heraka dates back to 2004, just after I had embarked on a Ph.D. programme at the Religious Studies Department in the University of Edinburgh. One night, I stumbled upon the Heraka in a book titled *A Pilgrimage to the Nagas* by Milada Ganguli (1984). I remember reluctantly carrying her book to the United Kingdom in my suitcase, as I felt it would be a helpful introduction to those wanting to know more about the Nagas. The book remained on the shelf, unopened and unread until that night. Upon reading the first few pages, I happened upon this passage,

> Her [Gaidinliu's] cousin Jadonang founded in 1929 in Tamenglong subdivision in north-western Manipur, adjoining North Cachar in Assam and the Naga Hills a religious movement called the '*Haraka* cult', a reformed kind of the old animistic religion of three related tribes: Zemi, Liangmei and Rongmei Nagas, inhabiting that area . . . Jadunang abolished sacrifices to minor gods and spirits and ordered his people to worship and make human and *mithun* [semi wild bison, *Bos Frontalis*] sacrifices to the god creator *Tingwang*, and in turn god would give them plenty of food and restore them their freedom. His cousin Gaidiliu was made priestess in the North Cachar Hills in Assam. (1984: 19)

Upon discovering this curious text, I immediately trawled through the library, internet and my family at home for information to find out more about the Heraka. It was still a mystery as to why, growing up in Nagaland, I had not heard of the Heraka movement. I was born in Nagaland and spent most of my childhood there before I went to boarding school in Darjeeling. I grew up in a very Christian society that was very conscious of any non-Christian elements. I remember being told of the 'Hindus' and how we

Christians pray to one 'true God' while the 'Hindus' pray to 'false gods'. These distinctions would surface again and again in church meetings, yearly church revival programmes and visiting evangelical tours that would fill public grounds with contingents from America, Europe and India.

Immediately upon receiving my email, my father recalled that he knew the President of the Heraka Association of North East India, N. C. Zeliang. After a brief meeting with him, my father mailed me a small pamphlet, without a title, about the Heraka. The description of the Heraka was vague and almost mystical. It talked of the 'full moon day', 'bloodless sacrifices', 'prayer to one God'. Not only was I intrigued, but I also realized that not much had been published on the Heraka; and maybe finally I had found my research topic. I did not know; I had to find out.

Off to Fieldwork

I first decided to do a pilot trip for a period of one month from September–October to visit North Cachar Hills and Nagaland (see Map 1.2). I drove to

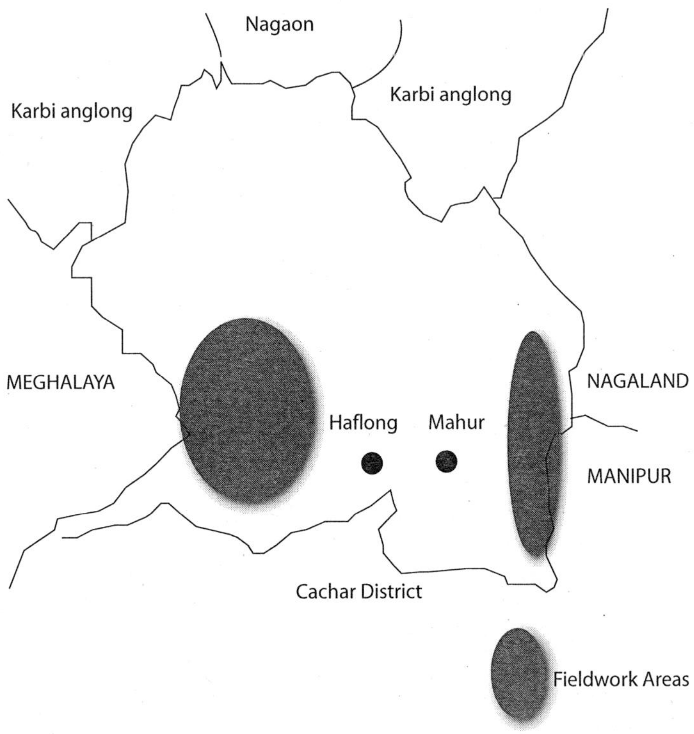

Map 1.2 North Cachar Hills District, Assam

Haflong, the capital of North Cachar Hills in Assam, in the month of September 2004, with a handful of contacts and a rough idea of the Heraka that I had received from the President of the Heraka Association when I met him in Kohima, Nagaland. I was still unsure if the Heraka movement was substantial enough for a study. When I met my contacts, one being the General Secretary of the Heraka Association of North East India, Ramkhui Newme, I was led by a common consensus to Hsongle village. But some help was needed especially with the language, as I was still new to Zeme (some of whom spoke English and others Hindi). I wanted to find a co-worker who could help me with the language and act as my guide for the long-term fieldwork.

By the time I had reached Haflong, news of my whereabouts and my enquiries spread quickly: I was a researcher wanting to know more about the Heraka. Curiously, that evening, an Australian anthropologist, Amanda, who had heard I was in town, came by to see me with her female co-worker, Adeule. In what was a fortunate meeting, they agreed to take me to Hsongle as they were going there themselves and Adeule would help me with the language and eventually help me find a long-term co-worker. The next day, we somehow reached Hsongle, amidst a downpour and the landslide between Ruham (a trading town) and Hsongle. Hsongle is a large village compared to the other Zeme villages. It consists of around 120 households with 'colonies' (localities) based on religious affiliation: Roman Catholic, Baptist, Presbyterian and Heraka. It has a relatively large market where people from the neighbouring villages come to trade goods. A frequent transport system (two buses) runs between Hsongle and Haflong almost everyday. From my point of view, its proximity to other villages would make it ideal for travelling for fieldwork, while keeping Hsongle as a base. The next problem was finding a place to stay.

Amanda and Adeule pointed out that I could stay in the hut Amanda had constructed with her own money on land belonging to the Baptist church. The agreement with the church was that after Amanda's fieldwork, the Baptist church could use the hut as they saw fit. Adeule approached the elders of the church and enquired if I could stay there when Amanda returned to Australia, a proposition they willingly agreed to. The arrangement could not have been better. Amanda was to leave in December, leaving the hut empty for me for January. My only hesitation concerned the appropriateness of staying at the Baptist colony while working with the Heraka.

I considered this from various angles. The Heraka colony had no free huts to lend me and suggested that I could stay with families during the time of my fieldwork. This did not suit me because I did not want to live with a family for a long period of time as this meant not only housing me but also possibly a co-worker. The second reason to avoid the Heraka colony was the periodic use of its 'medical centre' by the Indian army – sometimes for a few days or weeks – for patrolling the neighbouring villages and flushing out any 'Naga insurgents' operating in the jungles. This not only created tension in the village, but as a Heraka schoolmaster advised me, it might not be the ideal conditions for research work. Finally, I wanted my own personal space where I could reflect on the day's work and be slightly detached from the community with which I was working.

Not living in the Heraka colony, I realized, was not disadvantageous in any way. Their major rituals were only periodically celebrated which enabled me to plan ahead of time and attend; and the short distance from the Heraka colony meant that I was able to go to the Heraka colony night and day. I also realized that not sleeping in a Heraka household did not mean that my knowledge about the Heraka was inadequate. Rather, I realized that, due to the ideal placement of my hut, in relation to the market, and the different colonies, I had more visits from the Heraka, Baptists, Catholics and Presbyterians, than if I had lived on top of the hill. It also turned out to be advantageous because most of the Baptists were ex-Heraka, and they, more than anybody else, were critical of the Heraka in a reflective manner that allowed me to understand the position of the Heraka vis-à-vis the Christians, not only in Hsongle but also in most Zeme villages. Although the position of the Baptists is interesting since they have rejected the beliefs and practices of Heraka, their narrative is also 'positioned' and therefore, arguably, requires a critical view, recognizing that, as ex-Heraka, they may be especially likely to highlight differences/ boundaries important to their 'position'.

The importance of 'positionality' in fieldwork is important to the construction of discourse in relation to the community one is researching (see Geertz 1979; Clifford and Marcus 1986; Kirschner 1987). Although I was initially perceived as an 'outsider' with an open agenda to do research in the community, my status within the community evolved to that of an 'insider' with a responsibility to the people involved in my research. The dichotomies of 'insider/outsider' are difficult to transcend or even understand without positioning oneself in these circumstances (see Longkumer (forthcoming)). Rather than placing ourselves between two lines, I would argue that this problem is largely an interpretative one. Instead of clearly defining the lines between insider/outsider, it depends on the interpretative position of the insider as well as the outsider. For example, if I spoke the language and knew most of the people intimately, in some cases I would still be an outsider from the fact that I would eventually leave. These are surely complex issues. However, part of their acceptance of me was due to my status as a 'Naga', which was connected to a larger collective identity. The fact that I could speak in 'Hindi' or sometimes in 'Nagamese' with them, also made it easier for me to make direct relationships. The other point regarding my 'positionality' was religious affiliation. Although questions surrounding my religious faith did not come up, the Heraka assumed that since I was a 'Naga' from Nagaland, I was Baptist Christian. Drinking *zao* (rice beer) and not attending church allayed Heraka fears that I was there to convert them.

In a way, my hut became the enclosed space for different people and voices to interact without any presumed judgement on the accuracy or inadequacy of knowledge – and in my eagerness to learn, perhaps, some boundaries were effaced.

Walking and Writing

When I arrived in the North Cachar Hills for the second time (January–June) for my long-term fieldwork, with a new co-worker Tahulung, I expected to do a study based in one village. However, when I reached the eastern region of Hsongle village, that possibility became remote, as a vast network of knowledge, an aggregation of sorts, wired villages together. Enquiring about Zeme cosmology, for example, required travelling to three villages. Often, out of desperation, I would send word out to the person concerned, inviting him to stay with us for a day or two, but I would often receive a note saying that the person would only share his knowledge with me in his village. Sometimes, when people we wanted to meet came during market day (once a week), we would sit beside them talking during their trading; at other times, if they were hungry, we would invite them to our hut for lunch as a way of negotiating for knowledge. We would buy *zao* (rice beer) in exchange for conversation. But most often, we would divide our time between moving and talking, eating and sleeping as we traversed the vast range of villages tucked away from the world of official maps and designations.

I am reminded of Anna Tsing's account of her fieldwork in the Meratus Mountains of Indonesia; and how travelling became a feature of her ethnography as she negotiated identities, spaces and perceptions of her gender. Similarly, my ethnographic experience is dispersed, as each village requires a different point of 'arrival' and 'departure' (see Tsing 1993: 66). In a way, my journey constituted separable ethnographic pieces, each negotiated by what we heard, saw, ate, drank and talked. By journeying, I took on multiple identities, was known by many names, confused once over gender (because of my long hair), made various friends, negotiated on many levels and walked many miles. This journeying mediated between ways of knowing and ways of manoeuvring between the spaces (1993: 66–8).

Michel de Certeau, in his book *The Practice of Everyday Life*, provides us with a poetic analysis of walking, 'Walking the City'. Seeing a city from above, distant, 'seeing the whole', he says, is a voyeuristic attempt to totalize the experience without feeling the personal spaces a city offers. The ordinary pedestrian, on the other hand, lives 'down below', an ordinariness that is experiential; their knowledge of the city spaces are 'blind as that of lovers in each other's arms' which is 'migrational, or metaphorical', as they walk the city space also changes (de Certeau 1984: 92–3). My walking experience is similar (see also Ingold and Vergunst 2008). Maps were never used nor were they available. Destinations were used in the sense of near and far and not measured by any scale. Sometimes we stayed for a few hours, sometimes for days. In this manner, I learnt the act of walking and navigating vast walking trails, marked by a certain tree or a patch in the field, or the sound of a certain stream, from Tahulung.

Tahulung

Tahulung is a Heraka in his thirties brought up in the village until he went to Haflong town for his college education. He was very engaged with my research and many of our journeys were filled with conversations ranging from Heraka history, its present practice, to signs of the future. We walked and talked. Sometimes, we arrived unannounced in a village without knowing what lay ahead of us; at other times, a friend, or extended family would be told in advance of our arrival. At all times, we found a willing family to take us in, share their food and offer us *zao*, as medicine from the long day's walk. Often, due to my presence, we would be invited by many households wanting to share their *zao* and socialize: Where are you from? Is it cold or is it hot like the plains? We would sit there sharing sweets and biscuits I had brought along with me. Unable to leave due to our inebriated state, we would sit by the hearth and eat dried beef and rice, converse about the Heraka, before finding a bed to rest. As Tahulung and I got to know each other, his initial politeness wore off and he talked to me about the land, and stories he heard as a child: the brother who tormented and killed his sister and was cursed to become a bird, so that to this day he could be heard asking for his sister's forgiveness. 'Do you hear that bird?', he would say, 'that's him'.

At other times, he would ask me questions about my life and why I had come here. Soon, our conversations became straightforward rather than polite and complicated. Tahulung's knowledge of swidden cultivation was impressive. While walking through ashen slopes, he would stop and explain the different seasons for burning, planting and sowing; and how new cash crops like ginger were becoming popular among the planters. He talked of his education in Haflong Government College and his involvement with the Hemanki Integrated Wasteland Development Project (HIWDP), funded by the Government of India (GOI), as the secretary covering seven Zeme villages. His projects involve enabling people to form Self Help Groups (SHG) to conserve soil (terracing, vegetative fences to protect land erosion), harvest water (farm ponds, percolation tanks) and protect against land erosion (building dams). This job allowed him the flexibility to work with me at the same time.

Sometimes, deep in thought after a conversation, he would tell me about his memory of Rani Gaidinliu. 'She healed me', he told me one day when we were sitting on top of a rocky ledge. At the age of 5 he and his father met Rani Gaidinliu when she visited his village. Ranima immediately took a liking to Tahulung and recognized that he suffered from a weak leg. As Tahulung recalled, 'she rubbed a piece of ginger on her left thigh and told my father to cook the ginger with a cockerel. When it is cooked, she instructed, take the heart and give it to Tahulung to eat. After I ate the cockerel's heart, my leg eventually became better as promised by Ranima.'

Often Adeule would accompany us to the villages which enabled me to talk to women who were perhaps too shy to talk to Tahulung. Adeule, unlike Tahulung, is a Baptist Christian, a recent convert from Heraka. Prior to working with me, she had worked with Amanda who was working on the status of Zeme women. Adeule is a bright aspiring leader among the Zeme who, as a Heraka, attended a Rashtriya Swayamsevak Sangh (RSS) school in Uttar Pradesh, another state in India. She speaks impeccable Hindi and unlike Tahulung, is an extrovert. During our journeys, I would overhear Tahulung and her talk about the tense relations between the Heraka and Christians over conversion, and their own experience of being caught up in these situations. Through them I learnt most of my conversational Zeme, and though I was unable to speak Zeme proficiently enough for translation, my knowledge was enough to enable me to follow conversations. Most Zeme speak '*kacha* Hindi' (raw Hindi), and some English, so I had no problems navigating my way through their world. But it is above all Tahulung and Adeule who helped me understand the 'Zeme world' of recognition and *différance* as not only two ways of thinking but also two ways of living.

Chapter Outline

I have not organized this book in a historically linear fashion; I move back and forth between time and events because each chapter addresses a particular question. For example, I revisit historical events from Chapter 3 again in Chapter 6, considering them from a different angle. The thematic development is as follows:

Chapter 2 explores the pilgrimage to the Bhuban cave, the assumed starting-point of the movement. In this chapter I argue that the Heraka reform evolves through interaction with different religious groups in the Bhuban cave. Such encounters sharpen Heraka identity, and also emphasize religious boundaries as they erupt primarily in the 'cave ritual'. It also attempts to show how some Heraka ground the reform in intuition and experience.

Chapter 3 looks at the genesis of the movement in the 1930s and the impact it had on agrarian reforms, minimizing sacrifices, and altering the pantheon. I argue that these reforms gained momentum primarily for two reasons: (1) the misunderstanding by the British of the cycle migration associated with shifting agriculture and (2) the invitation of Kuki immigrants by the British to settle in land 'owned' by the Zeme. This created near famines and hostility towards the British and the Kuki immigrants. Attempts to alleviate the problem saw the introduction of a different form of rice cultivation, rice terrace cultivation, which also ended in failure. Due to these inadequate British policies, the 'Gaidinliu movement' in its millenarian form attempted to dislodge institutions that crippled the Zeme economy and rallied the people against dominant enemies. By initiating reform, the traditional roles of the landowner and priest were weakened, giving rise to a new village head (Paipeu), based on economic wealth. Removing the physical and symbolic aspects of the 'old' and replacing them with the 'new', brought about incremental change and the renewal of villages.

Chapter 4 focuses on how the cosmology – in this case the creation story – adopted one God, Tingwang as the macrocosmic entity. I examine the changes in cosmology and how the adoption of a healer, Herakandingpeu, had a vital influence on Heraka reform. The introduction of the Hingde Book as scripture for the Heraka also coexists with a new religious system that is increasingly separated conceptually and physically, by the adoption of the Kelumki, as both sacred and prohibited. This gives rise to a feature of the 'religious' as grounded in tradition, community and the individual.

Chapter 5 examines the larger notions of boundaries and how they define the Heraka through difference, both in position and conception. It appears that the 'Hindu' organizations and the Christians have a stake in how Heraka is perceived. Through the rhetoric of neo-traditional notions of Hindutva (or Hinduness) and their encompassing relationship with the *vanvasi* (jungle dweller) population such as the Heraka, 'Hindu' organizations are able to envision a unified 'Hindu' nation. Similarly, through historical precedent and the relationship with the GOI with regard to Naga nationalism, Naga Christians also inadvertently have a voice concerning who is, and who is not, Naga, based on religious affiliations (in this case Christian). These various positions of 'others' vis-à-vis Heraka identity are always formed by mutual articulation of difference. In this way, Heraka identity is always evolving.

Chapter 6 places the evolving history of the Heraka in Hangrum, the supposed centre of the Heraka. I examine the central question of community formation and how the Heraka community is constructed: whether along 'orthodox' or 'heterodox' lines? Although points of divergence are evident in Heraka practice, I suggest looking at community construction, following Anthony Cohen's formulation, community as 'aggregating device' (2003: 109), through the legitimation of the *heguangram* (free community) and *heguang* (agent of that freedom) in texts and narrative. This also situates the different traditions and voices in Hangrum which highlights the past, present and the possible future of the Heraka.

Chapter 7 concludes by offering us (1) the summary of the main arguments and insights, (2) critical reflection on what has been achieved and the limitations of the study, (3) future research directions and (4) wider contribution to scholarship research. In addition to this, I consider the role of ethnicity and nationalism as an important way to help us understand the Zeme Heraka. However, before we examine these questions, it is necessary to consider the origin of the Heraka reform. This brings us to Chapter 2.

Chapter 2

Circling the Altar Stone: Bhuban Cave and the Symbolism of Religious Traditions

I can see the hill top where the cave is from just below the stream. The sun has an orange glow, slowly receding from the hill top. Lush green vegetation reflects the glow before the light fades, blackening the hill.

Bhuban Hill is in the district of Cachar, Assam, about 50 km south-west of Silchar. Every year Heraka pilgrims from all over the region visit the Bhuban cave, situated near the top of the Bhuban Hill, during the month of February. For the Heraka, the Bhuban cave represents the point from where the reform began during the 1920s, where God Tingwang instructed the first reformers.[1] Why is the pilgrimage of such importance to the Heraka even after so many years?

I start this book with this question because in many ways the pilgrimage encapsulates the Heraka reform and the dialogue they hold with the many religious traditions around. This dialogue gives rise to themes such as identity, religious boundaries and the reform itself, which are discussed throughout the chapter and the book. A second reason the pilgrimage connects with the Heraka in such a powerful way is that it reiterates their bond with the 'essence' of what Heraka is: in the cave the blessing of Tingwang was bestowed upon Jadonang and Ranima (the first Heraka reformers) who were then instructed to teach the Zeliangrong people. Past pilgrims told me about the immense power of the journey, how their emotions were affected by the awe-inspiring presence of the cave, and its supposed miraculous effect on people making the pilgrimage. It is the journey I undertook with a group of Heraka pilgrims that is the main focus for this chapter.

I will examine the Bhuban cave pilgrimage as a representation of the way in which the Heraka reform movement is evolving. The ritual in the cave provides us with a clear illustration of how religious boundaries create a sharpening of identity and how the Heraka see themselves as both modern and traditional. In this chapter, I will first describe Bhuban Hill and the different symbols associated with it. Second, I will examine the cave ritual as revealing the way the Heraka respond to, and contrast themselves with the other religious traditions with whom they share the ritual space. Third, using individual accounts of Heraka followers, I will analyse how the reform is exemplified in the journey to the cave and how these experiences reveal both the imaginative and intuitive quality of what the reform represents. Finally, using Victor and Edith Turner's model of communitas, I briefly examine the notion of Zeliangrong with regard to the Heraka and Poupei Chapriak (see below) based on the Bhuban cave pilgrimage.

The Pilgrims: Do Categories Matter?

On this occasion at the cave, the Heraka pilgrims were primarily the Zeme from North Cachar Hills, who are also the largest of the Heraka groups. Probably due to the terrain and distance, not many Heraka adherents have come from Nagaland or Manipur. Bhuban cave is only now an increasingly important place for the Heraka and also for the Poupei Chapriak (a form of Rongmei traditional practice; see below) who contribute to the larger ethnic group known as Zeliangrong. Indeed, there has been a revival of the pilgrimage to the cave among the Heraka and Poupei Chapriak, who only recently have made the pilgrimage popular. There are also other religious groups who visit Bhuban Hill. For example, it is known for its Shiva temple (also called Bhubaneshwar temple), located above the Bhuban cave, and constructed by the Kachari kings: every year there is a Shiva *yatra* (pilgrimage) that is attended by hundreds of pilgrims.

Bhuban Hill represents various cosmic worlds to different religious traditions. With this initial description, we are immediately drawn to ponder the significance associated with such a natural symbol as the Hill. Why are people drawn to it? What is it that exudes such mystery and wonder? This Hill is not just a hill with its rocky terrain and its natural formations such as the cave and the deep underground tunnel or its tall trees and natural springs. The Hill also represents the human desire to relate to something they see as more than inanimate, as something sacred, etched into the memory of the people who walk on it, who worship it and who interpret it in various ways as it evolves. The balance between the natural and the experiential is felt through human relations with the natural world, and the metaphysical realities that bound their experience into a unique expression of their journey (see also Fuller 1992: 204–23). Because various religious traditions are associated with Bhuban Hill, it is easy to assume that certain names, practices or ideas derive from the dominant tradition with which they are primarily associated. This is so because identities are confusing; or to put it another way, there are no maps that indicate unambiguous religious boundaries (Oberoi 1997),[2] nor any list of defining characteristics which clearly divide one religious tradition from another.

For example, when I was thinking about these various possibilities, I realized that I was already mapping the terrain with certain limitations. I immediately assumed that this is a 'Hindu' pilgrimage and the local religious traditions, such as Heraka and Poupei Chapriak, are simply copying the order of a dominant structure. Just because certain assumed 'Hindu' systems are in place such as the temple, incense, flowers, temple bells, I fell into the same hermeneutic of suspicion, associating certain characteristics with being 'Hindu' rather than privileging local categories already in place.

These categories – Heraka or 'Hindu' – are unimportant in social situations (i.e. sharing of food, camp-site and entertainment) because the pilgrims themselves do not recognize them and the differences between the boundaries of each religious group, to the extent that they existed in the first place, become fuzzy. It is wrong to assume that these religious identities are fixed and that they in themselves represent identifying badges that signify their position and place in a hierarchy. It is only when religious traditions and their interpretations emerge, for example, in the sharing of ritual space in the cave with the Heraka and Poupei Chapriak, that boundaries of identity become more obvious and divisive, rather than unobtrusive and orderly (see also Chapter 5). This sharing of ritual space is examined below in considering the ritual of the cave. It is indeed more helpful to visualize Bhuban Hill as that which encapsulates all these world-views and therefore represents a macrocosmic world.

The Edge of the World

The motorable road to the Bhuban Hill ends at Kashipunjee, which is predominantly a Khasi village.[3] The last house on the bottom of the hill belongs to a Roman Catholic family, who willingly allow us to wash ourselves in their pond of water. Beyond this point, everything is steep slope, rock and jungle. The climb is uphill for two hours or so; and one usually has to employ *coolies* (porters) to carry most of the heavy load. As we walk up we meet other pilgrims climbing up to the Shiva temple, smoking from their wooden *chilums* (smoking pipes). The waft of a strong *ganja* (cannabis) smell combined with sweat leaves us feeling heavy under the sweltering heat. Once we reach level ground again, a sign nailed to a tree indicates that we have to take a right turn to the 'Naga Bishnu Cave'. This is the same as the Bhuban cave. The name 'Naga Bishnu' has been put up at least for two reasons: one, to indicate to the 'Hindus' and two to the non-Christian Nagas. It could also be assumed that this indicates a site for 'Hindu' pilgrims because of certain semantic similarities. The well-known image of Vishnu (Bishnu) reclining on a Shesha Naga (a very large snake) as he floats on the universal ocean with Lakshmi (Vishnu's consort and often known as the Mother of the Universe, goddess of wealth and wisdom among others) provides an obvious link to the name 'Naga Bishnu'. Indeed, some people attending the pilgrimage may interpret it as having some connection with the 'Hindu' Vishnu. For example, Zeliang (2005: 8–10) associates Bhuban cave with the abode of Vishnu by equating Tingwang (God for the Zeme) with Vishnu. However, in the present context it is important to privilege local categories over pan-Indian 'Hindu' ones. I am therefore hesitant to tie the name 'Naga Bishnu Cave' with the afore-mentioned point because, as we shall see, it is not that simple.

The Bhuban cave is below the Shiva temple and those interested in going further have another half an hour's climb before reaching the top. We make our way to the main camp rather than the cave. I am struck immediately by the throngs of pilgrims who have come to attend the 'mela'.[4] The evening sun is reflected in silvery steel cooking vessels, as people mill around waiting for their turn to wash their pots. There are small makeshift shelters of leaves and wood stitched together precariously with twigs, perched along the edges of the hill. Families, communities, villages, clutch their animals – goats, chicken, pigeons – as the road leading to the main reception area fills with people. It resembles a Saturday Bazaar, with Bengali hawkers selling sweet *jalebi* (deep-fried batter soaked in syrup) and *samosa* along the way.

The chill of the evening wind evaporates my sweat, and I quickly pull my jacket over me. I pass the main entrance to the flat top of the hill, where I am accosted by young men asking where I am from. 'I came from Haflong', 'oh, you must be Zeme Heraka then' they immediately reply. I nod half-heartedly and go past the huge banner that reads 'Heartiest Welcome to the 24th Annual Ritual Festival, Bhuban Hills, Cachar, Assam'. My half-hearted response was impulsive because their reaction to me coming from Haflong boxes me into a Zeme Heraka category. In physical appearance I am 'Naga' yet my association with Haflong could imply many things: that I am just passing through, that my point of departure was Haflong, or even the fact that I could be a Christian living in Haflong. None of this is taken into account by the folk welcoming us. The clear association of locality, ethnicity and religious belief is taken for granted and based solely on geographical location connected, in this case, with the Heraka. This is of course a widespread assumption, not only in Cachar, but also in other parts of North Cachar Hills and Nagaland, made particularly by Christians.

As I make my way to my allocated place to pitch a tent, I am hit by the heavy smell of burning meat coming from the huge fire lit in the middle of the main camp. My friends and I settle down for some tea while people below us prepare for evening prayers. Other Poupei Chapriak pilgrims are just making their way to the 'mela' and they carry with them animals and various birds such as pigeons and hens, as they line up outside the two Poupei Chapriak temples, 'Naga Bishnu Mandir' and 'Gairiemnang Memorial Hall', singing in unison (see Photograph 2.1). The two temples are revered only by the Poupei Chapriak.[5] They have obviously had a long journey carrying their heavy bundles. But their tiredness seems effaced by the sight of the gods inside the temples.

Photograph 2.1 Poupei Chapriak pilgrims outside the Naga Bishnu Mandir

They remove their shoes just as they approach the steps leading to the Naga Bishnu Mandir (temple) and place the animals, marked with pink dye, on the steps of the altar as a gift to the god. After praying, the *pujari* (priest) sprinkles water with a plantain leaf[6] on the pilgrims. A tiny bell is then rung as a completion of the prayer.

Temples and Myth: The Evolution of Bhuban

The Poupei Chapriak are Rongmei people who count Jadonang as their reformer. Poupei Chapriak literally means Poupei (ancestral), Chap (godly nature) and Riak. Riak has a variety of meanings: the existence of soul, mind; knowledge in the body and taking care of that body. The body and soul are kept holy by the power of our knowledge through introspection. This knowledge is known as Riak. The above glosses are generally classified by them as Poupei Chapriak religion, based on a locally held understanding, in common with the Latin '*Religare*', 'the zeal of trying to return towards where we come from'.[7]

The first temple which houses Bishnu is called 'Naga Bishnu Mandir' and the other one is 'Gairiemnang Memorial Hall'. Both these temples, according to the Poupei Chapriak, were built on 'original' sites; what these 'original' sites represented is not clear. But one general assumption is that these sites were venerated as holy places by the Poupei Chapriak since time immemorial, and the temples were built to signify and preserve the holy place.

According to the myth, Bhuban god begot a son called Gairiemnang. He was given all sorts of powers: talent, wisdom and beauty. At that time, there was a belief among the Zeliangrong people that a 'king' will come to bring peace and rule over the Zeliangrong people. People thought that Gairiemnang was the prophesized one. But instead of living up to his promises, Gairiemnang squandered all his talents and became a womanizer. All his blessings were withdrawn from him and the Zeliangrong people waited for the return of another 'king' who would bring in peace and rule over the Zeliangrong people. What the notion of this 'king' implies remains elusive to this day. Some say that Jadonang fits in with this image, but his premature death and the ascendancy of Rani Gaidinliu as the leader creates counter-claims, supported by texts, that Rani Gaidinliu was chosen over Jadonang to lead the people.

Both the temples are cared for by Poupei Chapriak *pujaris* (priests) who rotate every three months. Inside the temples, the figures of Bhuban and Gairiemnang are adorned with full Rongmei regalia in the traditional red, white and black body cloths. A Rongmei spear is erected beside them and a few *trishuls* (tridents) are also placed behind the spear. As worshippers approach the altar where incense and candles are lit, they kneel down to offer their *pujas* (a form of reverence or worship; in this case fruits and animals are offered) and pray. After their prayers, they ring the bell as a completion of their prayers and the *pujari* sprinkles holy water (taken from the Bhuban cave) with plantain leaves on the worshippers. This signifies the completion of the prayer. The *pujas* of fruit are used by the *pujaris* for consumption and the animals are sold off in the market or used for a meal, the money used for the upkeep of the temples. Whether animal offerings connote sacrifice or not is uncertain; but most people assume that a gift is a sacrifice. Sacrifices are a double-edged sword. Their connotations vary according to whom one talks to. For the Heraka, sacrifices of any form are now sacrilegious, while for the Poupei Chapriak they constitute a gift to God in exchange for their prayers being answered. This exchange is done by the person not out of compulsion but voluntarily. The relationship between the two is examined in the example of the ritual in the cave, which I discuss below.

The main temple, Naga Bishnu Mandir, houses Bishnu, who is also known as Bhuban. The semantic variation is figured in the different oral and written accounts where names or even spellings change to suit their context. This demonstrates the difficulty of defining categories and their evolution. The various languages of the area hold vital symbols representing particular world-views. For example, Bishnu has gone on to incorporate various changes that reflect how local world-views assimilate the larger ones or vice versa in processes called 'parochialization' and 'universalization' respectively (Marriott 1972: 197–201, 211). Bishnu is the Rongmei spelling; in Zeme he is called Munseniu (sometimes spelt as Mishnu). The Zeme Heraka say that Munseniu resided in what is now called Bhuban cave. J. C. Higgins, the Political Agent of Manipur during the 1930s, suggests that 'Buichenu [Bishnu] – lives in Cachar, on the Bhuban range (obviously Vishnu)'.[8] Jadonang, on the other hand, claims that 'Kangrellung, the god of the Bhuban Hills, appeared to him in a dream . . .'[9] In another account, Gaidinliu is questioned by J. C. Higgins in 1932 about Jadonang's affairs after she is captured. She replies, in response to a query, she 'also went to Bhuban to worship the god, in order to obtain prosperity, because Jadonang said he was going, and because the people of the plains worship there'.[10] This claim suggests that there have been local 'Hindu' influences in the way Bishnu is represented and adopted by the people. Moreover, the name

Bhuban initially may have come from the Shiva temple called Bhubaneshwar temple situated above the cave site and perhaps originally Orissa, which was built by the local Kachari kings. There is a possibility of the reformers hearing of this temple and visiting the site as 'the people of the plains' were doing, perhaps to give some sort of legitimacy to their reform message. But to refer to the Bhuban of Bhuban Hill synonymously with Munseniu/Bishnu can be quite complicating. Clearly, in this case, Bishnu seems to be semantically similar to Vishnu and the connection between Bhuban and Munseniu/Bishnu is probably a later identification brought about by the reformers who had access to Bhuban Hill. However, there is no obvious acknowledgement by the Poupei Chapriak or the Heraka that this is the case. For them, Bhuban/Munseniu/Bishnu are clearly the same as well as local.[11] Therefore, in what seems to be an odd but interesting appropriation of the word Bhuban, they simply use it to make the connection with Munseniu/Bishnu. So Bhuban, Munseniu/Bishnu are used interchangeably (see Figure 2.1).

There are various possibilities that emerge from this discussion. Generally, there is much 'Sanskritic' terminology used by the Heraka and Poupei Chapriak (Bishnu, Bhuban, pujari, Bhagwan, etc.). Clearly, at some period there has been a Brahminic, Vaishnava and/or Shaiva influence on what was a more ancient site. The Nagas could have been involved before or after this. If before, they seem to have accepted the identification of local gods with pan-Hindu deities and then made some attempts to relocalize them. If after, they attempted to associate with powerful external gods, such as Vishnu, who possibly represented an almighty presence, similar to their own God, Tingwang (god of the sky) or Tingkao Ragwang (Supreme God).

The Cave Ritual: Life, Death, Life

Early the next morning, at 5 a.m., we make the trek towards the cave. The cave is a short distance away from the camp-site. When we reach the cave, there are two entrances to cross to get to a level ground in front of the mouth of the cave: one of them has been closed off, while the other one is open and this is the one used by all pilgrims.[12] We remove our shoes and place them just outside this entrance adding to a large pile of the most colourful footwear. We squeeze into the oval shaped opening (the entrance of Rani Gaidinliu) and into the large space outside the cave. The crowd has already gathered there facing east, towards the entrance of Rani Gaidinliu. People are dressed in their traditional attire, sombre, huddled together

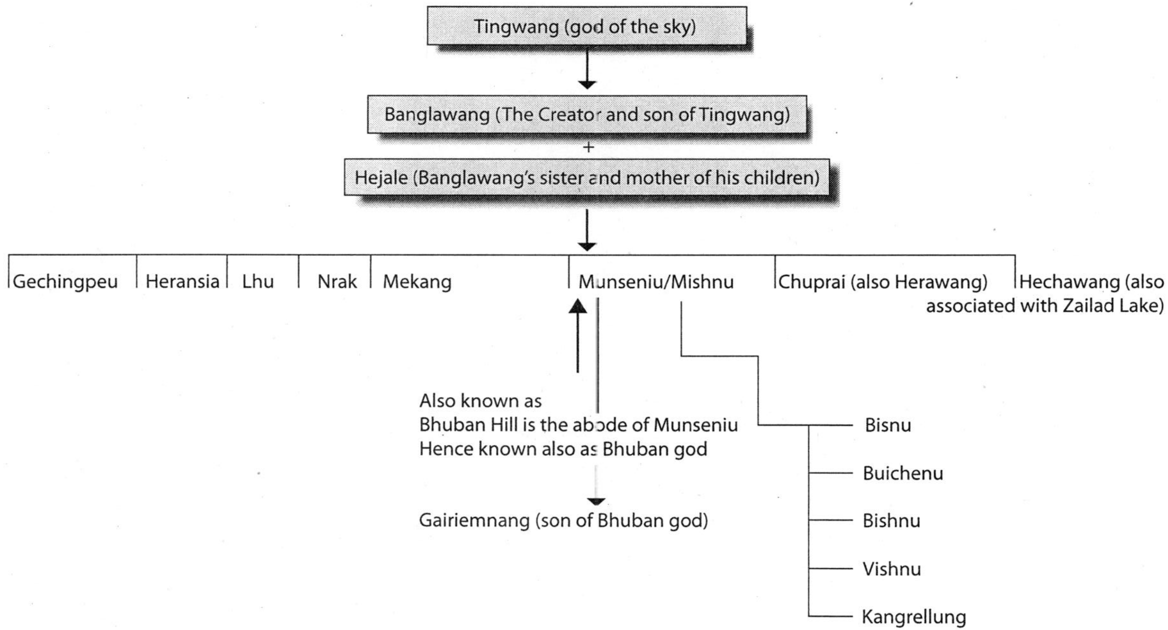

Figure 2.1 Zeliangrong gods: A Zeme Heraka version

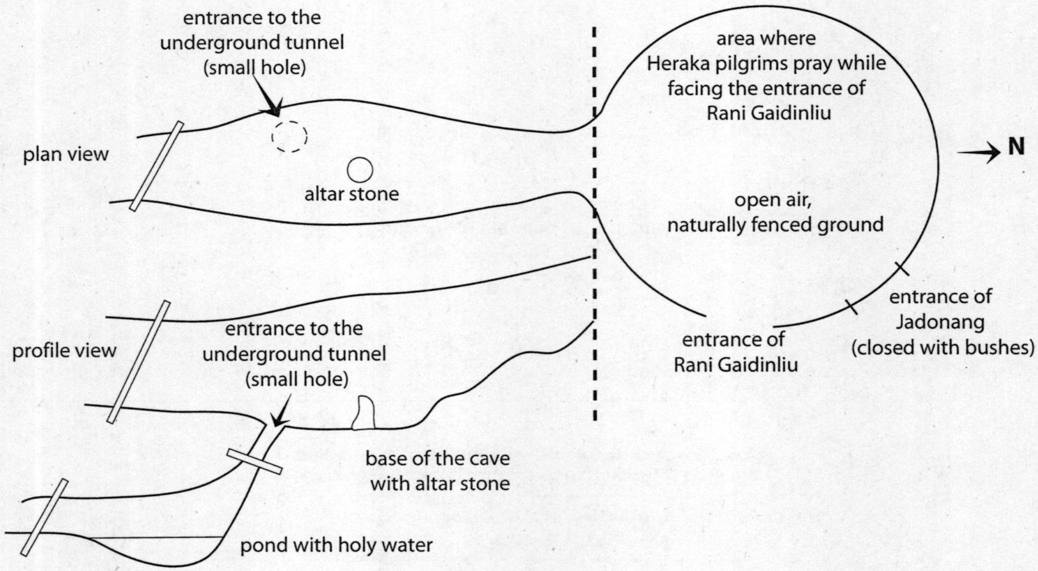

FIGURE 2.2 Bhuban cave area

Photograph 2.2 Heraka pilgrims outside the Bhuban cave during the Sunrise Prayer

as they let the morning chill pass over them. The sun slowly rises above the hills as drops of light splash onto the oily black hairs of their heads, one by one. People gather their thoughts while the giant mouth of the cave provides a contrast with the light. It appeared to me to be a blackened surface, open, welcoming, embracing (see Figure 2.2).

The sunrise prayer (*naimik kakelum*) begins with three young boys dressed in traditional Zeme clothes as they 'salute to the sun' (an interesting RSS and 'Hindu' connotations) (see Photograph 2.2). It resembles a physical drill, a slowly choreographed jumping-jack routine with a military style salute. The people sing 'Cheham Rani'[13] three times, signifying the process of rebirth, life-death-life (*keringbe-kechaibe-keringbe*). When the song finishes, the Paipeu (elder) steps forward away from the people and says a prayer with folded hands. Then, they slowly turn around and facing the cave, sing the song 'Ai Liangrina Bhuban Ragwang Gaiye'[14] three times.

After the prayers have been said, people start milling around the entrance to the actual cave. Below one can see an unknown figure dressed in orange sitting on the flat stone at the base of the cave. He slowly rises from his seat, and starts walking upward. The crowd light their candles and make their way down the cave.

There are no easy paths down the cave; one has to step on protruding rocks, moist ground and bat excrement. Drops of water fall from the roof of the cave and bat excrement, with its pungent smell, forms white etchings on the rocks, providing the only colour to the earthen surroundings. People whisper about the orange clad 'sadhu'(holy man) now making his way up effortlessly. His hair is a mass of matted locks, his face is unwashed and marked with what seems to be black paste smudged below his eyes and on his cheeks. He walks meditatively, perhaps aware of the throngs of silent people passing by, perhaps preoccupied with the blissful quiet of the abyss. One feels a sense of trepidation, perhaps a benign threat, as one ventures into the depths of the earth, as if sucked into a womb. Such fear is alleviated as the hundreds around walk in the solemn realization that they have come here not only to confront some fear but also in an awareness that something might be gained. Old, young, men, women, walk hand in hand as we reach the base of the cave.

Those who reach first start lighting candles and incense on the big stone which is used as an altar. Some women bring flowers, others money: all put them on the altar situated in the middle of the cave, believed to be the place where Rani Gaidinliu prayed to the God Tingwang on her visits to Bhuban cave. Once most of the people have gathered below, each one of them takes a candle and circumambulates the large altar three times, representing the notion of life-death-life. They move anticlockwise while saying a silent prayer. The pilgrims believe that one of the most important and auspicious events for the Heraka is the pilgrimage to the cave: ideally, it should be done three times over a lifetime. Because of the effort involved in accomplishing the pilgrimage, it is believed that prayers will be answered for rewards relating to the arduousness of the journey (Daniel 1984). The circumambulation of the altar represents completion, a ritual pattern that signifies what the Heraka promise. There is life after death, symbolized by the circling of the stone. Once they complete the cycle, they offer their prayers again in front of the altar. When the prayers have been said, the younger people get ready to go down to the bottom of the cave through a tiny hole leading to an underground tunnel and the pond below. The water of the pond is supposed to be miraculous and a potent healing agent for sicknesses and ailments. They refer to the water as 'talau ndui' (holy water). The young men and women gather their water jugs, large plastic canisters, and make their way through the tiny hole. This is an effort as, once they pass through the small opening, they have to climb down with the roof touching their backs for another 1 km, before finally reaching the pond. The pond is around 20 metres in length and 10 metres in breadth. The pilgrims fill their jugs with this water while standing knee deep in the pond; most people carry water back for their respective villages that will be used for special ritual occasions.[15] They return to the camp-site after four or five arduous hours.

Enumerating Ritual Space: Poupei Chapriak and Heraka Dynamics

As most of the young people go down to retrieve the holy water, I stay back with the elders to talk about the importance of the cave. While we are conversing, a group of young Rongmei Poupei Chapriaks arrive at the cave altar with some live hens. They say their prayers and then attempt to offer the hens to the god of the altar. A Heraka elder is standing beside the altar collecting the money left by the Heraka pilgrims. When the Poupei Chapriaks approach to put the hen as a gift on the altar, the Heraka elder absolutely refuses saying 'this is not our [Heraka] custom'. The Poupei Chapriaks argue for a while saying that there is nothing wrong in giving a gift to God by placing it on the altar; the Heraka elder retorts by saying that 'in our custom we do not follow any form of sacrifice or even gifts of animals to be placed before God.' Annoyed by the situation, a Poupei Chapriak places the hen on his forehead and lets go of the hen as an offering, watching it flutter over the altar, to the obvious consternation of the Heraka elder.

It is almost 8.30 a.m. in the morning and we have been here for around three hours. More and more Poupei Chapriaks are coming down to the cave to perform their ritual before the altar. The Paipeu (Heraka elder) decides to leave the cave. He gathers those remaining in the cave and together they say the benedictory prayer 'Dinkiuming' before making the climb back to the top of the cave. As they are leaving, a Poupei Chapriak *pujari* storms into the cave; he comes running down hurriedly uttering something in Rongmei. Behind him, his disciples are shouting 'don't leave, don't leave' in Hindi. It is obviously addressed to the Heraka. The remaining Heraka people ignore the plea and leave quietly. The Poupei Chapriak *pujari* stands in the altar and strikes his spear on the ground five times, angered by the refusal of the Heraka to listen to him. He stands there fuming, clad in his Rongmei traditional clothes and covered in necklaces of prayer beads. For a moment he just stands. He then orders his disciples to clear and clean the altar area with water. The Heraka people have left candles, incense and paper (from the candles), which the *pujari* considers a mess. A Poupei Chapriak disciple later told me that '*Bhagwan* [god] has gone inside his [*pujari*] heart; he has come from far away and *Bhagwan* has gone inside him . . . We [referring to all of us] need to ask for forgiveness as we have committed a grave sin, that is why we asked the Heraka people to stay behind.' He also said that the Heraka had left a mess and desacralized the holy space. They then lit a fire with the wood they had brought and as people came down, the Poupei Chapriak ritual began.

Analysis: Reform and Discourse

While the cave represents wholly different things for the various religious groups, the disputed space and rituals associated with it are deep seated, embodied in the processes of history and its subsequent interpretations. While the Poupei Chapriak maintain their 'original' status by declaring the preservation of 'traditional' culture, the Heraka, on the other hand, argue that the origins of Heraka preceded those of Poupei Chapriak and that Poupei Chapriak is but a corruption of the original Heraka. It is the Heraka who are 'original'. The process of returning to the original state is the goal of the Heraka. For example, the rejection of sacrifices on the altar of the cave by the Heraka is not only connected with the gradual economic reforms which led to village reorganization during the mid-twentieth century but it also envisages a state of purity where no sacrifices are necessary. The Heraka reform encouraged the change from complex agricultural patterns to a simpler form that reduced sacrifices connected with the efficacy of crops. The change entailed revising Zeme history. To do this, the Heraka have resurrected key folk heroes and gods to make their history viable against that of the Poupei Chapriaks, and to position their argument for legitimation effectively within the Zeme world-view. For instance, it is believed that after the death of Herakandingpeu (a mythical and renowned folk healer), humans were corrupted by vicious and bloodthirsty gods who constantly demanded sacrifices. The Heraka hold the view that the latter stage is embodied in the Poupei Chapriak practice (see Chapter 4).

The disparity in their religious tradition becomes evident within the setting of the cave. For instance, the Heraka rotate around the big stone altar three times, anticlockwise, while the Poupei Chapriaks rotate five times, clockwise. The authority of the *pujari* for the Poupei Chapriak is absolute and they are singular in their devotion, while for the Heraka there is no priestly figure that wields such authority. The only veneration is for Ranima. 'For us the cave is important because it is from here that we got our message', the Heraka Paipeu in the pilgrimage told me, 'but there is no such importance for the Poupei Chapriaks in Bhuban cave. The only reason they come to the cave is because of Ranima and since she is Rongmei, now, the Poupei Chapriaks want to absorb her teachings into their religion and make it popular.'

This tug of war between these two opposing groups raises important issues about the nature of revivalism and reform in religious communities. Such processes attempt to address questions of ethnicity, religious affiliations and influences, and where national loyalties lie. These loyalties are tested every time the pilgrimage gets under way, which, among the 'Nagas' occur once annually during the month of February. The 'mela' often carries with it 'Hindu' overtones; but both the groups deny any links with Hinduism. Due to their geography (being in Cachar district), the Poupei Chapriak are naturally influenced by Bengali Vaishnavism. They vehemently deny these links or the fact that they have been influenced at all by the Shiva temple. They claim that they are an 'indigenous faith' who count Jadonang as a prophet who reformed their practice. The Heraka similarly reject any connection with Hinduism and also claim Jadonang as their own. Despite the fact that both religious groups acknowledge Jadonang, their practice relating to him is very different. Part of the reason lies in the influence of Ranima on the Heraka, and the greater influence of Jadonang on Poupei Chapriak (it is difficult to speculate the reasons behind this). Another part is connected with the way reform has shaped the Heraka. They have become affiliated with various 'Hindu organizations' such as the RSS and Vishva Hindu Parishad (VHP) and adopted their reactionary rhetoric against Christianity. These constitute important points in the process of Heraka reform.

It must be stressed that the Heraka reform is not merely rhetorical or defined by the desire to exclude others, it is also grounded in human emotions and experiences. In this respect, people often recount the experience of going to the Bhuban cave as visceral in its depth and emotion. By drawing attention to the latter, I am attempting to explore what people think of their experiences during the pilgrimage. Their responses have led me to believe that such a pilgrimage resonates with how the Heraka reform is itself changing amidst the chatter of the world.

Cave Experiences: Coalescing Religious Traditions

I now propose to recount briefly two experiences to demonstrate the vitality of the cave and what it represents to the people in its imaginative and intuitive quality. While the cave represents the various practices and views associated with it, it also signifies pivotal landmarks for the adherents as they make their annual trips. Peule, a Zeme Heraka, recollects her experience:

> I have been to the cave five times. I first went there when I was 15 years old. During that time I was not in good health, and even the doctor could not heal me. So I asked the Rongmei Poupei Chapriak *sadhu* in the cave about this and he advised me not to marry immediately but to first be healed by visiting the cave five times. Following his advice, I visited the cave five times and I was healed. The *sadhu* then told me to marry; he said, as a human being, one must get married.
>
> When I visited the cave the first time nothing happened, but on the roof of the cave I saw a form of a tiger. The second time I saw a soldier but I can't remember what he was carrying. The third time, I saw a statue of a *sadhu*. A prophet from the Zeme community, Namke Kuame, told me that when we see pictures of saints, God will bless those who are witness to such an event and I was indeed blessed. The fourth time, I saw a *mithun* [also known as an Indian Bison]. The fifth time, I saw a statue of Ranima. On this visit, along with my friends we came down and took the ashes from the fire in front of the cave as a cure for our cough. At that time, the white bats inside the cave (who come out when people make too much noise) rushed towards us. Afraid of them we ran from there carrying the ashes. We then asked the Poupei Chapriak *sadhu* what the statue of Ranima represented, he told us 'God said, the visits are enough, it is too much for you.' That was the last time I went.

Interestingly, when I visited Peule again at her house in Hsongle, she organized a prayer meeting, because as she said, 'certain things were not going according to plan as my husband and I thought they would'. She told me that the idea for the prayer was organized by the Poupei Chapriak *sadhu* she met in the Bhuban cave. She later told me that she saw no problem with the Poupei Chapriak *sadhu* leading the prayer because they pray to the same God, Tingwang. A similar incident is recounted in the administrative reports when a Zeme goes to see a 'Naga sadhu', a 'Kabui [Rongmei] Naga of Jongkao who possessed 'healing powers'.[16] The present Poupei Chapriak *sadhu* comes from the same region, which shows how similar exchanges were taking place during the 1930s as well. I was curious how these two world-views interacted because most people from either camp see it otherwise: namely, that each represents different things in terms of religious worship and embodies a distinct identity through historical narrative. While they seem to share a common historical narrative of the cave, their ritual in the cave again highlights their differences. It makes it difficult for the Heraka to recognize that their reform is based on traditional Poupei Chapriak elements.[17] The Heraka accuse the Poupei Chapriak of being 'evil' corruptors of the original Heraka practice. This view of the Heraka is adopted by most of the Heraka and pits them against the Poupei Chapriak. They do not recognize the common thread that runs through both the Heraka and Poupei Chapriak. In fact, what is surprising in Peule's account is her acceptance of the *sadhu* as a holy person in whom she genuinely believes. Ideologies in this sense collide and then coalesce in an acknowledgement of each other's belonging in the cosmos, here represented through the imagery of the cave and the experience it engenders. However, this debate seems far from over as each religious claim affirms a certain history, and a certain religious practice that claims to be 'original' and, perhaps in the process, excludes others from that particular world-view. The juxtaposition of exclusion and inclusion, of change and tradition, is again reflected in the cave with its myriad symbols. These symbols are evident in the next account.

Heulung, another Heraka follower, told me:

> I went to Bhuban ki [house] twice. In 1982 when I first went, there was no proper way to the cave so we went through the jungle. When we reached 'Gairiemnang tingkun' which was near the present Gairiemnang Memorial Hall, I saw the wall made by the British Government. Near the wall, I saw eight mango trees and eight jackfruit trees. On that day, when we reached the place, there was heavy rain. We decided to pray for the rain to stop because we could not cook or sleep. So we sang *Ragwang Damtong*[18] and *Ndibangtu*.[19] After the songs, the rain stopped and the sky cleared. Early next morning we went to the cave and after going down to the base of the cave, beside the altar stone, a small pool of holy water, *talau ndui*, had collected from the roof of the cave. Behind the altar stone there was another stone shaped like an *almirah* [wardrobe]. In those days the stone altar was straight, but now it is slightly tilted. This I could see in my second visit, but the *almirah* was no longer there. Like the Bhuban ki that changes, humans also change year by year. When someone visited before, what they told me, I could not see or find. Though we do not meet Tingwang in the cave, with the changes in the Bhuban ki, we can know that Tingwang is there changing the world year after year.

> Not only do the Heraka visit the cave but it is also visited by all the humans of the earth. That is why, through them, we believe that Bhuban ki is a holy place.

In both these accounts, the importance of the reform is clearly highlighted. The Heraka reform has a way of accommodating practices and symbols that to an outsider might seem mutually conflicting or incompatible with being 'Naga'. This is clearly seen in the example of Peule's belief in the *sadhu* as representing a similar cosmology to that of the Heraka or Heulung's eloquent narrative of how the world is changing year after year, even though the Heraka are espousing the need to preserve tradition while also encouraging change. The strength of the Heraka reform lies in the paradox that it refuses to be boxed into a certain category, while looking to the past for stability and the maintaining of tradition. In both these accounts, the cave becomes the conduit for this experience of reform to be taken forward. It also highlights the imaginative and intuitive quality of their experience in Bhuban ki without necessarily abiding by codified Heraka laws of either/or; they profess multiple belongings that locate their experience in the body of the world.

Pilgrimage: Authenticity over Communitas

In this connection, I propose to draw attention, briefly, to Victor and Edith Turner's seminal work on the understanding of pilgrimage as a re-enactment of communitas (1978). I want especially to question the understanding of communitas as a celebration of common humanity through the 'emergence of the integral person from multiple personae' (1978: 34; cited in Eade and Sallnow 2000: x). Michael Sallnow, in particular, questions the validity of the applicability of the notion of communitas in pilgrimage because, according to him, the Turners have divorced pilgrimage from the larger cultural and political agenda. In his study of the High Andes of Peru, pilgrimages 'stimulate neighbourhood factionalism, foster inter-community conflict, and generate new ethnically-based hierarchies of control' (1981: 180). In effect, says Sallnow, 'when people converge in pilgrimage, meanings collide' (Eade and Sallnow 2000: 137). In the pilgrimage to the Bhuban cave, a similar scene unfolds. Though there is relative calm at the sharing of the camp, when it comes to the religious enactment inside the cave, the scene is loaded with meaning, and is open to tension.

The rituals accompanying the pilgrims in the cave question the very fabric of Zeliangrong as a composite ethnic group who struggle to understand the Heraka and the Poupei Chapriak reform. It appears that both have a particular history which posits either Jadonang or Gaidinliu as their main inspiration. In fact, according to Gaidinliu's account she is clearly chosen over Jadonang by Tingwang to lead the Zeliangrong people (see Chapter 6). Communitas, in the way the Turners envision it, never occurs, because the religious rituals constantly question 'authenticity' and the triumph of 'tradition' suppresses the feeling of communitas. In this sense, the notion of the Zeliangrong is fractured. We need to contest the Heraka claim that it represents all the Zeliangrong people, as religious meanings in the cave alter any notion of communitas by giving rise to division into ethnic claims of 'authenticity'.

Conclusion

At the centre of the Heraka reform is the notion that somehow it has not fundamentally changed. Opponents, on the other hand, say that it has changed completely and has embraced Hinduism – the Heraka adherents are often known as 'Hindu'. Some also hold the view that it is a completely alien religion implanted from the imagination of a select group of people. It appears that these challenges are inevitable for a reform movement like the Heraka who are peeling the layers of the onion and trying to uncover the 'original' core. What the original core represents is ambiguous, but by displaying an inherent sophistication in dealing with what 'original' is, by referring to Zeme history and the presence of the Heraka since time immemorial, they are equipped to argue that they represent something in its earliest and therefore 'purer' form. In common with Christians and 'Hindus', this process reveals the discourse by which a reform movement like the Heraka is contesting, redefining and revising opinions. This makes the Heraka an expression of a changing world amidst the cacophony of dominant religious groups like the Christians and the Hindus. Maintaining a balance between the influences of the latter two religious traditions while drawing attention to their own traditions, makes the Heraka a marginal yet significant religious movement. That is why, as Heulung recounts, the Heraka are not caught up in the trap of rigid traditions that refuse to change. By using the imagery of the cave and its changing nature, they are able to envisage a changing world in which the Heraka are not only bystanders but are also changing through participation, and whereby a new agency is affirmed in the process. This change has repercussions for the debate on religious modernization, ethnic constructions and boundaries that are central to the study of any reform movement (Oberoi 1997; Sen 2003).

From the mouth of the cave to the outside world is where the next chapter will take us. I have already pointed out the significance of Bhuban cave as the point of genesis for the Heraka. Indeed, through the years it has undergone numerous changes and phases that were both a response to and agent of change. This is an ongoing process that is analysed in the following chapters. However, the point of impact of the Heraka reform is first felt in the early 1930s in North Cachar Hills, Assam. The popularity of Gaidinliu provided the base for this change. This is the focus of the next chapter.

Chapter 3

Millenarianism and Refashioning the Social Fabric

The Gaidinliu movement or the Heraka, as it came to be known in later years, spread in the North Cachar Hills, Assam, from 1930s onwards. It had a reformist message which aimed to alter the rituals associated with the swidden (or 'slash and burn') agricultural cycle, locally known as jhuming. I will argue that the reforms were mainly in response to the scarcity of food, and to alleviate what Michael Adas calls feelings of 'frustrated hope' (1974: 202–3). The Heraka called for a reduction in animal sacrifices associated with various agricultural rituals. For villages governed by the rituals of agricultural cycle, altering the latter in any way not only altered the lives of the villagers but also affected their world-view. I argue that the necessity for change was primarily due to two interrelated reasons: cycle migration and Kuki immigration.

The Zeme practice of 'cycle migration', first, refers to migration from one village location to another – as opposed to swidden cultivation which involves a shift of only cultivated sites – cultivating and then abandoning the site to return to it over a period of time for obtaining optimum agricultural yield. It was a common feature of Zeme agriculture (see also von Fürer Haimendorf 1946: 78–93; Hutton 1969: 72–84). It was also a protection against any diseases that an older site might have been associated with. Second, the settling of Kuki people in Zeme land at the behest of British colonial officers, who were not aware of the Zeme system of 'cycle migration' and agricultural practices, caused land shortages which affected Zeme economy.[1] Paucity of new sites for swidden or *jhum* cultivation, and an inability to return to the older sites (which were now occupied by the Kuki people) were responsible for low agricultural yield and ensuing shortage of food. This gave rise to widespread dissent which the Heraka movement was able to capitalize on by suggesting alteration of rituals and promises of a 'golden age' of material prosperity. This alteration of rituals affected the village organization and the social hierarchy, as I shall discuss below. Consequently, this effected a reinterpretation of tradition over the years. The Heraka, the successor of the Gaidinliu movement, became the embodiment of this new system of religious attitude in relation to economic realities. To espouse an integrated economic system on a par with the reform message, the reorganization of the Heraka village was also necessary. This was done by renewing the village according to Heraka Hingde (rules governing everyday life).

In this chapter, I will consider two examples to demonstrate this point. The first example argues that by changing the name of the village, the village is renewed and cleansed of the past. It also examines how the Heraka negotiate with the Paupaise (ancestral practice) in forming a distinct Heraka practice when establishing a village. The second example examines how the Heraka use history as a tool to indigenize the past and make certain claims. This is done by using the rhetoric of reform, and attempting to project a world that is changing. Both these examples illustrate that the reform the Heraka were espousing was not a wholesale abandonment of former practices, but a gradual movement embracing both the traditional and the modern. First, however, we start at the beginning of the movement.

Beginnings: Jadonang and Gaidinliu

Between 1929 and 1931 a series of entries were made in the Administrative Reports of Manipur and Assam regarding Jadonang, a Kabui Naga, and his cousin Gaidinliu. They were accused of plotting a rebellion against the British and the Kukis settlers.[2] In these Reports Jadonang is referred to as 'messiah', 'healer', *maiba* (priest), 'king', 'spirit king' while Gaidinliu is called *maibi* (priestess) and later as a 'sorceress'.[3] They professed to establish a 'Naga Raj' by ousting the British and massacring the Kukis, who were seen as the enemies of the Kabui and Kacha Nagas. The enmity between Kuki and the Kabui (Rongmei) and Kacha (Zeme) Nagas can be traced back to the Kuki Rebellion (1917–19), which erupted primarily against the British on the issue surrounding the recruitment of Kuki manpower for the Labour Corps during the First World War. Under the pretext of the Rebellion, some Kuki villages allegedly attacked Kabui and Kacha villages to settle 'old scores'. This gave rise to ethnic tensions in the late 1920s and early 1930s fuelling the 'Jadonang movement' (Singh 1992; Parratt 2005). From 1930–1 the 'Jadonang movement' pronounced certain measures against the British as well as the Manipuri King such as the non-payment of house tax to the colonial administration, the rejection of the *pothang* system of labour,[4] and disobedience towards the *lambus* (government appointed interpreters). However, the movement claimed that the house tax and *mithun* (semi-wild bison) should be given to Jadonang, who claimed to be the new King or 'Raja' (Kamei 2004: 152–3).

Jadonang, was born in Kambiron, a Rongmei (or Kabui) village in Tamenglong district, Manipur, around 1905 (Kamei 2002a: 14). Jadonang claimed miraculous powers and divine ordination from *Tingkao Ragwang*, the Kabui supreme being. Jadonang professed he had 'visions' and 'trances' during which he could commune with *Tingkao Ragwang* who 'took him to heaven' and showed him 'many of the secret things [rituals?] done by people before his time' (Pamei 2001: 39). Claiming divine sanctions through the visions, and also from his visits to Bhuban cave in Cachar district, Jadonang devised rituals based on traditional Kabui religious practice. It is claimed that these practices were closer to the Vaishnavite traditions of the dominant Meitei community of Manipur; Jadonang claimed to be a *maiba* or priest in Meitei (Manipuri) religious tradition. During this time, Christian missions were also gaining a foothold in the region. For some Zeme, Christianity was the answer to escape the burdens of ancestral traditions and for others it was Heraka. Perhaps in a response to Christian missionary activity, Jadonang also advocated adoption of *Tingkao Ragwang* as the only god, encouraging the abandonment of the minor, local gods (see Chapter 4; also Eaton 1984: 1–43).

Jadonang built temples for worship and claimed closeness with the Hindu God Vishnu. These temples were destroyed by the British in their attempt to halt the movement. J. C. Higgins, the Political Agent of Manipur wrote in his reports that he was told that destroying the temple did not interfere with the Kabui practice of 'animistic religion' as it was not their custom 'to have temples for their gods'. These temples, Higgins continues, appeared to have originated in the brain of Jadonang (see Chapter 4).[5]

The progress of the 'Jadonang movement' initiated by Jadonang came to a halt when C. Gimson, the Deputy Commissioner of Cachar, arrested him in Lakhipur. He was transferred to Manipur where he was later executed in Imphal jail on 29 August 1931. He was charged with the murder of two Manipuri traders who were allegedly sacrificed to 'his god'. Gaidinliu, Jadonang's cousin, a young girl of 16, is said to have escaped to the North Cachar Hills where she found refuge and support among the Zeme Nagas.[6]

Gaidinliu was born in the same district (Tamenglong) as Jadonang, in the village of Lungkao on 26 January 1915 (Kamei 2004: 157). Gaidinliu was also Rongmei. She apparently came into contact with Jadonang around 1926 or 1927 during her visit to Kambiron to get her dreams interpreted by Jadonang. This meeting, recounts one historian, was the 'beginning of a master and disciple relationship' (2004: 158). Gaidinliu was apparently impressed by Jadonang's teachings and his healing powers, while Jadonang admired Gaidinliu's steely determination and her devotion to his teachings. As to their relationship, we gain some insight through Gaidinliu's biography, but generally it remains rather sketchy (see Chapter 6).

Generally, we hear of Gaidinliu only in relation to Jadonang during the early stages of the movement. She is often portrayed in administrative reports as a *maibi* (priestess) and Jadonang as a *maiba* (priest) within the Meitei tradition, while local historians locate them within the tradition of seers or shamans (see Kamei 2002a: 18). For example, in his statement before the Political Agent of Manipur on 23 March 1931, after Jadonang was arrested on 19 February 1931, he says,

> I have been a *maiba*, God anointed priest, for four years. Kangrellung, the god of the Bhuban Hills appeared to me in a dream and told me to become a *maiba*. I do not know if the Kabuis call me a god: I am not a god. I built temples because the Bhuban god told me in a dream that there would be prosperity and good health for every one if I did so, although it is not our custom to build temples.[7]

The role of a *maiba* is an important part of the Meitei cosmology, especially when it comes to understanding the relationship between the deities and the people. Arambam and John Parratt (1997: 18) observe that the *maiba* (priest) and *maibi* (priestess) are still crucial in establishing a connection with the pre-Hindu Meitei religious culture. This is effected through the current ritual of Lai Haraoba (pleasing of the gods) which is interpreted by some as a revival, opposed to the resurgent Brahminical 'Indianise Manipur' movement.[8] It is the *maibas* and *maibis* who operate as oral transmitters and are responsible for preserving the wording of the Haraoba. Besides this, their other functions are offering gifts and sacrifices to the gods in their role as priest and priestess. Indeed, their role as mediums between the deity and the human is their most significant contribution (1997: 19, 34–5). However, it is usually the *maibi* who is privileged over the *maiba*. This is because the *lais* (gods) take more pleasure in women, who are far more likely to be possessed than men. For instance, when a man does get possessed by the *lai*, he traditionally wears the female *maibi* apparel and is referred to as a 'male maibi' (1997: 33).

Maibas are generally male and they have a different function within the Meitei cosmology. They are 'traditional physicians' who cure people of their physical, psychological and spiritual illnesses (Brara 1998: 143). This tends to support the idea that Jadonang was recognized as a *maiba*, and Gaidinliu as *maibi* in the Meitei tradition. Where Jadonang's function as a *maiba* is concerned, he says, 'Kangrellung . . . appeared to me in a dream and told me to become a *maiba*'. The identity of Kangrellung is elusive; though, there seems to be some suggestions that Kangrellung could be a form of the God Vishnu (see Chapter 2). The importance of dreams was a vital part of the local cosmology which clearly interacted with Jadonang's activities as a *maiba*. For instance, on one occasion, it is said that, the entire village in Puilon (in the Tamenglong district of Manipur) was affected by scarcity of food owing to the failure of crops. After 'dream consultation' with *Tingkao Ragwang*, he instructed the villagers to sacrifice a *mithun* as an appeasement to God. After some hesitation, the villagers sacrificed a*mithun* and, as prophesized by Jadonang, they were blessed by a prosperous harvest (Zeliang 1998: 7; Kamei 2002a: 21). A thorough consideration of the sources reveals that dreams play a significant role in determining many of Jadonang's activities. For instance, he dreamt of a 'fakir' (a person who survives on alms) whom he later met; certain prayer and worship rituals were revealed to him in a dream; similarly it was in dreams that he learned that sacrifices of *mithuns* would lead to prosperity in rice and money; the meeting with Gaidinliu occurred because she wanted her dreams interpreted; finally Jadonang was led to Bhuban and Zailad, a lake god, by 'Raguang' (God) first in a dream.

Jadonang's dreams were viewed as coming from 'gods he has invented' – a declaration on his mental capacity made by the Civil Surgeon examining him during his murder trial. The surgeon believed that while his mental state during his dreams and visions was abnormal, it was normal during his actions at the time of the murder. Further, his activities are seen as those of a high priest, whose stock-in-trade is visions of gods. Jadonang is alleged to combine this with the 'lucrative profession of medicine man and interpreter of dreams, the interpretations being communicated to him by his gods in these nocturnal visions'.[9] Reported statements by Jadonang may give the impression that the accusations are not unfounded, for he himself confesses that 'I cannot dream unless I have *zu*, rice-beer'. Further, he says 'I get Rs. 4/- for praying for the dead, a bottle of *zu* for interpreting dreams, and Rs. 3/- for treating the sick, when the patient recovers: if he does not, the money is returned'.[10]

This is followed by the statement 'I do not know if the Kabuis call me a god: I am not a god.' Although Jadonang himself does not believe that he is a god, some statements corroborate the view that he was indeed considered a god,[11] a *maiba* and even a messiah or a Naga king.[12]

Millenarian Songs: The World has Changed

The historical trajectory of the 'Jadonang movement' is difficult to follow considering the various adjectives attributed to him (messiah, priest, shaman, healer, prophet, king, spirit king). However, Jadonang's successor Gaidinliu, on the other hand, gave a clear millenarian direction to the movement. There is a plethora of definitions concerning millenarian activities, but Kenelm Burridge's classic definition corresponds closely with my analysis of the Gaidinliu movement in its psychological, political and sociological as well as economic aspects. Burridge defines millenarian movements as

> the adoption of new assumptions, a new redemptive process, a new politico-economic framework, a new mode of measuring the man, a new integrity, a new community: in short, a new man. A precondition of this regeneration is dissatisfaction with the current system. (Burridge 1969: 13)

For some the arrival of a 'hero' is the first step to finding a 'messiah' or 'prophet' for this 'new redemptive process' (Burridge 1969: 3, 11–12).[13] The way this 'new redemptive process' is considered to unfold can vary. It can be seen as a process of 'revival' or 'revitalization' (Wallace 1956: 264–81) rather than just a responsive function to the present condition. For others, the notion of 'nativism' (Linton and Hallowell 1943; Norman Friedman 1967) that attempts to revive aspects of a 'golden past' as a reaction against the dominant cultural discourse seems more attractive. Other movements like the 'cargo cults' focus on the anticipated millennial event that will bring abundant Western cargo (Burridge 1969; Worsley 1970). Some view millenarian activities as the basic or archaic form of class struggle (Lanternari 1963; Hobsbawm 1965).

The Gaidinliu movement fits several of these paradigms. It incorporated myths of a 'golden age' that sought to attract people who were experiencing famine and loss of land as a result of population pressure on land caused by Kuki immigrants (see below). The movement promised prosperity by praying to *Zailad*, a Zeme Lake god, and to Zeme sky god, Tingwang. The movement claimed that signs of this 'golden age' would appear when taxes formerly paid to the British government were instead paid to the Gaidinliu movement, and when the Kukis were driven off Zeme land. Songs were used as a medium of spreading this new message. Strands of what Wallace calls 'revitalization movement' – as 'a deliberate, organized, conscious effort by members of a society to construct a more satisfying culture' (1956: 265) – are evident here.[14] These songs cleverly wove together powerful themes and stories of mythic heroes to evoke a sense of the 'golden past', which would mobilize the villager (see also Scott 1976: 234–40). For example, a popular song during this period was titled 'Kedeirei Se Keli Wang Jeu' (The World has Changed). The song contained references to folk heroes (such as 'Amang' an ingenious orphan) and sacred landscapes such as ponds along the river Barak which runs through most of North Cachar Hills.

These visions and themes continued to be important even after Gaidinliu was arrested in 1932 and imprisoned for 18 years. The reforms were carried forward by Gaidinliu's followers, some of whom claimed miraculous healing powers, thus attracting a large number of people to them. The British administration, however, did not see anything positive coming out of these 'mediums' or 'prophets'. J. H. Hutton, the British Political Agent, was of the view that, if anything, these uprisings only provided false hope to the villagers.[15]

Inventor of Religion

The British viewed the activities of Jadonang and Gaidinliu with suspicion. They saw this movement as practising a sort of 'debased Hinduism' that murdered four traders to be sacrificed to the 'Gods of the religion of which Jadonang was Priest and Gaidiliu [*sic*] Priestess and present features of a peculiarly brutal character'.[16] In fact, the British questioned Jadonang's mental faculties when he was interrogated for the murder of the four traders. The Civil Surgeon concluded that:

> The only uncertainty as to the propriety of convicting Jadonang of murder arises from the question as to whether he was mentally responsible for his actions at the time of the murder. It may be assumed that no inventor of a new religion is normal, for the reason that normal men are content with the religion of their fathers, or some existing religion. Jadonang's mental abnormality is further exhibited by the fact that he claims to receive visits from the gods which he has invented, in his dreams. But these gods never appear to him, except in dreams, and their alleged appearance is not improbably part of his stock in trade as high priest, with which he

> combines the lucrative profession of medicine man and interpreter of dreams, the interpretations being communicated to him by his gods in these nocturnal visions.[17]

The British officials did not know what to make of Jadonang and his activities and they remained doubtful of the seriousness of the 'new religion' Jadonang allegedly invented. The dismissive attitude of the British is further evident in their assessment of the Gaidinliu movement. J. P. Mills' report of 1932 mentions that its methods are 'nebulous' and that 'it depends on superstition and fear'. Its aims look towards the coming of a 'Naga King' who will subjugate the Kukis and disperse the British. The report further mentions that the immediate aim of Gaidinliu is 'undoubtedly notoriety'.[18]

The death of Jadonang, accused of murdering the traders in 1931 and the eventual capture of Gaidinliu in 1932, ends one chapter of the Jadonang and Gaidinliu movements. The spread of Gaidinliu's message in North Cachar Hills among the Zeme would not be extinguished, as people still loyal to her and her teachings would continue the reform until her release from prison in 1954. The movement then takes another turn. The religious reforms going on in North Cachar Hills and some parts of the Naga Hills would finally coalesce to form the Heraka in 1974 under the leadership of Gaidinliu. Thus begins yet another chapter of the Heraka reforms.

Understanding the Problem

The Gaidinliu movement appealed to the people by combining emotional appeal with the devising of practical reforms which reworked the Zeme ancestral rituals. To manage the reform, they had to focus on Zeme religious practice and economic problems. Thus reforms focused on rituals connected with the agricultural cycle comprising a series of animal sacrifices and 'non-working' days (*nrei*).

The sacrifices were made not only to appease the various deities and ensure a good crop. They were also undertaken to perform feasts of merit (*ka hingkuibe*) after the harvest. The performance of a series of such feasts earned a husband and wife social status. However, the rituals also required *nrei*, that is, a restriction on movement of people outside the demarcated geographical area (such as the family house, the village ward or the entire village). Such restrictions seriously limited the mobility of villagers. When education was introduced in Zeme areas such restrictions became a problem, as schools were located outside the village boundaries.[19] The Gaidinliu movement responded to this problem by eliminating the tradition of animal sacrifices and with it the restrictions on physical movement. This was one of the reasons that people converted to Heraka. As Heraka, they could venture out of the village, get education and find jobs. They also related the ensuing economic success to the blessing of Zeme sky god Tingwang.

The Burdens of Social Rank and Communal Wealth

Since the 1930s the reform message of the Gaidinliu movement has spread into most Zeme villages. Earlier physical symbols of Paupaise (ancestral religious practice) were replaced by new ideas brought in by the reform. Voicing her obvious displeasure, Ursula Graham Bower (later Ursula Betts), who spent a long period with the Zeme in North Cachar Hills during the 1930s and 40s, wrote, that monoliths, traditionally important in Zeme society, were being destroyed 'at the instance of Gaidiliu' [*sic*].[20] For the reformists, these represented the 'old' way of life, which they saw as a hindrance to their message. This illustrated the massive dislocation to the traditional world-view as symbols, such as the monoliths, which once made their world coherent and orderly, now represented disruption and chaos.

The monoliths were erected during major celebrations and feasts of merit. The aim of a feast of merit is to enable a person to gain social status by sharing his wealth with the rest of his community (von Fürer-Haimendorf 1946: 52). For instance, in traditional village organization the wealthiest person would perform feasts that required the construction of large houses called *kumarumki, kapeoki* and *hekuiki.*[21] These houses could only be built in sequence, the second only after the first was completed and so on. This required large expenses as each house usually took a year to complete; the performance of feasts also conferred status and prestige on the donor in his village.[22] The feast served a double function. The person gained merit through the feast, but at the same time, because of the excessive expense incurred by the feast, his economic wealth was reduced to that of the common villagers, thus reintegrating him into society (Stirn and van Ham 2003: 102; see also Betts 1950: 67–72). This reintegration is connected primarily with the economic aspect and not necessarily with the status gained during the feast.[23] In this sense, feasts convert material wealth into social rank, though we could also imply that the reverse is true.[24]

Associated with the feast were sacrifices that transform the feast into a work of merit (Hutton 1969: 345–50) and *neube* (usually a rite carrying certain prohibitions on particular social functions, such as abstinence from sexual activity, abstinence from travelling). A *neube* is often linked with a sacrifice of some kind and usually precedes it. A sacrifice is a 'purchase' from gods, who set the price on animals (Mauss 1990: 16), through a shaman or priest. This can involve a chicken, cow or *mithun*, depending on the occasion or the gravity of the illness: the rule is that the greater the need, the bigger the sacrifice.

With the advent of education this prohibition became a problem, as most of the schools were located outside the village boundaries. As I mentioned earlier, this was one of the reasons that people converted to Heraka. As Heraka, they could venture out of the village, get education and find jobs. Being Heraka eased the social burdens that being Paupaise entailed. In this sense, I was told, 'the Paupaise were ill equipped to deal with the changing world'.[25]

The performance of a feast of merit depended on the agricultural yield which in turn was associated with performance of various fertility rituals for a good crop. The traditional Zeme agricultural cycle required around 80 *herateube* or divinations by a shaman (female: *herakapui* and male: *herakapeu*). These provide omens as a guide to performance of rituals in a year. The divinations required a prescribed number of sacrifices intended to enhance the efficacy of the ritual. These sacrifices were an attempt to appease the gods, and a failure to carry them out or to do them incorrectly could have dire consequences for the village. Such failures would then require further sacrifices to resolve the problem. Consequently, such sacrifices demanded a huge investment which people could not afford during the 1930s, because of the pressure on land due to the British land policy and Kuki immigration. Therefore, Gaidinliu's reform banned sacrifices of larger animals while strategically allowing continued performance of those involving fowls.[26]

The Pau Cin Hau movement in the Chin Hills (present-day Mizoram and Myanmar) in the early 1900s took a similar approach: due to economic hardships it adopted a new God who required no sacrifices. Pau Cin Hau first meets this God in a dream who tells him that he is the one 'who made heaven and earth, men and animals, the sun, the moon and the stars and who has power to cure all sickness'. He recounts why he believed in this God:

> I had faith in him and in a moment was cured from my illness of fifteen years. During those years for the cure of that illness I had paid the sum of Rs. 400 in making sacrifices of various kinds of animals to the nats or demons. The cure of God was complete and cost nothing. (Census of India 1933: 217–18)

The abandonment of sacrifices due to its costliness and the ineffectual response of the 'nats or demons' became the initial impetus of this movement in the Chin Hills. Pau Cin Hau further reiterates the success of the movement:

> One wholesome effect of my teaching is that where formerly many who had nothing went into debt to obtain sacrificial offerings and so could neither afford to buy food nor pay their taxes, my followers being free from such expenses are in much better circumstances. (Census of India 1933: 217–18)

The relation between sacrifices and economic realities is quite common in the early phases of conversions to Christianity as well. In the 1950s, Barbara Boal similarly observes that the Konds of Orissa chose Christianity over their 'old religion' due to sacrifices being too costly:

> We are wearied of the never ending sacrifices.
>
> So much ritual-observances was destroying us; we couldn't afford it any longer.
>
> We exhausted our money without any profit whatever.
>
> The priest kept on telling me to sacrifice a pig. I sacrificed every pig in the village, and still I was sick.
>
> The cost of appeasing the spirits was ruining us – and our children still died anyway. So we came to try 'the new laws'. (1982: 194)

The economic benefits evident in the above examples were also attractive to the Zeme, as they realized the cost effectiveness of abandoning sacrifices. But in altering sacrifices as an important way of propitiating the gods, the structures to deal with these reforms also needed similar attention. The ban extended to installation of monoliths as symbols of status and those who were connected with it, that is, the landowner (*kedeipeu, kadepeo*) and the priest (*tingkopau*). This meant Gaidinliu's reformists had to devise a way to replace the 'old' system of landowners and priestly power.. This was effectively done by creating a new non-hereditary position of the Paipeu or 'village elder' based on the wealth of the individual.

The Organization of a Village: Habitats and Conditions

In the pre-Heraka era the landowners (*kedeipeu*) maintained an economy that subsisted through the use of multisited fields and shifting village sites by a system of 'cycle migration'. Along with the priest (*tingkopau*) the *kedeipeu* maintained a strict ritual regimen which legitimized the importance and pattern of land ownership.

Paupaise villages were established by the *kedeipeu* as the first settler and thus the owner of the land. *Kedeipeu* belonged to the dominant clan of Nriame.[27] The office was hereditary and upon the death of a *kedeipeu*, it was passed on to the oldest member of the 'extended patrilineal family' (*tsami*) (Betts 1950: 36–45). The *kedeipeu* must have considerable wealth to maintain his status within the village, as he is entrusted to entertain guests and must be judicious in order to maintain office. A *kedeipeu* receives no payment for his services rather he 'has to pay for the prestige that the position bestows upon him by increased hospitality' (1950: 48). The office of the priest, on the other hand, was not hereditary and the incumbent was chosen on the basis of his knowledge of ritual and traditional practices. Only the priest had the authority to perform ritual sacrifices on behalf of his clients. The economic costs of these animal sacrifices were substantial as they were also made at the time of contingencies such as illnesses. In spite of this, the people were often willing to sacrifice in order to avoid divine anger. The reform movement thus sought to alleviate the economic costs by doing away with the rituals.

An early account of the Zeme economic woes was recorded by Bower who situated their beginning in the 1920s (Bower 1952).[28] The failure of crops and ensuing poverty was directly linked with British policy of allowing Kuki immigrants to settle in those fallow lands that were part of the Zeme agricultural cycle. The economic decline and continued Kuki migration directly contributed to the increasing popularity of Gaidinliu movement.

Cycle Migration and Kuki Immigration

So far we have seen how traditional symbols of social rank were largely connected with displaying material wealth on a massive scale. Connected with this were sacrifices, *nrei* and *neube*. The regulation of this system was legitimized by the land owner (*kedeipeu*) and the priest (*tingkopau*). Abolishing sacrifices also meant that the role of the priest was recast in the Heraka reform. The reason for the above changes was largely due to two factors that gave rise to most of the economic problems in the Zeme areas: namely (1) the sheer size and scale of cycle migration practised by the Zeme population was an important factor in economic decline and along with it, the availability of land and (2) not only did this create a failure in terms of agricultural production but also it inevitably affected Zeme village life. This can be seen in the near famines experienced in the villages and by the inability of the British administration to do anything about it.

By the early 1940s, or thereabouts, cycle migration was disappearing because of the occupation of land by Kuki immigrants. Indeed, as Bower mentions, the Zeme are the only ones with this unique system in the Naga Hills. But what necessitated such a system to be adopted, when many of the neighbouring tribes relied on ordinary swidden, or wet terrace cultivation, to sustain their economy?

Even now, the particular kind of swidden cultivation undertaken by the Zeme is hazardous in the extreme. If one stands in a Zeme village such as Hsongle or Hangrum and surveys the area, one discerns clearly that the villages are built on hilltops that plummet suddenly but recover steadily, as the rough rocks form a piedmont when they touch the valley below. The steep ridges form a continuous chain that is covered in thick jungle, and from a distance one can see earthen winding footpaths etched along the vertical drop. When the swidden cycle (cutting, burning and planting) starts, cultivators must walk sideways to the slope, balancing on the ashen grey hillsides after the burning. The stream below and the summit above, are almost equidistant from the point where the cultivators crawl upwards, as they dig and plant the ginger or chilli (mainly cash crops), clearing fallen branches. The danger becomes almost trivial when compared with the impact on their livelihood if this is not done or even worse, if it fails. Such are the risks.

Much of swidden cultivation which required clearing and burning of forests was situated at a distance from the actual site of the Zeme villages. Owing to the steep mountainous terrain, limited land was available for cultivation and the swidden fields were scattered over a large area at a distance from the village. The distance from the village to the fields was considered impractical for the security and sustenance of the village. The answer to this was cycle migration, that is, moving the whole village to the new site for swidden cultivation, leaving the land fallow for a number years before returning to it.

The ritual associated with the establishment of an 'original' village would be conducted in the new village also and the original leaders reinstated according to customary land ownership. After some time the village would move on in search of another habitat with fresh land. The old site was not abandoned but kept fallow with all the signs of past human habitation such as defences, house platforms, monuments (Betts 1950: 122).[29] When the present land was exhausted, the same pattern was followed: either they searched for another piece of land or reoccupied the previous one. Depending on the size of the village, they could have four or five such sites which they used in rotation as the village population grew.

From the mid-nineteenth century onwards, the Kuki began to occupy the fallow land, under the presumption that the land had been abandoned by the Zeme. The Kuki themselves practised a form of swidden cultivation that constantly required new lands. The subsequent encroachment on land and deforestation caused many disputes between the Zeme and the Kuki. There were rumours that the Kukis would also be massacred along with the British, an event predicted to herald the 'Naga Raj' – a sort of paradisiacal state that would confer freedom on the Heraka and their practices. In this report, the Kukis are reported as 'interlopers' by the Nagas.[30]

This over population, Bower observes, caused serious difficulties. As she says,

> The result was serious. The land which had just sufficed for the Zemi was now carrying a bigger population than it could support. Progressive over-cultivation followed, with endless encroachments, land disputes, tribal friction, and steady deforestation and degeneration of what jhum-land there was. (Bower 1946: 52)

The Zeme blamed the government and the Kukis for reduction in cultivable land, because of which the villages began to be disbanded. For example, Bower writes that in 1920 in Asalu village, a bad harvest followed by famine was blamed on exhausted land that could no longer sustain the community. The looming threat of starvation, coupled with high infant mortality, caused by malaria, convinced the village to move. Eventually in 1936 they went to the older site of Gareolowa which belonged to the *kedeipeu* of Asalu. However, the site had been already occupied by Kuki settlers which complicated the situation. Some Asalu villagers moved to Impoi, after permission from the Sub Divisional Officer (SDO), a neighbouring village where the land was more fertile. Meanwhile, those who stayed back in Asalu experienced crop failure, and with no regenerated land available to them, the village disintegrated (Betts 1950: 128–33).

In an attempt to help the Zeme, the British colonial government introduced wet rice terrace cultivation (as was practised by the Angami people). However, the logistics of wet rice cultivation, which requires intensive labour in the building and maintenance of rice terraces, conflicted with the traditional Zeme system of labour which was organized on a reciprocal basis.[31] Each member of the community worked according to the traditional customary pattern of shared labour. But as most Zeme villages were small, they had to depend on hired labour for terrace cultivation for which they either bartered or took out loans. Many Zeme also opposed this new system in the belief that untoward supernatural consequences would follow the alteration or abandonment of traditional agricultural practices (Betts 1950: 126).

The increased demand for water for wet rice cultivation was taken as a bad omen by the Zeme, who believed that springs of water in a field caused the owner to die from dropsy. Another reason wet rice cultivation failed was due to the limited availability of land suitable for terracing. Most Zeme villages abandoned the project halfway through (Betts 1950: 137). However, the Kuki, on the other hand, availed themselves of the government training for rice terrace cultivating and applied it to the newly acquired land. Driven by famine and low fertility of land the Zeme people began working as farm labourers on rice fields owned by the Kuki and Kachari, another neighbouring non-Naga 'tribe' (Bower 1952: 140). 'To keep his family alive', Bower says, 'an Asalu man must work all day and every day in his employer's fields, never seeing his own, and so in the following year had no crop and must work again, unless some wealthier kinsmen could redeem him' (1952: 140). Bower warns that the situation is progressively deteriorating and that by the next generation or so the community will not be able to sustain itself adequately (Betts 1950: 137, 139).

View from Afar

The colonial view was that the Gaidinliu movement was simply a 'racket'. Gaidinliu's followers, says Bower, sold 'Gaidinliu water' as potent elixirs and did her 'patent infallible magic ceremonies' for the sick (Bower 1952: 44). This 'racket' was turning out to be profitable. In the words of a district administrator, J. P. Mills, 'fame and offerings are pleasant things' for those involved. Indeed, J. C. Higgins, another administrator, while touring the villages during the 'Gaidinliu affair' makes a similar remark when assessing why various prophets and 'mediums' keep turning up in the region. The British assumed that the Gaidinliu movement depended on superstition and fear and that the utmost secrecy and loyalty was required of every villager. According to the British, villagers were told that any form of disobedience would lead to harm coming to the family. They would not be able to share in the blessings that would unfold in the immediate future for those following the Gaidinliu movement.[32]

J. H. Hutton, the District Commissioner of the Naga Hills, in 1932, similarly makes an assessment after the Jadonang and Gaidinliu uprisings. Hutton comments on the lack of administration and personnel in the region and notes that some of the villages have not been toured in six years. In some of the villages assessment could not be made properly, Hutton says, because of such extreme poverty. This condition, he suggests, could have been one of the reasons that the 'agitation' caught on so rapidly; or for that matter, he ruefully speculates, any movement proclaiming some sort of hope or prosperity from their present circumstance would have easily caught on. He says,

> Since the slump they have been able to get nothing for their cotton and chillies, and many more than before have had real difficulty in raising the petty cash for their house tax. Any prophetess who promised prosperity and affluence would be bound to take on, and at first there was not necessarily anything seditious in endeavouring to profit by sending presents for a blessing.[33]

Was this a protest against the colonial government or was it the widespread dissent caused by the growing agricultural and immigrant problems?[34] I want to suggest that the two are connected. For example, Bower, writing a report in 1945, points to the failure of the government in understanding the cycle migration. She also argues that 'apparent disregard for Zemi needs and rights helped to form fertile soil for Gaidiliu's [*sic*] rebellion'. 'Though it was quite unwitting', Bower continues, 'the Zemi thought the alienation deliberate, with unfortunate effects on his attitude to Government'. She thereby proposes certain measures that might help redeem the Zeme's regard for the British government and to curtail the vast numbers of destitute in Zeme villages: provide free rice for a year or so to every household, transfer some Kukis settlements to other areas and return Zeme land for further cultivation, and for a long-term solution to this problem, Bower suggests, introduce wet terrace cultivation again.[35] Although these grievances were simmering, the message proclaimed by Jadonang and Gaidinliu – to stage an uprising against the British and Kukis – ironically never came to fruition. These threats were perhaps designed to mobilize the crowd, or to find some release from frustrated hopes and disillusionment. The Gaidinliu movements certainly achieved this latter.

Rebellions, uprisings and protests, says Michael Adas, are viable ways to stage a revitalization of culture, in the local idiom of the people (1987: xxii–xxiii). Their aim is to usher in a new socio-cultural order, in response to the ambiguities of the modern world, Christianity, new systems of governance and taxes, brought in by the colonial order. These systems create ideal conditions for such movements to arise under the guidance of prophets, messiahs and leaders. But these were not just millennial 'flashes in the pan' – over before one could even feel their heat. These movements reveal a certain theoretical logic because they concern everyday resistance that seems quixotic but actually involves the 'constant, grinding conflict over work, food, autonomy, ritual . . .' (Scott 1985: xvi).[36] This attitude of 'every day forms of resistance' became the hallmark for the reformers as they tangled with traditionalists, priests and hostile crowds, persuading them of the need to embrace these changes for survival. The reformers realized that having a *laissez-faire* attitude to an economy in dire conditions would only cause widespread famines. They effected change by slowly reforming the traditional notion of sacrifice and *nrei* and *neube* to curtail expensive rituals. This meant fewer sacrifices to the many local gods and the adoption instead of one God, Tingwang – universal, effectual and accessible. The religious and the economic are inseparable.

Large-scale changes were occurring over the years which meant that the Zeme were becoming educated, mobile and urbane. This also meant that newer ways had to be developed to expand their 'limited horizons'; seeing beyond immediate kin, family, village. They needed to adapt to the changing politics and different environment of urban life, to deal with markets, itinerant merchants, centres of learning and the growing indigenous elite. This meant that society itself had to change to respond to the needs of the people (Adas 1987: 81). The Heraka provided one such response.

Heraka: Religious Modernizing?

It is perhaps a naïve misunderstanding of Max Weber's famous thesis that Puritanism caused capitalism (Andreski 1983: 3). Rather Weber was proposing that there is a relationship between the promise of heavenly rewards and the work ethic of everyday life (Weber 2003: 13–31), or, as in the Heraka case, of a promised prosperity through a relationship with Tingwang. However, this uneasy marriage of heavenly belief and the work ethic was not evident in the early parts of the Gaidinliu movement. Itinerant preachers, I was told, proclaimed that 'grains would fall from the sky', that 'one will become educated by using a book as the pillow' and that 'one must abandon work and instead pray to Tingwang for untold blessings'. These 'superstitious beliefs', I was assured, were accepted by some people and deterred them from seeking education.

Weber considered 'magical and superstitious' beliefs a hindrance to economic exchange and production because it ran counter to the 'rational' mode of thinking (1965: 207–22). Protestantism, as a 'rational' religion, was outwardly free of magical and superstitious traits (Weber 2003: 105). Weber thought that for modernity to emerge, it was not enough just to eliminate magic. Rationality had to be routinized, embedded into a 'life of good works' (2003: 117).

The changes entrenched in aspects of Heraka reform mirror in many ways the shifts from the 'superstitious' to the 'rational' theorized by Weber.[37] For instance, at first Heraka workers displayed 'indifference to wage incentives' (Taussig 1977: 130–55), preferring to stick with what Weber called 'traditional production' or 'primitive traditionalism' (1977: 132–3). The Heraka reformers, on the other hand, now argue that if economic transformation was to occur, some 'superstitious beliefs' connected with sacrifices, restrictions (*nuebe*) and agricultural practices would have to be discarded to prepare the way for the 'rationalization of economic life'. Thus the Heraka's simpler cosmology, which gave primacy to one universal God who inherited all the attributes of the other lesser gods such as *Chuprai* (the god of grain) and *Zailad* (the god of prosperity), and its marginalization of the role of the priest in favour of that of the Paipeu, the village elder, promoted economic change.

Centrality of Power: Concentrated Wealth[38]

This latter reform was, in turn, part of another Heraka initiative – the reworking of the village offices was hierarchized with the Paipeu given the biggest share of responsibility for village welfare. And the rules of office-holding were changed too. Unlike the *kedeipeu* which was a patrilineal hereditary office, the office of Paipeu was opened up, theoretically, to all – though, in practice, the honour usually fell to the wealthiest man of the village. Also, while the person who held the office of Paipeu could change, the status associated with the office remained the same.

The new importance of the Paipeu within the village organization was significant for several reasons. First, by streamlining the power base, and placing it primarily in the hands of the Paipeu, a system of competition within the village was created. The moral was that the villagers needed to compete if they wanted to become wealthy. Second, the elevation of the Paipeu signified a shift from a largely subsistence-based agrarian economy to a market economy. This was connected with several factors: first, the fact that the land did not generate much income, with most of it occupied by outsiders; second, the emphasis on education and literacy which moved people away from the land; third, the shift from collective farming to individual enterprise. With the reorganization of the village these bourgeois values were nurtured and encouraged.

Finally, in order to maintain uniform Heraka practice, authority needs to be vested in the Paipeu, which he then may delegate. By being the arbiter and at the same time interlocutor between his village and the other organizational leaders, he is given the right to disperse orders that come from the organizational centre. By doing so, more power is vested in the Paipeu. The social order is thus hierarchized into one that the collective leadership can deal with directly.

But how does the organization of the village change overnight? In the next section, I want to illustrate just how this is done: by steadily reorganizing villages according to Ranima's principles and using powerful metaphors and Zeme myths in song that justify the changing of the Zeme cosmology. By altering history and highlighting notions of progress, prosperity and abundance through the use of popular folk heroes, such as 'Amang', they are able to portray their economic reform as the way forward and effectively play on the various themes of the reform: curtailing of *nrei, neube* and prohibition of sacrifices, all associated with freedom.

Summary

The above analysis shows how the interconnections between Kuki immigration, failed colonial land and administrative policy, the emergence of the 'Gaidinliu movement' with its message of reform, and the important role of the Paipeu affected the way pre-Heraka notions of land ownership and agricultural production were connected to the village organization led by the *kedeipeu* and *tingkopau.* The Heraka provided a practical remedy for the dislocation brought by contact with the 'outside world'. The Paupaise failed to adapt to the changing situation. The Heraka, on the other hand, successfully reworked their social fabric – and in turn found willing followers – not simply because of some exemplary motives, but by addressing the fundamental issues that affected Zeme village life.

The Heraka, and to some extent, Christianity, proved to be more suited to deal with the change the outside world was bringing.[39] This, as we have seen, is by attempting to eradicate sacrifices and *neube* that had an effect either on economy or mobility, that is, villagers being unable to attend school or employment outside of the village, due to the sacrificial restrictions. A shaman recounted the burden Paupaise *neube* can have on the people even nowadays. She said, 'when my father died, my village was conducting a ritual, *pukpet,* so I couldn't see my father because we were observing a *neube.* So I was crying outside the house. I wanted to give some clothes for my dead father, but I was restricted. So yes, sometimes we have too many *neube.* But it is okay because customs dictate so.' It may only be a matter of time before the Paupaise succumb to the flexibility, and sophistication of approach that the Heraka reforms engendered.

With the change in agricultural practices and the different rituals associated with it, the psychological mood also required a certain shift. In other words, the need to renew villages meant not only changing certain aspects of Paupaise life, it meant that literally, physically they had to 'scrub its exteriors'.

Rubbing off History?

There is a tendency in Heraka villages for people to dissociate themselves from the Paupaise past. In a crude way – to borrow a Heraka metaphor – it washes them clean of a ghostly exterior by scrubbing the interior of the village. The metaphor operates in two different ways: internal and external. The internal metaphor could indicate possible Christian resonances, of cleaning the heart, or washing oneself of sins, and the external metaphor could indicate a Heraka motif of cleansing the past, in this case blood sacrifices. The altering of the *hezoa* and the cleaning of the village could indicate the latter possibility. Belongings such as pots and pans are washed, floors scrubbed, and the ritual cleaning of the village begins at its heart, the *hezoa.* In Paupaise the *hezoa* is the ritual centre of the village, where God dwells.

In the North Cachar Hills district, there are at least three Heraka villages – Nchubonglo, Hegolo, Hereilo – that have cleansed their villages from Paupaise ways, in line with the teachings of Ranima. In this process, they believe that the new is ushered in and the old swept away. In Hereilo, a village which based its religious centre on the teachings of Ranima was established by the Nriame (or Riame) clan. But in establishing a new centre, one notices that the 'old tradition' is not quite swept aside. It rather continues to form a part of a village tradition, as a continued (and constantly created) point of reference, a counterpoint of dialogue. The representation of this system is displayed in the narration of history that simultaneously debunks a 'previous history', along with constructions of the contemporary system in a way that justifies it.

Oral Narratives: Making of a New History

Renewal of a village is concerned with situating oral narratives in the context of history. Whereas scholars in the 'West' would differentiate history and myth, the Zeme 'story' (*rasam*) conflates them into one seamless flow of narrative. Therefore, there is the sense that in the narration, sung histories and memories are negotiated thought-streams between difference and legitimation. Oral history in this sense provides for the Heraka the crucial axis of ongoing negotiation on which their reform can function.

Jan Vansina in his magnum opus *Oral Tradition as History* puts the question of oral history into perspective. He says, 'oral traditions make an appearance only when they are told' (1985: xi). Oral history is told in the present not only as a form of recalling the past, but also as a means of shaping the present, while at the same time embodying the past. It exists in two tenses simultaneously. Indeed, oral traditions are the 'documents *of the present*' which is based on memory as an active recreation of what once was (Vansina 1985: xii, 147; see also Tonkin 1995; Thomson and Perks 1998).[40] But 'what once was' is a difficult notion to establish when the Heraka narrates the past. Inherent in their narratives is an intent to ground their message of reform. This constitutes a recreation of past narratives, with the past itself as the enemy. In a sense, the present not only modifies the past, in its ability to recreate, but also projects back the past from the present. This is justified by what the Heraka conceive of as necessary change, which reforms society and identity. In this way the Heraka are seen as representing 'progress', 'advancement', yet being grounded in 'past tradition'. This is negotiated by processes of inclusion and exclusion. The anthropologist, Elizabeth Tonkin, an advocate for oral history, points us in the right direction:

> We also try to shape our futures in the light of past experience – or what we understand to have been past experience – and, representing how things were, we draw a social portrait, a model which is a reference list of what to follow and what to avoid. The model is part of the processes we live in and call 'group', 'family', 'institutions', 'society' and it helps to reproduce or modify them. Sometimes these processes and structures from the past are overturned; then there is a social revolution. (1995: 1–2)

In the following paragraphs, two examples are presented to bring to light the above arguments. The first example is situated in Nchubonglo village that highlights the importance of negotiating identities between the 'past' and 'present' by employing notions of naming and hygienic practices. This is done by altering the symbols associated with the past, and renewing the 'old village' to give rise to a 'new village'.

Revival of a Village: Name is Everything

This representation of the present and the past was narrated to me by the Heraka preacher (*hingde pame*) in Nchubonglo village, in the western part of North Cachar Hills. He said as follows: 'During Paupaise most of the people were sick and eventually died. Wild animals also plagued us and ate our livestock and grains. So we realized that it was time to change our practice and follow what Ranima and Jadonang taught. So after we became pure Heraka, 25 years or so ago, all these things which happened during the Paupaise have not reoccurred. We have our livestock and have no trouble at all. And, the population also increased after we became Heraka. This is because we renewed our village according to Heraka Hingde' (see also Chapter 4).

'On the day of renewal, we washed all the things in each house with water. We also changed the stone of the hearth and made bamboo jars to carry the water. All the firewood was gathered and, along with the bamboo jars, we put it on the *hezoa*. We changed the altar stone of the *hezoa* as well and plastered the floor of the houses. Before sunset we went outside the village boundary and constructed temporary huts to sleep in for the night. We carried a laundry basket (*nsung*) with our valuables like money, jewellery, ornaments, dress, *dao* [a hacking knife], spear and utensils (only the ones needed for cooking). We cooked outside the village and slept in the temporary houses.'

'As soon as the sun rose (the day of the ritual), from the North side of the village, we sang a song "Ndi Pumkuna Wangra Chimak Keheu Kum". The meaning of the song is 'before we did not know about Tingwang, but now we know about the creator'. So, on this day we asked for blessings on our present generation, our livestock and agriculture. We sang this song and marched to the *hezoa*; and then we stopped the song and put the new altar stone in the *hezoa*. The priest (*tingkopau*) was standing behind the stone and praying. In his prayer he asked Tingwang to bless this generation, livestock, agriculture, wood, trees, water, to bring wealth, care for the needy and also to keep the wild animals away. After the prayer was over, each and every family of the household gathered near the stone of the *hezoa* and lit a fire using the wood already there, carrying the bamboo jugs and fire to their houses because man cannot live without water and fire. The women carried the water and men carried the fire (fire and water are the signs of renewal). Once the fire was lit in every household, we cooked, ate and drank.'

'After the lunch, if any important matters needed to be discussed, we would gather at the *hezoa* again and discuss how to maintain the village; if we needed to change the Paipeu or the person in charge of the *hangseoki*, we would do it during this time. After this renewal ritual, I saw that the prayers had come true – the village had improved.'

'When the village was originally established, we settled here from the village Ramchiram. No ritual had been performed, but we continued with our *jhum* [swidden]. At that time it was Paupaise, and the village had ill health, was very poor and had no paddy. Priests also had a short life. We thought that these problems could have arisen because no proper ritual was conducted when the village was established. So, a renewal ritual was advised by the Heraka preachers (Heurangbe, Dihungbe, Heluileing) and by also Heunsambe.'

'We heard about the ritual from the preachers, so I decided to ask Ranima if we could renew the village in this way. I went to Ranima at Lsong and asked her. The villagers contributed 10 Rupees to give to Ranima. This renewal was around 1987. Ranima blessed the 10 Rupees and she told me to remind her again in the morning. Next morning, I went to her and asked for the ritual and she said to me, "the founders of the village did not have the ritual for foundation. That is why you are having these problems". I also asked her, "should we follow what the preachers have said?" So she said, "yes, you can follow as the preachers have suggested". She said the same thing as the preachers had said but she said when you pray for the village say "Nchubonglo" [a new name] and not "Bolosan" [the old name]. The renewal was necessary because the village had been made dirty by the Paupaise practice and we might have displeased Tingwang somehow. Also, we hadn't prayed to Tingwang [sky god] but to *Tingchura* [god of stone] and evil spirits. So, the ritual was performed to ask Tingwang to forgive us for our mistakes because this ritual symbolizes what Heraka is: to overcome evil spirits and *to erase the memory of sacrifices and evil spirits*' (emphasis added).

The Past is Made Present by the Future

Sitting inside the spacious hut in Nchubonglo, warmed by the constant flickering of the flame from the hearth, it became strangely apparent that I was inhabiting two worlds as my host talked about Bolosan in the past and

Nchubonglo in the present. What occurred to me as merely a linguistic preference of Nchubonglo over Bolosan was, for the speaker, a significant change in which the latter with its reference to *Tingchura* and evil spirits was seen as pejorative. The time-shift is a debate that persists: Christians who have come from Nchubonglo would refer to their village as Bolosan, because that was the name associated with ancestry. On the other hand, the Heraka prefer Nchubonglo because they are trying to erase the memory of sacrifices and evil spirits associated with the Paupaise and hence Bolosan. The naming of terrain is thus not only linguistic but also ideological in its form. Hence the tension over it. With the change in names, the village has also changed.

My host is proud of his village and the vast troves of 'tradition' he says his village still preserves. From the vantage point of the hill where his hut is placed, we can see the long bamboos as they jut out from the massive building made from the biggest and longest of trees – the remnants of the *hangseoki* (male dormitory) and its 'tradition'. This may indicate the shift away from age cohorts, a sign of growing 'individualism', or of different sexual mores. Now it is largely empty, used only rarely for special rituals and occasions. How do we maintain and use such a large structure for the future, he asks me? During these conversations, I realize that 'tradition' still persists in unspoken past time in reference to Bolosan over Nchubonglo. The past was Bolosan, the present Nchubonglo, while the future is a combination of both – what we shall leave for our children is something that inhabits a world of change as well as 'tradition'. And, in a strange way, the metaphor of the 'ghostly exterior' still persists.

Illness and Renewal

The renewal of Nchubonglo village is tied in with the role of hygiene, and illnesses associated with its lack. Part of the problem is the habitual patterns of Paupaise life that, as a Heraka elder said, managed to keep the village dirty. Removal of dirt, as I was told, functioned within the village like any other daily routine, informed largely by the priest. For example, it was prohibited (*neube*) to sweep the floor on certain days, or it was *neube* to use water on certain days to clean the plates. So most people would lick the plate clean with their saliva and prop it by the wall. Animals, children, people, would come and go and the 'dirt' and 'bacteria' would naturally collect until it caused disease and illness, which people then attributed to an evil spirit troubling them. Through reinterpretation of these processes, the Heraka have managed to preach hygiene as a crucial tenet in upgrading or 'advancing' their lives in a sustainable and healthier way. Indeed, the Victorian adage, 'cleanliness is next to godliness', could be applicable to this context.

Considering the connection of notions of purity and danger in society, Mary Douglas examines them in relation to ideas of cleanliness and dirt. The former gives society a sense of order in contrast to the disorder represented by the latter. In cleaning dirt, an attempt is being made to control the environment positively (Douglas 2003: 2). The disorder that is dirt, is also, in this case 'backward', while cleanliness is order and 'advancement'. In this sense, the notion that dirt was present in Paupaise life, clearly represents a system where dirt was 'matter out of place' (2003: 36). Now the Heraka system distinguishes itself by removing dirt, leaving matter in place. By sweeping floors and using water to clean the village or the plates, the new system is seen as orderly, an elevation of personal and collective hygiene and therefore 'advancement' from the previous life of disease and disorder. By using water to wash the dirt, a renewal takes place. Writing of the religious symbolism of water Mircea Eliade discusses a common South Asian phenomenon.

> Breaking up all forms, doing away with the past, water possesses this power of purifying, of regenerating, of giving new birth . . . Water purifies and regenerates because it nullifies the past, and restores – even if only for a moment – the integrity of the dawn of things. (Eliade 1958: 194; quoted in Douglas 2003: 162)

The 'hygiene' metaphor is important for understanding how cleanliness signifies 'advancement' to the Heraka in a way that clearly breaks from the past. This is evident in meetings such as the 'Telung Ndui' (cultural meetings),[41] where mostly women and children are taught how to cook, clean and minimize the use of water while also achieving maximum cleanliness. The preacher told me these hygiene practices, in hindsight were common sense, yet they are credited to Ranima and her teachings. Of course, what worked so effectively is that the reform, side by side with safety and hygienic rituals, safeguarded the community from further illnesses. Following this logic, this in turn eradicated the need for sacrifices, for not only was disease less, but it was believed that these changes happened because their religious lifestyles had been altered for the better.

The Village and Its Heart

It is surprising, as the preacher points out, that no proper foundation ritual for Nchubonglo village was originally held. It is almost inconceivable that such an important ritual like the founding of the village would be neglected. But the omission gave them a reason to re-establish the village according to the Heraka teaching. The changing of the *hezoa* stone is a crucial step in discrediting the older traditional religious centre and replacing it with a new one. In this action an entire epoch has been decentred with a single sweep. It is not merely on a symbolic level that the old has been dispensed with and given way to the new; the heart of the village has altered. By claiming a radical change, the reformers had in mind that such a move would not be possible without keeping cultural and traditional symbols intact – the numerous accoutrements used to maintain the 'old system' remain. But instead of spilling blood over the altar, they simply kill the animal with a heavy stick; instead of praying before the sacrifice, they pray after the kill;[42] instead of the priest chanting prayers, a song is sung collectively to recognize the village as an entity that is praying to one God – there are no longer clan taboos, individual house gods, or displeased ancestors and evil spirits roaming around (see below). The entire ideology has radically shifted to the one God, a monotheistic triumph.

How one indigenizes the past to suit it with current contexts is an important question that needs addressing especially in relation to the Heraka reform. The second example attempts to answer this question by examining key events in Hereilo village.

Constructing Villages

The dialogue between the larger representation of 'official' Heraka history and the loosely constructed placing of this in a local context (or vice versa) revolves around the notion that there are multiple ways of narrating. The tying of oneself and others into a fixed place and claiming ancestry there legitimizes their own use of history. This connects up with the present, giving order to the sequence of past events (see Tonkin 1995). Such vibrant narratives offer an insight into the workings of Heraka belonging and how they create a niche that indigenizes, by constantly reconceiving and conveniently reifying their context. The ethnographic notes below demonstrate this indigenizing of the past. The narratives which follow describe the formation of the village, the proclamation that 'the world has changed', and explains the macrocosmic recreation of the world within the microcosmic village. This narrative has been set in Hereilo village in the eastern region of North Cachar Hills.

'Before 1600 CE', Heuhulung narrates, 'our forefathers were settled here, and in 1952 we resettled here again. We forgot how long we left this place, but it had been sometime. We resettled here to preserve this ancient place. The Kuki people were settled here and we negotiated with them and the Kukis said, come and settle here together with us and you can also preserve this ancient site. Since the Kukis were few in number, they needed more inhabitants, and a proper village according to Government standards was already established. The Kukis came here in the late 1800s.'

'We don't have any records about the Naga village (in the 1600s) but their grandchildren were still alive and they recounted their stories as proof. One of the Kuki leaders, from Khongmoul, got recognition for the village by the District council Haflong, but some Kukis from Nagaland opposed the fact that Zeme Nagas were settled here too. Khongmoul was the recognized name, but it later became Hereilo. In 1963, Naga-Khongmoul was formed and recognized by the district council. During the one Khongmoul (where both Kuki and Zeme lived) there was conflict, but after separation of Naga-Khongmoul and Kuki-Khongmoul, there was peace. And, eventually Naga-Khongmoul changed into Hereilo in 1995. During the 1950s we asked Ranima what to do with the Kukis and she told us not to fight with them as "those who don't want to stay here will leave". In 2005 when a commemoration stone was unveiled for the founders, we realized that Ranima's sayings were true – that the Kukis have left and this is Tingwang's blessing on us.'

The World has Changed

'In 1956 when we relocated to the upper side of the village we performed a ritual that was based on the renewal of the village (as recounted above), and on this occasion we sang "Kedeirei Se Keli Wang Jeu" (The World has Changed)'.

The song exemplifies Heraka reform. By revitalizing village organization according to Heraka teachings, they managed to make the message of the reform central to their progress. Fed by the new religious ideology, they used old myths effectively to legitimize their movement.

The world has changed,
The effect is because of Heratingrangpui.
Let all people come!

My Jau is like the Barak ponds.
Even if we distribute the piece of meat, it will not finish.
Children of Maileng, there are no *neube* in the name of my father.
It is like having Amang's Jau.

Heratingrangpui, popular mainly in the Eastern Zeme area, is the goddess who gives birth to creation. The first two lines have a double function in its narrative construction because they equate the 'original' goddess to Ranima. The world has changed due to the effects of Heratingrangpui; but she is used here more as a symbolic metaphor representing the changing world in the real person of Ranima. *Jau* (also *zao*) is an alcoholic rice drink of religious, therapeutic, social and cultural value that cannot be separated from being a Zeme. The song also, in effect, supports its usage in rituals and, hence, it is viewed as a gift from God. To compare it to Amang's *jau* is an honour because of Amang's status as a folk hero. He is idolized as a poor orphan, who managed to become rich by hard work and wisdom; it is often said that during this time humans received their culture and birds their names. Instead of condemning those who mocked him, he welcomed all of them to share in his wealth (see Chapter 6).

In a similar vein, this song welcomes all to share in the new found wealth and freedom; by invoking Amang, those who are in the periphery can similarly gain ascendancy. The Barak ponds (from the Barak River) are important in the Zeme landscape and thenceforth tie their identity to a specific geographical location, which revisits many traditions. For example, it is believed that Hejale (the god of creation Banglawang's sister) laid eight eggs (who each became gods) on the eighth step of a cave – which is believed to be the source of the Barak River. The invocation of this ideal paradise, with an ample supply of *jau* and meat for all, attempts to create a place in this world for the coming of Ranima.

The birth of creation is a result of the ingenuity of Maileng who weakens and numbs Heratingrangpui's toothed vagina with 'the world's most sour fruit' (*hiangbutchi*), lest it snap at his penis. By deceit and rape, out of necessity, Maileng impregnates Heratingrangpui and the children of Maileng, the Zeme, are born into the world along with all of creation. Now, in the name of Maileng all the *neube*, which placed such a burden on the people, are abolished. There is now paradise, 'it is like having Amang's Jau'.

In our generation, Tingwang, we follow our mother's words
It is good, freedom, it is for the good, for the good
Come and worship God.

Good! Because of the goodness, we will have to worship God.
The great and good life is only for the Nagas.
Ranima has made it simple to lift us up, lifted up by Ranima
The source of Barak River is straight
And the waters come together
Those, my neighbours, who are searching for grain
Come to Zeliangrong, my big lake.[43]
No one can fight us.[44]

The way the Heraka situate themselves in the cosmos is through the use of different generations. Indeed, it is a helpful way to embellish as well as justify their position within the evolution of Zeme society into what it is now. Zeliangrong history consists of five generations, and it is in this way that the official history of the Heraka as recorded in the Tingwang Hingde (popularly known as Hingde Book; loosely translated as Law Book) begins. Each generation has a particular function within the cosmological scheme of things (see Chapter 4). Thus the function of the Heraka generation is to abolish sacrifices, *nrei*, *neube* and pray to one God, Tingwang (Newme 1991: 4–11), all of which has been brought about by the teachings of Ranima ('our mother's words').

Associated with the supposed eradication of sacrifices and *neube*, there comes enormous freedom, from the burden of pleasing every god through sacrifices, thus lifting huge economic burdens from the people. This goodness, this 'lifting up' of the people from oppression and debilitating economic conditions creates added incentive and gladness. This condition, where there is freedom from past burdens, may constitute a turning point, where the reform really gains momentum.

Enumerating History

The narrative of the founding of this village is important for several reasons. Though historical accuracy can be contested – for example, the attempt to establish an ancient pedigree through a linear calendar date 1600 CE – it nevertheless bases the village in a particular place which, when discovered, establishes legitimacy in the present. All this is said to occur as Ranima told them and with Tingwang's blessings. But the organization of the village is incomplete without performing certain rituals prescribed by the teachings of Ranima, under the reform she was propagating. Yet, in a symbolic way, by establishing a village, not only do they construct their own history from 1952, thereby creating an empty period that sets aside the pre-1952 phase, they also effectively eradicate a – presumably – lived 'tradition' by hypothetically insinuating an arbitrary date. Their presence has been acknowledged and the memory of them – 'we don't have any record of the Naga village in the 1600's' – is gone, the purpose it served of authenticating this site as theirs by evoking the ancient footprints of the past no longer being necessary (see also Sundar 2006). Thus begins the process of disremembering the past and creating a present that is made to appear as if it has no connection with the past.

Assessing the Field: Reworking Village Organization

The revival and re-establishing of the village has a dual function. It reiterates the reform motif as well as addressing the economic resurgence of the Zeme villages. While the traditional elements are still vital, the way it has been reworked is familiar and at the same time subtly placed within the Zeme system. Over the years the *hezoa* has given way to the Heraka *kelumki* (prayer house) as the centre of the village. Blood is often associated with the Paupaise; and to distance itself from the Paupaise the Heraka ritual is reversed. The animal is killed then prayer is said to give the impression that it is not a sacrifice. The animal merely symbolizes the prosperity of the village blessed by Tingwang. During the harvest ritual (*heliengi*) in Hsongle, the people had to wait until the animal was killed to offer prayers in the *kelumki* (see Chapter 4). Such strict procedures are followed to avoid mimicking the Paupaise social structure.

Conclusion

Perhaps it is fitting to refer to J. P. Mills to understand this process. Writing on the excluded areas of the then Assam Hills, he says,

> Fires light the village dancing ground on such nights, and the old men sit sipping their rice beer and within the waving plumes of the bucks and the swaying bodies of the girls. 'Let everything be done as it always has been done' is the burden of their talk. Change will inevitably come to them, but 'twere well if it comes, not with deadly speed, but with kindly slowness. These virile races are bound to play their part in the India of the future. They will play it all the better for standing aside and watching how.[45]

J. P. Mills was well aware of the reform movement, the Heraka (then Gaidinliu cult), during his tenure as an SDO, and later District Commissioner. Perhaps, he was not far off the mark when he wrote this in 1926. In fact, his predictions have mostly come true. Change has happened, but with 'kindly slowness'. The quote also juxtaposes the two central elements for the Heraka: reform from what and reform into what?

The initial millenarian activities spurred on by the Gaidinliu Movement gave rise to frustrated hopes and yearning for a 'golden age'. Yet by altering the village agricultural cycle, reducing the use of sacrifices and inculcating the notion of one god, the Gaidinliu movement laid the foundations for the later Heraka movement which took the further step of reforming village organization to accommodate the economic aspect without neglecting the religious. In this respect, the earlier millenarian activities lent an emotive gloss to the reform process while the Heraka provided it with an element of 'rationalization' – one that could help the Zeme adapt to the changing world beyond their villages.

While this was going on, the Heraka village organization also changed, shifting from a largely egalitarian structure to a more hierarchical form of power that rewarded the wealthy with key positions within the village. The need for this move arose from the desire of the reformers to replace success in the old system of cultivation according to a yearly agricultural cycle with a market economy relying on communal labour laws. Now, thanks to the Heraka, individual wealth is valued over communal wealth, as is clearly shown by the symbol of the Paipeu.

While this change has been positive on many levels (flexibility and mobility in terms of education and urban employment), the Heraka have also seen what change can do to the 'traditional' forms of knowledge, values and gender relations. The reordering of history and the way the village has been organized also reveal the way in which the Heraka are able to maintain a level of 'tradition' while at the same time looking for change. In this way, they find ways to reinterpret a new 'tradition'. The way this is done, by utilizing myths, symbols and metaphors, does not disconnect the people from their identity, but merely reorders it to bring home the need for change, as well as embracing and embellishing it.

This balance between the 'old' and 'new' is precisely what the next chapter will highlight, especially the way the Heraka incorporates changes in the world as changes in its own cosmology. With the basic structures of the 'old' Zeme life altered, the change in cosmology highlights the various ways by which the Heraka reform is moving towards engaging with the world.

Chapter 4

Changing Cosmology and the Process of Reform

The central focus of this chapter revolves around Heraka reform. What is Heraka reform? How was it done? By focusing on these questions, the chapter highlights certain historical factors that fashioned a systematic religious system which became increasingly separate from the Zeme Paupaise (traditional practice). By distinguishing and differentiating between the various practices of Zeme Paupaise, particularly emphasizing the *mirase* (my-god-practice) reform, there are now noticeable distinctions between the various sections of community life where previously there were none. How were these distinctions created? In other words, how does a society, once based on traditional practices, envisage something more viable as a way of making the transition from the local to a more open and global scenario?

First, I examine the process of 'dismantling the gods' from 'religion bound societies of the past' as a step to incorporate 'the triumph of autonomy' (Hervieu-Léger 2000: 1). Once this dismantling was done, the Heraka reintegrated and systematized the cosmology with the adoption of a single God. Second, to establish legitimation the Heraka grounded their reform in elements of tradition that justified their position within society. Therefore, to this effect, the Heraka have argued that for every new generation a change in *hingde* (rules governing everyday life) is also required. Third, the adoption of the Tingwang Hingde (or Hingde Book) and the power of literacy have enabled the Heraka to codify their teachings into one that is ethical and didactic, enabling them to project a view that is increasingly seen as 'religious'. Finally, with the establishment of the Kelumki (prayer house), the Heraka have carried over the idea of *neube* (prohibition) from Paupaise in relation to their Kelumki which is 'set apart'. The systematization of a Heraka religious system is an incremental process that involves a range of these practices, eventually formulating a religious system that is on a par with the other major religious traditions in the region. It is this process of reform set over and against the traditional domain that merits attention. I shall deal with this first.

The Past

To help us understand the reform process better, let us briefly highlight what this traditional domain was with regard to the Paupaise practice. It is impossible to construct a 'pure' Paupaise past, as the Paupaise itself is a twentieth-century construction. With the introduction of Christianity and Heraka into Zeme culture, distinctions were made to differentiate one from the other. The classification of Paupaise began only under the retrospective carving out of a separate 'traditional' form of practice, now labelled, literally, 'grandfather-grandmother practice' (Paupaise).[1] This implies that their grandparents did x, y and z, in the past, some of which still continues to this day. The core identity was Zeme, *zemena* (human): being Zeme meant was to be governed by *hingde* (rules governing everyday life). Now the Christians have a different *hingde* and so do the Heraka. The non-Christians and non-Heraka Zeme bring forward Paupaise as an identity which, out of necessity, they now have to embrace. In the arena of religious traditions, these classifications became a tool for difference. As Durkheim said, 'religion'

> extended to everything; everything social was religious – the two words were synonymous. Then gradually political, economic and scientific functions broke free from the religious function, becoming separate entities and taking on more and more a markedly temporal character. (1984: 119; cited in Hervieu-Léger 2000: 20)

In fact, the character of Paupaise centred on 'rules' (*hingde*) and 'action' (*mitulung*) that governed their lives, alongside rituals to gods (*mirase*) and the importance of the house and family (*mikise*).[2] These four basic characteristics were interrelated and revolved around the yearly agricultural cycle. These principles governed their cosmos, as this was what made them Zeme, and there was no alternative for a 'human'. In one sense, for Paupaise to be Christian or Heraka is to stop being a Zeme or to become *perua* (empty) (see Chapter 5).

From scattered oral and written accounts (Betts 1950; Bower 1952), and the presence of a Paupaise village, we can gather some knowledge on the rituals and customs. The Paupaise world was a cosmos inhabited by innumerable *hera* (gods and spirits) associated with natural surroundings, illnesses, wealth, birth, death, harvest, and so on. According to Bower/ Betts, *hera* is a 'spiritual being which is not a ghost and has never inhabited a body'. It is the *hera* that causes the most sicknesses and are the ones that require the most sacrifices (Betts 1950: 143). A similar reference is made to the Garo in the Garo hills of Meghalaya by Robbins Burlings. He points to the fact that the Garo use a general name for supernatural beings, *mite*, which incorporates both 'god' and 'spirit'. The latter 'bite' the people and cause diseases. Propitiation must be made to the *mite* to remove the source of illness (1963: 54; cited in Karlsson 2000: 164). Bengt Karlsson working among the Rabha of West Bengal offers a similar insight regarding the role of *bai*, which is similar to the Garo *mite* (Karlsson 2000: 164).

However, in most recent translations and understanding *hera* is understood as god while *herui* is spirit. One could suggest that the understanding of *hera* and *herui* evolved over the years to create a separation between god and spirit, while in the traditional understanding gods as well as 'spiritual beings' could have been referred to as *hera*. In this context, I will use the word *hera* to mean god and *herui* to mean spirit as it is used today. It was not only a *hera* that can attack a person: sometimes the recently dead can also do so if adequate respect is not paid to them (e.g. failing to honour them by pouring libations of *zao* every time family members drink). The only way the living escape the wrath of the dead is the separation of the living from the dead at the end of the year during the ritual of *Hekak-ngi*, where after the ceremony of sacrificing an animal, the lower gate of the village is closed by the *tingkopau* (priest) to signify this separation (Betts 1950: 144–5).

Central to their village formation was the role of a *kedeipeu* (landowner) and *tingkopau* (priest). The *kedeipeu* was the person who founded the village, and his relationship with the *tingkopau* was vital, as the village itself could not be established and maintained without a *tingkopau*. Within this system were the *herakapeu* (male shaman) and *herakapui* (female shaman) who were responsible for divination. The shaman could divine everything concerning the well-being of the village, its inhabitants and their relationship with the natural elements. Although the shamans also sacrificed, it was the *tingkopau* who performed all the major and large sacrifices. In this regard, animal sacrifices were central in maintaining the status quo with the many gods and spirits.

Animal sacrifices underpinned the Zeme Paupaise relationship with their gods and spirits. An animal sacrifice was seen as a gift to them. The exchange was mutual: if someone were ill, the gift (animal) to the gods and spirits would cure the illness. All propitiations were tied up with a *neube* (prohibition) and *nrei* (period of observance or non-working days). Within the period of the ritual (*nrei*), certain restrictions were maintained (regarding food, exchange of sexual fluids, abstention from *zao*, rice beer, for example). This meant that for any propitiation to be efficacious, a ritual had to be a communal affair. If all did not join in, it was not efficacious. Any anomaly, deviation, disrespect or mistake was treated with great gravity. The ritual usually had to be redone, to avoid further grievances from the gods. When Christian missions were spreading, a strict separation was needed between the Christian and Paupaise villages as a precaution to avoid conflict arising due to the two separate world-views (see also Chapter 5). The Paupaise propitiation to the gods was a compulsory communal affair while for the Christian and Heraka (to an extent), any ritual is largely seen as voluntary.

With the Christian presence in the ascendant and the Heraka slowly spreading, the whole Zeme Paupaise life governed by *hingde* ran into collision with these forces. I would suggest that the early Heraka reformers had no intention of altering basic Zeme Paupaise practice; all they intended was marginal reform, to address the issues of animal sacrifices, and propitiation to the many gods. They saw their reform as a continuation of Paupaise, rather than a distinct break. However, with alterations to the major ritual, animal sacrifices, and therefore relationship with the gods, it became more and more likely that a Heraka system was evolving separately from that of the Zeme Paupaise.

With the presence of Paupaise, and now the Heraka and the Christians among the Zeme, the landscape became a complex set of relationships culminating in the formation of competitive boundaries between various religious groups, brought about by British administrative policy, conversions, education and economic change (see Chapter 5).

Beginnings of the Reform: A Cosmology in the Making

The separation of communities into ethnic slots for administrative purposes became the hallmark of British administration in the Naga areas as early as 1832. People rarely conceived of 'self-identity' in terms of 'ethnicity' because, although belonging to a certain polity, they mixed with a world where boundaries shifted and were redrawn accordingly (Ranger 1993: 72–3). In a sense, this 'construction began in classification' (1993: 68). Such classification was important for the British because religious movements, which were thought to spread across tribal boundaries, 'confused categories' and created fear among the colonial powers of a pan-tribal alliance. These movements were seen as a new threat, and 'as subversive of "traditional society" as of colonial order' (Ranger 1993: 69). This was certainly the case when Jadonang and Gaidinliu started causing a stir during their reform of traditional practice. Jadonang was accused variously of 'inventing a religion', which was a 'debased form of Hinduism', while Gaidinliu was cast as a sorcerer and the new priestess of this 'cult'. Regardless of colonial suspicions, the reforms gained momentum around the Kambiron area (Manipur) and in the surrounding regions of North Cachar Hills and the Naga Hills.

When the reforms initiated by Jadonang and Gaidinliu were becoming popular, Jadonang used 'civilizational symbols' (Thapar 1989) from the 'Hindu' pantheon, such as Bishnu and Mahadeo, to crystallize and evoke a sense of awe through the appropriation of these powerful symbols to further the reform. This could have elevated Jadonang's status as a *maiba* (priest), healer, shaman, God. Gaidinliu also started invoking Soraran, a sky god, associated with the Meitei (Manipuri) religion, who, Gaidinliu said, communicated with her.[3]

Jadonang and Gaidinliu also built temples to exhibit their power and prestige in the region. J. C. Higgins records that Jadonang's temple was intricately designed. It had two levels, five round black stones (used to bring good luck), a sacrificial altar that was 'caked in blood' and it borrowed items of dress and gods from the neighbouring areas. Hats, an idea taken from the plains of Cachar, were worn by 'maidens', as Jadonang preached and prophesized. Clay figures of the God Bishnu and his wife along with a smaller figure of a *mithun* (semi-wild bison) were well modelled, dressed in traditional Kabui clothes and placed in shrines. These powerful symbols were probably adopted by Jadonang and Gaidinliu to seek authority and legitimation. For example, Jadonang tells Higgins that he got these ideas from a 'Hindu fakir' in the Bhuban caves. The caves frequented by Hindus from Cachar, also became important for Jadonang and his disciples, and more recently for the Heraka, as an annual pilgrimage.[4]

Once Jadonang was hanged and Gaidinliu escaped to North Cachar Hills in 1931, the reform took a different turn. Gaidinliu and her followers wanted to unite the Zeme (North Cachar Hills), Liangmai (Naga Hills) and Rongmei (Manipur) into a united front against the British and Christianity. The situation in the region was such that the three groups were fragmented politically. To achieve unity, a common symbol had to be found to bind them. I suggest that, by appealing to a macrocosmic system, the new cosmology was one outcome of this desire to seek unity.

The Great Transformation

An important essay by Robin Horton (1975), based on African cosmology, contends that cosmologies reflect the functioning of social relations. In connection to a two-tier cosmology comprising of a microcosm (lesser gods) and macrocosm (Supreme God), Horton examines how these relations affect those bounded within a certain locality, on the one hand, and those with access to the wider world on the other. In traditional society, particularly one with subsistence farming, the boundaries would be more defined and contained. Local deities, or lesser spirits would figure more prominently (microcosmic reality). On the other hand, if the scale of social relations were wider in terms of long distance trade and marriage, the social life would be geared more towards a supreme being who cut across boundary lines (macrocosmic reality) (1975: 220). I will return to this point later with regard to the Zeme Heraka.

Terence Ranger (1993) is critical of Horton's argument. He shows how Southern African traditional religions ranged over a much wider territory through marriage, trade and hunting, or as Ranger remarks, their world was one of 'economic change, social dislocation, and regrouping' (1993: 72). Southern African religions accommodated 'macrocosmic realities' through their territorial fluidity and flexibility. Indeed, Ranger is critical of studies on African traditional religions that posit a tribe as a bounded subject, without any interaction with other tribes or groups (1993: 71).[5]

Mirroring a Cosmic Reality

While accepting Ranger's argument that exchange (in all forms) is seminal to a cooperative world between people, as can be seen in the adoption of macrocosmic realities even among small communities, such notions are not so clearly formulated in the Zeme context. The earliest source we have on Zeme cosmology by Soppitt in 1885 mentions four gods: Siberai (the head god), Moushini (god of crops), Songhu (protector of the village) and Gaja (god of war) who 'work for the good of mankind'. There are also numerous evil spirits presided over by Songkam (god of death). Propitiation is made to all these gods and spirits by offering blood sacrifices (Soppitt [1885] 1969: 423).

Noteworthy is Richard Eaton's conversion theory concerning the Sema, Ao and Angami Nagas. He says that the Sema, because of their migratory way of life, relied more on one supreme deity, Alhou, who transcended local deities. The macrocosmic deity, Alhou, could therefore easily fit in with the notions of a Christian high god, which made conversion more acceptable. The missionaries could easily supplant Alhou with the Christian high god. Both conveyed a similar idea of an all knowing and all powerful deity (1984: 38). Among the Ao, Lungkijingba was so remote (he dwelt in the sky) that when missionaries wanted to translate the Christian Jehovah into Ao, they chose instead the word *tsungrem* (spirit) with a capital T as the most likely term to fit into a macrocosmic reality for the Ao due to the latter's closeness with the everyday world of the Ao Nagas (Eaton 2000: 61).

Among the Angami Nagas, the above process proved to be more elusive. Unlike other Nagas, the Angami are rice terrace cultivators and not shifting cultivators. Therefore, they are generally fixed to particular places. Eaton argues that, due to the importance of land and agriculture, both their deities were female: Ukepenopfü and Maweno. The Christian message was therefore slower to penetrate because the missionaries could not find an adequate translation for the Christian high god and ended up using a foreign word, 'Jehovah'. The Angami case is interesting because, as Eaton remarks, a close affiliation between land and their fertility cult could have hindered assimilation of newer identities, that is, Christianity (2000: 70). Failing to have any impact on the Angamis for five years, the American missionary, Rivenburg, returned to America in 1892, exhausted. In 1918, J. E. Tanquist, the fourth American missionary, supervised a translation of the entire Bible, replacing the word Jehovah with Ukepenopfü, without realizing that 'pfu' was a feminine suffix. It was later that he realized this and changed it back to Jehovah, by which time Ukepenopfü was undergoing change from female to male (Eaton 2000: 71; Hutton 1965: 181). It was only in 1983 that the Angami Christians reinstated Ukepenopfü, the traditional goddess, to represent their Christian high god (Eaton 2000: 72). These issues raised by Ranger and Eaton are certainly important. On the one hand, Ranger argues that one must not assume that 'tribal' societies were closed systems that did not interact in any way with the outside world; in fact societies could have ranged over a wide territory and easily incorporated a macrocosmic deity. Similarly, Eaton shows, in the Sema, Ao and Angami (to a slower degree) case how the supplanting of local deities with macrocosmic notions parallel to the Christian high god helped speed up conversions.

On the other hand, Richard Eaton's argument, however, is limited in that it concentrates primarily on the ability to translate the Christian God into the local language with an effective fit. In this way, the importance of translation was primarily considered one way (see also Karlsson 2000: 190).

Against the background of these interesting cases, I now turn to the Zeme and how the Heraka managed their reforms.

Rationalization of Cosmology?

As explained in the previous chapter, when the first reformers, in North Cachar Hills, started preaching in the 1930s against the 'old way of life', attacking specific institutions that crippled Zeme economy, they did so by altering traditional cosmologies. These changes were seen, by the reformers, as altering certain institutions (animal sacrifices) which hindered Zeme development in relation to the modern world. Were these alterations seen as conversions? Certain limitations inhibit the application of a strict 'conversion' model to the Heraka. First, when the Heraka message was spreading in its nascent form, it appears that the reformers were conscious of maintaining the status quo prevalent in the region. Therefore, becoming Heraka was seen as a fluid transition from one system to another and not as 'conversion' in the sense of exclusivism. In fact, what we see is incremental replacement of the traditional cosmology with one which, I was told, 'was more effective and attuned with present conditions'. Second, it is difficult to suggest that the reformers were exclusivist in the sense that one is either Heraka or Paupaise (although they did harbour reservations about the Christians). This exclusivist attitude is regarded as the hallmark of Christianity, which, even today, sees itself as the true religion. Becoming Heraka did not require its adherents to profess their faith or announce certain doctrines. It was seen simply as changing with the times. Nowadays, however, it is becoming more like Christianity in professing its faith.

But what do I mean by changing with the times? According to the Heraka and Christians, Paupaise was seen as expensive, outmoded and too cumbersome. It involved innumerable sacrifices to the gods and spirits of the village, prescribed for illnesses and to ensure good harvests, rain, and so on (see also Boal 1982). It also required restricted movement, within the village boundary, and any excursion outside required a ritual that, if not done, made the traveller vulnerable to evil spirits. These conditions meant that venturing outside for government jobs, education and trading made life expensive and tedious. The Heraka reform provided the needed relief, as did Christianity: it made everything 'lighter and easier'.

Religious change, in the Zeme Heraka context, is something that did not happen consistently or evenly; it occurred in some aspects but not so in others (Hefner 1993: 18). For example, the Heraka thought that the reduction of animal sacrifices was a viable way to move from 'superstitious behaviour' to something simpler and more elevated. The reason for this shift occurred on various levels. First, the adoption of a cosmology that was well organized and espoused a high level of integration was paramount in the establishment of a new religious system. Second, since the Paupaise gods and spirits were relatively fixed to their localities, the new cosmology helped the Heraka become more mobile, a feature which ties in with developments such as education, employment and trade. The cosmology took on a monotheistic and hierarchical structure. This is evident in the representation of one high god Tingwang (who is active) and other smaller gods (who are ineffectual). The latter remain in the cosmology for legitimacy based on the Zeme tradition. This image also conveys an idea that the Heraka god Tingwang is positioned over, and to an extent encompasses, the smaller gods of Paupaise.

Creation Stories

According to present available literature on the cosmology of the Zeme, Liangmai and Rongmei people, there are some similarities in the way cosmologies have been arranged. In the Rongmei account, the creators are known as Dampapu (the male deity who creates the universe) and Dampapui (the female deity who creates the earth). They are commanded to create the world by a supreme deity but no account of the nature of the creation is given (Hodson 1911: 127). Recent literature stresses the importance of a Supreme God, Tingkao Ragwang (sky god) (Kamei 2004: 24; Makuga 1994: 1–2). The adoption of Tingkao Ragwang would probably explain the desire to find a 'metaphysical conception' for the 'creation of the material world' (Hodson 1911: 127). In the Zeme and Liangmai version, there is more of a similarity. Creation is attributed to Heratingrangpui (a goddess) (in the Liangmai, Charahsingrangpui) who gives birth to creation (see Figure 6.1). In the Zeme narration, Heratingrangpui is raped by Maileng (the Zeme are often known as children of Maileng), and then gives birth to all creatures, while according to the Liangmai narration, Charahsingrangpui lays eight eggs by the river bank and gives birth to the eight gods. In fact, according to one creation account collected by a British administrator in 1926, Charahsingrangpui and Jiberai (Chuprai/Siberai) are the two most important gods.[6] As already mentioned, C. A. Soppitt's account of the Kacha Naga (Zeme) of North Cachar Hills in 1885 gives a quite different account. He says Sibrai is the head god and Moushini (god of crops), Songhu (protector of the village) and Gaja (god of war) are the other, perhaps minor, gods ([1885] 1969: 423).

These scattered and divergent stories, with their fluctuating array of gods and narrative plots, come together in a more recent rendition of the creation story that borrows freely from the above accounts (see below). As I have mentioned, most of what we know regarding the identity of the gods and their role is sketchy at best. It is difficult to say whether such a 'high god' among the three ethnic groups traditionally existed. The quest for an active high god as the effective enabler for pan-ethnic binding through time and space is largely a modern conception. Indeed, such characteristics of the presence of a high god are evident in Christianity, Heraka and neo-traditional groups such as the more recent Tingkao Ragwang Chapriak (see glossary).

But why is this pan-ethnic binding important in the context of these three tribes? The Zeme, Liangmai and the Rongmei, it is said, share a common ancestry. Their tradition, custom and language have such similarities (Johnstone 1896; Hodson 1911; Hutton 1969: 352) that in 1947 a pan-ethnic conglomeration was formed stressing this identity, known as Zeliangrong (see Chapter 1). Therefore, the Heraka creation story is often known as Zeliangrong creation story.

One of the most important changes in the cosmology of the Heraka is the different ways the role of the gods has been recast since the reforms began in the 1930s. The variation and changes are complicated. For example, there are two different versions of the creation narrative within the span of a few years, both recorded by Bower.

First Creation Narrative

In Bower's first narrative of the creation story recorded in the late 1930s, her entry states that a *herapeo* (shaman) is the reason for the birth of eight spirits, who later go on to become the eight gods of the Zeme pantheon. She says,

> Once there was a herapeo who lived alone, and he dreamed that if he cut off two of his fingers they would become a wife and a sister (her name was Zale). When he woke he cut off two fingers, and a wife and a sister they became.[7]

Upon seeing her brother and his wife having sex, Zale had the sudden urge to lay eggs. She laid the eight eggs by the cliff of the hill, Tallaurok, leaving them to hatch.

Second Creation Narrative

In Bower's second narrative, written during the early 1940s, the story takes on more of an organized form. She says that Banglawang descended from heaven and created the world; Banglawang replaces the *herapeo* and takes the more definitive role in the act of creation. Banglawang is an odd insertion into the Zeme creation story. Bangla-ong, as the deity was known among the Kabui, lived inside the earth (Hodson 1911: 128). The transition from living underground to becoming creator is an interesting twist to the story, but one that merits more discussion. This will be elaborated on later as we will see.

The mention of Tingwang, a minor god, in yet another narrative also gives the impression that insertions into the creation story were already taking place. By the 1970s when von Fürer Haimendorf visited the Zeme areas, he reported that Tingwang was the most important god, followed by Kedewang (god of the earth) and Chuprai (god of grains): he also notes there are no female deities.[8] In the following paragraphs, I would like to examine this process, as the 'fashioning of gods' allows us to understand more about the Heraka reform.

The following Heraka creation story mixes many themes and plots from the three ethnic groups and attempts to unify them (e.g. see Kamei 2004; Miri 1991; Bower 1952) . It is interesting that over the years this creation story is generally taken to be the official one across religious traditions among the Zeme. This is associated with the desire to project a strong cultural identity connected with a coherent and stable past. Such a rendition does precisely this. The Zeme are also able to place their cosmology, alongside other systems, in a way conducive to ethnic pride. Such ruminations are common – 'oh, we also have an Adam and Eve story, we also have the story of Noah, we also have the story of Babel' and so on.

The Heraka Creation Story[9]

> One day Banglawang, the son of Tingwang – the King of the universe – was very lonely, so he went to ask his father if he could go down to the earth and rule. Banglawang approached Tingwang and said: 'Apeu [father], I am your son Banglawang; I am here to request you to let me be king on this earth'. Tingwang replies, 'Didn't you see the water on the earth, I was unhappy with the Manshai generation [see below], so I filled the earth with water'. Banglawang replies, 'Yes, I saw that, but I want to be

king'. Again his father replied, 'You cannot go down as the earth is filled with water; you will find no place to rest'. But Banglawang was persistent so his father finally allowed him to go down. However, his father warned him: 'if your feet touch the water, you cannot be king'. Banglawang descended to the earth using an iron ladder, and as instructed by his father, he hung onto a tree called Chigenebang (red fruit tree). But after a while Banglawang accidentally loosened his grip and touched the water with his foot.

Banglawang saw a *tezikiempui* (an insect) sitting on a yam leaf and asked him if he had seen dry land. The insect told Banglawang that he could not see dry land anywhere and instead he should ask the earthworm king when he comes up to the surface every two months. When the earthworm king came up, Banglawang asked him if he could bring the earth from below. After three months, the earthworm king came up with the mud he had eaten and spewing it out, he formed the land.

When the land was formed, Banglawang saw a crow and asked him if he could level the earth by flattening the rough areas. However, the crow could level only parts of the surface, thus some of the earth is flat while other parts are hilly and rugged.

Banglawang then approached the serpent, Ramtegie. He asked Ramtegie to crack the earth so waterways could be formed; water flowed into all directions and thus rivers were formed. Banglawang then chopped some thatching-grass (*ngai*) and scattered it on the river, and fishes were formed. To add to the beauty of the river, Banglawang put down some stones and placed crabs under them. He still felt that something was lacking so he planted trees by the riverside and on the land. Birds and animals of all sizes appeared on the land and added to the beauty of the place. (Pame 1996: 96–7)

Birth of the Gods

After all of this was completed, Banglawang was very lonely. One day, he cut off his thumb and split the severed digit into two pieces. One became his sister, Hejale, while the one beside him became his wife, Jegale. One day, Banglawang and his wife were having intercourse when Hejale walked in on them. When Hejale saw the couple having intercourse, she also conceived, as Jegale and Hejale were from the same thumb.

This was a problem, as the sister was to conceive the brother's child. So she was sent to an island. Hejale took a Hulu (a black monkey), a bunch

> of bananas and a *dao* (a hacking knife). There she laid eight eggs on the eighth step of the cave: this is believed to be the source of the Barak River (a popular river in many Zeme stories). After laying the eggs, she left the island. Seven of the eggs hatched and men came out, but they were blind. Seeing this, the monkey started to eat a banana without sharing it with the seven. Mishnu, being the cleverest of the seven, however, found the bananas, cut the bunch with the *dao* and gave one each to his brothers. They then decided to cut the hand of the monkey, as he was eating all the bananas. When they cut the hand of the monkey, the blood spilled into their eyes and they could finally see. They pushed the eighth egg into the lake and he became the God of the lake, the python king Hechawang. The eight were: Gechingpeu, Heransia, Lhu, Nrak, Mekang, Mishnu, Chuprai and Hechawang.[10]
>
> The seven decided to go and look for their mother, transforming themselves into crows. As they were flying, their mother spotted the crows and started counting them; she counted only seven. When Mishnu noticed a woman counting, he immediately realised that she was their mother. They transformed into humans again to meet her. When she saw them, she asked what happened to the eighth. They told her that they had pushed him into the lake. The mother replied 'the brother you pushed into the lake was to be the strongest and cleverest among you'. Reunited with their mother, the brothers eventually settled down in and around the Barail range.[11]

According to the second narrative of the creation story that Bower collected only two gods are mentioned: Gechingpeu and Chuprai. Gechingpeu is seen as the oldest while Chuprai the great and clever one. In this version, the honour belongs to Mishnu. The importance of Mishnu is connected with the symbol of Bhuban (who is allegedly the same as Mishnu or sometimes as Bishnu) for the Heraka reform. In Soppitt's account, no god figures prominently at all in the creation narrative, and the story of the eight gods are not even recorded ([1885] 1969: 433–4). The final story quoted above brings about the downfall of Banglawang and the ascendancy of Chuprai as the undisputed god of the earth.

The Match

> Soon the seven brothers were introduced to Banglawang. It was agreed that whoever beats Banglawang in a wrestling contest would become the

> next King on earth. Chuprai, the youngest among the brothers was the favourite of his mother and she arranged his marriage with the daughter of Banglawang and Jegale, Kamadile. Supported by his mother and wife, Chuprai was the favourite to win.
>
> During the wrestling match between Banglawang and Chuprai, the earth shook for five days and nights. Seeing the agony of the fight, Chuprai's mother gave Kamadile a magic tuft of hair and asked her to choose between her husband and her father. Out of confusion, and seeing that her husband needed help, Kamadile took the tuft of hair and threw it catching Banglawang's legs. He twisted and fell.
>
> However, Chuprai, out of respect, refused to become King. But Banglawang replied, 'An agreement is an agreement, the spit by which we made the pact cannot return to my mouth.' Having said this, Banglawang went underground, taking all the good creation with him. There he became god of the underworld, leaving Chuprai to become the king over the earth.[12]

Unable to live without the 'good creation', Chuprai requested his wife Kamadile to go underground and plead with her father, Banglawang, to part with some of the 'good creation'. Banglawang finally gave in to Kamadile's request, but loaned the 'good creation' only for a short period of time every year. A storm at the end of winter symbolizes Kamadile's descent underground to collect the 'good creation'. Her ascendance with the 'good creation' is marked by spring.

Divine Hierarchy: An Analysis

Max Weber has contributed much to an understanding of what he called 'traditional religion' and 'rationalized religion'. This distinction is seen in his argument that 'traditional religion' espoused a bounded view of lesser gods and spirits attached to their settlements while 'rationalized religion' 'favoured the primacy of universal gods; and every consistent crystallization of a pantheon followed systematic rational principles to some degree' (Weber 1965: 20, 22). Clifford Geertz expands Max Weber's view usefully. He says,

> Traditional religions consist of a multitude of very concretely defined and only loosely ordered sacred entities, an untidy collection of fussy ritual acts and vivid animistic images . . . Rationalized religions, on the other

> hand, are more abstract, more logically coherent, and more generally phrased . . . [and] they become conceptualized as universal and inherent qualities of human existence as such, rather than being seen as inseparable aspects of this or that specific event. (Geertz 1973: 172)

Weber's view has been challenged by scholars (Tambiah 1990; Ranger 1993) who argue that this characterization of 'traditional religions', as narrow and bounded, is too restrictive: they can in fact be flexible and accommodating of a systematic world-view (Hefner 1993: 15). Peter Worsley offers a different critique of what he identifies as Weber's association of 'traditional action' with 'irrationality'. He says, 'traditional action . . . may not appear irrational if one examines its application in a particular situation; the extent to which the action is efficacious in practice will show how far it is based upon a correct theoretical understanding of reality' (Worsley 1970: 268). With the Heraka cosmology, the view is not one of rationality or traditionalism in its extreme forms, but one of negotiation. The reform itself suggests a progression, an improvement on the traditional order. And, for historical legitimacy, some aspects of the traditional cosmology are also incorporated.

The creation story also evokes a sense of symmetry and elegance that the other scattered accounts lack. The creation story not only presents a coherent world-view in terms of the hierarchy of the gods, a single high god acting on behalf of the world, but also a creator who is seen as benevolent and involved in everyday actions. It provides the crucial axis upon which the supreme deity, Tingwang, is portrayed as omnipotent and universal, which is further reiterated in the Tingwang Hingde (also known as Hingde Book) of the Heraka. It says that Tingwang created the 'Sun, Moon, Stars, Earth, Water, Air, Human, Animals, and all living things' (Newme 1991: 4). Though it contradicts the role of Banglawang as creator, it nevertheless establishes the primacy of Tingwang over Banglawang and over all of creation.[13] What is interesting, however, is that in Soppitt's account, Sibrai (Chuprai) is the head god and is seen as the creator. He sits on an elevated hill and creates the world, which is 'covered with one vast sheet of water' ([1885] 1969: 433). But why this monumental shift in the role of the creators in the span of 30 years or so? I suggest that this shift happened for several reasons and was consciously amended by the reformers to reflect their reform and, latterly, to legitimize a new religious system.

The story first suggests two important points for the Heraka cosmology. The story asserts the continuing importance of Chuprai through his victory over Banglawang. In most of Zeme Paupaise understanding of their cosmology, Chuprai was an important god, due to his status and connection with the harvest, grain and rain. In the systemization of Heraka cosmology Chuprai is no longer seen as the creator (see below), but he is relegated to one of the lesser gods. In the Heraka reform the shift occurs in the diminished role of Chuprai, and the importance accorded to Banglawang. In effect, Banglawang is resurrected.[14] Finally, due to the large sacrifices offered to him, a cause of innumerable economic burdens, Chuprai, in all forms had to be denounced, replaced and forgotten.[15] And, by emphasizing Banglawang's return, the good aspects of creation are also returned to earth, which in turn emphasizes the renewal of the world.

In relation to Chuprai and Banglawang, the narrative of 'the match' is striking because, according to Soppitt's account, it is associated with the story of earthquakes. 'Bangla Raja' (Banglawang), Soppitt says, died and went to the abode of the gods. There, he fell in love with Sibrai's (Chuprai) daughter and married her. In time, 'Bangla Raja' set himself up as Sibrai's equal and a huge disturbance erupted. It was agreed that the only way to settle this was by having a wrestling match. The loser would be confined forever in the centre of the earth. A long struggle ensued and the result appeared doubtful, until 'the wife of the Bangla Raja, Sibrai's daughter, tied her husband's feet together with her hair'. Sibrai then threw his adversary down and according to the pact, confined him in the centre of the earth. The occasional earthquakes are his struggle to free himself (Soppitt [1885] 1969: 435). The role of the central characters in the two accounts have been inverted and even the choice that Sibrai's daughter makes is in support of her father and not her husband. In both accounts, Sibrai (Chuprai) appears to be victorious. Why does the narrative twist and turn and why are the stories inverted? Lévi-Strauss reminds us that myth undergoes transformation due to certain reasons: 'romantic elaboration' or 'historical legitimation'. Such history, he says, is of two types: 'retrospective – to base a traditional order on a distant past; or prospective – to treat this past as the beginning of a future that is in the process of taking shape' (Lévi-Strauss and Moore 1974b: 280–1).

It is most likely that the cosmology is a combination of the 'retrospective' and the 'prospective', legitimizing a new order based on the past, and using the past to recreate something for the present and the future. In this way, the reformers sought to distance themselves from the traditional cosmology, as they were proclaiming a new message. If the reformers had to downplay the sacrifices then Chuprai had to be replaced by someone who would carry the message of reform, which was one of a pan-tribal alliance, economic progress, development (education, agricultural reforms) and also a universal God. And the only way to separate from Paupaise was to differentiate.[16] Tingwang became the obvious replacement. This interesting inversion became clear to me when I visited the Paupaise village. They told me that Tingwang is a minor god, prayed to only once, at the end of each year, and when they look for a new settlement or establish a new village (a god perhaps that establishes community irrespective of the new locale theysettle in or encounter). Up to the present day, the most important god for the Paupaise is Chuprai, also known as Herawang (king of the gods).

The fact that Tingwang takes a monotheistic face could be attributed to the Christian influence in the region. It was probably the Christians who first started using Tingwang, as a way of addressing the high god of the Christians.[17] The Christian influence can be found in recent literature on the theology of the Heraka. It looks upon Tingwang as the 'root of all creation', and the belief in the 'worship of one Supreme Being, as practised by the Heraka, is the introduction of the concept of monotheism or belief in one God in the Zeliangrong religion, which is traditionally a polytheism, belief in many gods' (Zeliang 1980: 7). The treatise written by N. C. Zeliang, the past-President of the Heraka Association, is cluttered with Christian passages, Christian ideas and philosophies that makes one question his stated intentions.[18] But this perspective, primarily that of the elite, holds the view that 'Heraka is not a departure from the traditional Naga people but a rational improvement on it' (1980: 9).

It is interesting to note that not only is Banglawang reinstated but the other god, Hechawang (python king), who was largely forgotten is also given prominence. He symbolizes wealth, freedom (often associated with *heguangram*) and bounty of grains. He is now known as Zailad god, after Zailad lake in Manipur, and it is believed that the seed of the rice grain comes from Zailad and is called Zailad *nreu* (see also Chapter 6). Bhuban god is also vital because he is largely seen as the one who first drew Ranima there to be inspired by Tingwang to reform the Zeliangrong religious practice. His place, known as Bhuban ki, is the annual pilgrimage site for the Heraka, because of its mysterious and consuming power discussed in Chapter 2. The underlying importance of a creator god, Banglawang, and the reform motif of individual wealth (associated with Zailad and bounty) represent the growing importance of embracing a changing world. Chuprai, who represents the localized and microcosmic god, is replaced by Tingwang, all unifying and macrocosmic, a change from the agricultural economy to the market economy.

Summary

From what we have seen so far, a clear picture of the initiation of the reform emerges. Missionaries focused on the translation of an indigenous high god into a Christian high god to initiate conversion among the Sema, Ao and Angami by supplanting local gods with the notion of one god. This made the transition easier and more persuasive, especially in the case of the Sema and Ao. To return to Horton's argument regarding the two-tier cosmology, I would like to emphasize how, in the Heraka case, it is not a question of a neat demarcation between the two but rather how microcosmic gods can be conflated into the macrocosmic system (Tingwang and Banglawang). In this regard, the Heraka also reconstructed its local cosmology to have a high god, perhaps partly to combat Christian influence. This is an interesting theoretical point. It could suggest that the presence of a high god enable one to resist Christian conversion, and make one vulnerable to it as in the case of the Sema and Ao. However, the difference is that the Heraka have retained local deities into their reform when those deities are not in conflict with the central message – that of change, economic reform, and so on. The change in the versions of the creation story both *reflects* this shift towards a high god *and* the ability to incorporate lesser gods. The use of the creation story to reflect this shift is a demonstration of a reform movement 'reconstructing' the past of the traditional order to (1) provide base for their reform, (2) incorporate the religious practice of the people and (3) to move the reform on by developing ideas from old ideas such as the creation story. This is, as Lévi-Strauss argues, both 'retrospective' and 'prospective', as a way of basing their cosmology on some traditional framework and of moving forward at the same time. But what happened to the rest of the reform?

In the following sections, I will explore and explain how the reform targeted certain aspects of Zeme Paupaise life and thus shaped Heraka life. Through this process, it is important to examine the formation of a religious system that negotiated the various levels of the 'sacred' coupled with secular elements, trafficking ideas and sentiments on a reciprocal basis. The process of this change for the Heraka is tied in with the growing access to the modern world and how inevitably 'the changes in concepts articulate changes in practices' (Asad 2003: 25). In other words, in the case of changes from the reform, the salience of these concepts must be examined not in isolation but in tension with the wider world that helps form a body of practice constantly engaging with the world and not withdrawing from it.

Note on Concepts

Before we proceed, let me clarify the use of certain words that are important in the Zeme Heraka context. When I asked the Zeme Heraka about their reforms, they used the word 'Hingde' to denote the Heraka practice, as in Heraka Hingde.[19] Hingde (with a small h) literally translates as 'rules governing everyday life', and sometimes loosely as 'rule' or 'law'. (Nowadays, Christians substitute 'commandment' or 'law' with *hingde.*) In Paupaise, *hingde* regulated the rules for eating, drinking, wearing of clothes, rituals, animal sacrifices, agricultural, and so on. *Mitulung* (my-nature) was the action that embodied these rules into habit. The relationship between the two regulated Zeme life, and provided them with a framework needed to govern their lives. Even clan and household taboos and *neubes* were dictated by *hingde* (certain families could not eat frogs, or tigers according to their clan totem). Therefore, as we understand it, without *hingde* there was no Zeme life.

Nowadays, the Heraka speak of their *mikise* (my-house-practice), their *mirase* (my-god-practice), their *hingde* (rules governing everyday life) and *mitulung* (my-nature; as in that which I do) as separate categories, because the reform has already made certain distinctions between them. I suggest that this noticeable separation happened with the *mirase* reform. By initiating changes and adapting a new *mirase* (the old *mirase* was connected with sacrifice) with the sacralization of the Kelumki (prayer house) as the embodiment of the Heraka Hingde, the landscape was conceptually altered.

Abolishing Gods and Sacrifices

The Heraka are adamant that they are the torchbearers of Zeme tradition and by reforming they are merely establishing an original link with the past. By attempting to provide a new Hingde, they summarily replaced the old Paupaise *hingde.* This is a central part of Heraka reform. The Heraka claim that only the *mirase* (my-god-practice) has been reformed. Small gods associated with animal worship, within the *mirase* system, have been eradicated. But these Heraka reforms could no longer be accommodated within the Paupaise practice, and the Heraka had to break away and form into a distinct group. This was done in several ways. First, they grounded changes in different generations as a method of navigating through past narratives of Zeme history and legitimizing present ones. Each generation has a prescribed Hingde, or divine rules, and therefore the Heraka suggested that different generations require different practices, which in this current generation is influenced by the recovery of the Hingde Book (officially known as Tingwang Hingde). Second, they have resurrected a key healer, Herakandingpeu, in Zeme tradition and pitted him against the Paupaise cosmology.[20] By resurrecting this healer for their reform message, they were able to project the Paupaise generation as 'evil'. Finally, in order to reform the *mirase* (my-god-practice), the establishment of the Kelumki (prayer house) became necessary. This gave rise to a wider problem: the tension created between *mitulung* (my-nature), which embody the actions, and the ever-widening Hingde, which are the rules governing those actions.

Generational Change

For the Heraka, a helpful way of establishing continuity as well as change, since the creation of the world, is by distinguishing between generations.[21] Each generation supposedly receives a new Hingde, through the regeneration of time. This happened for the Heraka according to Tingwang's will. Each generation, in the following narrative, is provided with a prescribed *hingde.* These narratives about generations therefore constitute an important part of Heraka tradition. This generational story can be narrated thus:

> *Aman mi* (dream fire) was part of the first generation. This dream fire burnt the world. After this generation came Manshai,[22] who was King and ruled the world. He could read a mysterious scripture called Hingde Book and could heal using this. Thus, people did not need to sacrifice to any animals and were free from dependence on the bloodthirsty and evil gods. One day he went off to the field and left his Hingde Book in the *nsung* (laundry basket). But once he put it inside the *nsung*, it was *neube* (prohibition) to take it out again before any illness occurred. Finally, one day, Manshai himself got ill and asked his wife to bring out the Hingde Book. When she reached for the basket, it had disappeared; Tingwang had come and taken it away. Since he did not possess the secret codes for healing found in the Hingde Book, Manshai turned to the *herakapeu* (shaman) to prophesize. The shaman mediated between him and the god and found out what was making him ill. Thus came about the *kemeume* generation (prophecy generation). During this time people suffered immensely as they did not have the Hingde Book; they had to depend on these bloodthirsty gods. It was during this time that the flood came to the world and destroyed everything. Only Emobai was saved as he built a boat

according to God's instructions. When this generation was also wiped out, Banglawang (the creator) came and recreated the world. During this generation another great healer Herakandingpeu came. But he was also killed by the *kemeume* generation, and the world became chaotic and was ruled by evil spirits. Then Jadonang and Gaidinliu came and now we are in the Heraka generation after receiving the *hingde* book from Tingwang in Bhuban cave.[23]

Interpretation

The narrative of the generations explains the existence of the Heraka book at an ancient time, and its renewal by Ranima and Jadonang in the Bhuban cave. It is also clear from the above narrative that Christian influences are interlaced in the narrative, particularly with the story of Emobai and the flood. From this narrative one can discern a familiar thread: Manshai generation clearly reflects the present Heraka reform in their rejection of animal sacrifices and their reliance on their own Hingde Book as mediating between Tingwang and humans. The Hingde Book lost during the Manshai generation was subsequently found again during the Heraka era in the Bhuban cave. The motif of a lost book is found among many people in Southeast Asia. For the Karen of Burma, for example, European missionaries bearing the Bible were seen as the return of the 'White Brother' bringing the Karen's lost 'Book of Gold' (a mythic text of the Karen). The coming of the missionaries was seen as the divine intervention of God; and in some cases these legends were invoked to explain conversion (Stern 1968: 309; Kammerer 1990: 282). One can apply a similar framework to the Heraka, and, in their case also, the idea of a lost book retrieved invokes a higher status for their religious reform. The reference to the Hingde Book in the narrative seems to be a retrospective, selective insertion on the part of the Heraka to justify a link between the 'old Hingde Book' and the present one.

The importance of writing can be traced back to Gaidinliu (see below) and how literacy was valued as a symbol of power. The writing of the present Hingde Book suggests a link with the past, both with Gaidinliu's and Manshai's writing. The *kemeume* generation, associated with Paupaise, is highlighted on two occasions when they are accused of suppressing a time of harmony and freedom from sacrifices. These idyllic times are associated first with Manshai and the Hingde Book, and second with Herakandingpeu. The Heraka talk about Herakandingpeu as the paragon of the Heraka reform and his summary killing by the bloodthirsty god,

Chuprai (god of grain). I therefore suggest that Herakandingpeu's Hingde mirrors the Heraka Hingde, a view also supported by Pautanzan Newme, the General Secretary of the Heraka Association (2002: 6). In the following paragraphs, I explain the importance of the Hingde Book and the role of Herakandingpeu as a vital symbol of the Heraka reform.

Hingde Book

When the British captured Gaidinliu in 1932, J. P. Mills confiscated her notebooks. In Mills' description of the notebooks, he says,

> Magic books of the sorceress Gaidiliu [*sic*] captured with her other property in March 1932. The writing is apparently nothing but meaningless scribbling. She is a Kabui girl of no education at all and taught herself to scribble. Her 'literary' power gave her immense prestige and she used to send written messages to her adherents – with verbal messages to say what they meant.[24]

When I examined the books, some pages had writing that resembled the Meitei and Bengali alphabets while other pages had random lines, circles and drawings. Overall, the writing was very cryptic. The meaning and the knowledge of the script are shrouded in mystery. One writer suggests that the script is the ancient Naga script found by Jadonang; he apparently used it widely to compose hymns. Furthermore, some claim that this script has been deciphered (Pame 1996: 104). When I was doing my fieldwork in North Cachar Hills, I was often asked if it was possible for me to retrieve the notebooks of Gaidinliu's from Oxford, for their keeping. Secret coded messages which are valuable for the founding of the *heguangram* (a free community) were allegedly inscribed in the notebooks (see Chapter 6). Whatever the reasons for Gaidinliu keeping the notebooks or their efficacy in the minds of the Heraka, the important fact was that the writings represented a form of 'literary power'. These writings were, according to Gaidinliu's account, received in Bhuban cave. She recalls that the walls of the cave were filled with writing. They transmitted an aura of the written form that she allegedly took down in detail: the notebooks are the only probable remnants of her writing. People who visit Bhuban cave narrate visions of words appearing suddenly and then disappearing again. Indeed, the narrative of Manshai and his Hingde Book and the current writing of the Hingde Book, taps into the power of the written word and indicates the eventual systematization of a religious system that puts one on a par with the 'religions of the word'.

We may ask why there is this strong need for the Heraka to adopt a holy book? Is it, as Maurice Bloch reminds us, the need to adapt to a world system increasingly influenced by 'world religions'? Among the Merina of Madagascar, Bloch sees this as a growing phenomenon. He says,

> The Merina had previously not distinguished between their politics and religion, because their culture . . . did not separate these aspects . . . But the effect of the attack presented by Christianity on the Merina state meant, ironically, that the Merina were forced by the dialectic of the situation to talk of 'their religion' and 'their custom' as though they were distinct entities. This was partly for internal consumption, so that something could be contrasted and valued against the foreign import. It was also partly for foreign consumption, in order to convince outsiders that the Merina were not lacking in religion, and in order to impress with the splendour and coherence of their cults. (1986: 20–1)

With the need to 'impress with the splendour and coherence' of their religious practice, the Heraka have 'canonized' their holy book as a guide for daily living. The Hingde Book is didactic and peppered with ethical insights such as how to live according to Tingwang's will, or the codification of birth, marriage and death rituals, which become 'sacred repositories of the word of God, which in themselves remain unchanging, eternal, inspired by the divine and not by man alone' (Goody 1996: 6). According to Goody these 'religions of the Book' (1996: 1–4) transpose their beliefs into a corpus of writing that transcends generations and retains the essence of the 'religion'. In the Heraka narrative, finding some connection between the current Hingde Book and that of an eternal past, enables it to proclaim its own present as existing since time immemorial.

In recent years literacy has become particularly important for the Heraka, not only to convey its message to its members, but also to maintain a uniform religious practice in the face of a plurality of views within the Heraka itself. Despite the publication of the Hingde Book, its impact is far from certain, as are its consequence in the lives of the Heraka, whose population is mainly in the villages where levels of literacy remain low. For literate societies, Goody argues, the problem thus becomes one of 'universalism'. By adopting a written form of codification, the 'word' becomes more 'abstract', 'generalized', and formalized; and to some extent replaces the contextualized oral tradition (1996: 12, 15).

In the attempt to encourage the reading of the Hingde Book another problem arises: the privileging of hierarchy. The educated and the elite clearly have the upper hand when disseminating knowledge. This creates a chain of command and a centralized leadership which trains *hingde pame* (*hingde* preachers). They then travel from village to village preaching about Heraka Hingde and interpreting the religious text. This encourages a relationship between the *text* as 'determinate' with the 'power to bring about particular beliefs' (making the reader passive), while the *reader* is 'taken to be actively engaged in constructing the meaning of texts in accordance with changing social circumstances' (making the text passive) (Asad 2003: 11; italics in original). If Talal Asad is right, the relationship between the 'divine text' and 'human approaches to it' must surely be pertinent in forming a community of believers around the religious text (2003: 11).

With the Heraka the relationship between the text and the reader is even more ambiguous. The preachers encourage its adherents to read the Hingde Book, to quote passages in their daily life, to have a Hingde Book training session (akin to the Christian Bible study) as the way forward in religious development. These characteristics are evident with some Heraka youth referring to the Hingde Book and reciting passages that inspire them, or stories they hold dear. The older community, on the other hand, are largely uninterested with the Hingde Book, possibly due to literacy constraints. For them, Hingde is not informed by any leader (or text) but by Tingwang; its practice is therefore implicit and must be centred on the community and not dictated by certain individuals. This dependence on text, they allege, leads to too much power in the hands of a few. This creates a hierarchy of knowledge, rather than a horizontal dispersal of knowledge. Orality is able to dispense the latter while writing tends to hinder it. The older generation feel that when knowledge is passed down through writing, customs are naturally weakened, as the youth do not refer to their elders' knowledge anymore.

Respect is thus being quickly lost, literacy bringing with it a learned arrogance, as the rural people see it, that drives a wedge between those who can read (developed) and those who cannot (backward).[25] These notions are becoming more pronounced and the privileging of literacy over orality is a growing trend. Moreover, the relationship between the text and the recipient is largely passive because of low levels of literacy. Even though the Hingde Book attempts to codify a religious doctrine that has highly didactic overtones, oral narratives (in villages) are the preferred method for transmission of knowledge. In this sense, this codification discredits the

Heraka claim to be an extension of the Zeme way of being human; it is becoming the modern way of acting. In this connection, the story of Herakandingpeu is worth examination, for the oral transmission of knowledge is still privileged on a wider scale, especially in the villages that see the story mirroring Heraka Hingde.

The Healer: Herakandingpeu

There is a difference, the Zeme Heraka say, between Herakandingpeu as healer and Ranima as mediator. This difference is in the manner they operated. Herakandingpeu healed by using plantain leaves, grass and roots like ginger. He was extremely intelligent and knew how to communicate with animals and gods, and possessed magic that could heal humans and animals. But herein lies the difference. Before Herakandingpeu died, the only thing he taught humans was to cure by using ginger. Therefore, the people eventually had to revert to the bloodthirsty gods for their grievances. On the other hand, they say, Ranima possessed much more knowledge. Her intimate relationship with Tingwang made it possible for anyone to be healed by just singing a song from the hymnbook or singing one of the prayer songs. There are no codes or special privileges; everyone is equal in the eyes of Tingwang. Even after Ranima's death, not only are her followers free but they themselves possess all the grace and knowledge to be makers of their own destiny.

The story of Herakandingpeu is important for the Heraka because they say that Herakandingpeu did not sacrifice any animals, not a single drop of blood was shed. He was so clever and astute that the bloodthirsty gods were jealous, angry at being deprived of any blood. The gods therefore planned to kill him. Chuprai, the god of grain, was the chief conspirator.

> Chuprai disguised himself as a poor boy and approached Herakandingpeu and questioned him about his immortality. After incessant questioning, Herakandingpeu finally told him: 'I will die only if a wagtail (*dui rui*) wounds me in my navel.' Chuprai then approached the council of gods and it was agreed that Chuprai disguise himself as the wagtail and wound Herakandingpeu. The next day Herakandingpeu was out fishing and in his fishing basket (*hebua*) he found a small, curious looking bird. He thought to himself that this would make a good present for the children. He tucked the bird in his belt around the navel. As he was making his way home, the bird suddenly bit his navel and flew away. Immediately, Herakandingpeu fell ill and rushed home. He instructed the men of his

village to go and fetch a particular herb from the jungle. When the men reached the outskirts of the jungle, the gods disguised as men told them that Herakandingpeu had died and to return to the village immediately. When the men returned, Herakandingpeu was still alive. Realising their foolishness, another group of men were sent. The same thing happened again and again, until finally, he sent a young boy to go to the jungle. The young boy cleverly went past the gods but before he returned with the medicine, Herakandingpeu had died. However, before he died, Herakandingpeu told the village: 'I will put my spittle on this ginger, and whenever you are ill or meet with an evil spirit, ask the ginger for help. I will put my spittle also on this bamboo, and when you want to know [about certain illnesses], ask of it also.'[26]

Interpretation

The killing of Herakandingpeu is associated with Chuprai and the other bloodthirsty gods who are in turn identified with Paupaise (the *kemeume* generation).[27] Chuprai is obviously the target for the Heraka. Any blood sacrifice is associated with Chuprai and his posse of gods, while Herakandingpeu's era is associated with 'purity' in the sense that no blood sacrifices were made, which in turn mirrors the current Heraka reform. With the story of Herakandingpeu, the Heraka are able to establish continuity with the past, which is in turn interpreted as a new Hingde.

Heraka Hingde

As explained earlier, Heraka Hingde claims to mirror the era of Herakandingpeu which in turn is the model for the new Hingde. But the problem for the Heraka is that this Hingde is not regulated and therefore has a weak hold on its adherents. They argue that Muslims have the Qur'an which they read or the Christians have the Bible: both are supposed to discipline their lives according to its teachings. Therefore, the Heraka is similarly attempting to systematize religious belief and practice. For example, the Hingde Book speaks about eight steps that encapsulate Heraka Hingde. They are as follows:

1. Tingwang created the earth and will destroy it again, but believe in him and sing his praises and pray to him.
2. Respect your parents and elders and preserve the good Zeliangrong culture.

3. Have a disciplined mind and a clean body. *Heleuraube* (selflessness) will make your image wonderful and you will become the son/daughter of Tingwang.
4. In all speech and work your mind must be truthful. Search for knowledge and light but breed not jealousy and enmity.
5. Love all of Tingwang's sons and daughters and search the way for happiness and peace.
6. Observe *Jalua* (full moon day) well.
7. Set up a Kelumki (prayer house) and pray with an empty hand (i.e. stop animal sacrifice).
8. Have faith in rebirth.[28]

This codifying of rules is an attempt to organize Heraka society under the rubric of Hingde. In fact, nowadays, people are encouraged, like the Baptist Christians, to talk about their faith and belief in order to project themselves as having a testimony – a transformative experience. There is intense competition with Christianity. Working under the shadow of the Christians makes the Heraka seem vulnerable and dispossessed. The organization of a viable system is therefore essential if the uniformity and integrity of the Heraka Hingde is to be maintained.

Mirase

In addition to regulation, the reforms were targeted at changing the way *mirase* was conceived. According to Heraka reformers, sacrifices to the many small gods were primarily in the realm of *mirase*, and by changing the *mirase*, every aspect of culture would subsequently alter, due to their interrelatedness. This is because the 'new Hingde' was making a break with the 'old hingde'. The change of *mirase* necessarily incorporated this 'new Hingde'. But it also gave rise to different sets of problems associated with the previously unfamiliar conceptual–ontological split between the various sections of social life.

The Heraka have eventually replaced the system of animal sacrifice, associated with Paupaise *mirase* (sacrifices to small gods), with the Heraka *mirase* of Kelumki (prayer house; prayer to the one high god Tingwang). In fact, an analysis of the relationship between the *mirase* reforms, the establishment of a Kelumki and the *neubes* associated with it illustrates how the Heraka have managed to carve out something 'sacred' and separate from everyday life. They have done this by also incorporating Paupaise notions of ritual and *neube*. The Paupaise reject the Heraka's piecemeal excising of *neube*, however.

The Sacralization of Space

When I first visited a Kelumki (prayer house) my ignorance of its ritual specificity was accepted as a sign of me being an outsider (see Photograph 4.1). As a result, my actions were treated with politeness rather than indignation. As I became accepted into the Heraka community, my ignorance of the Kelumki was no longer treated as naivety but as disrespect. Through trial and error, and the constant reminder of my Heraka friends, I became familiar with the strict ritual regimen inside the Kelumki.

My analysis of the Kelumki is centred primarily on the Heraka villages in and around Hsongle. *Jalua* (full moon day), *Heleingi* prayer (prayer before the harvest), *Hepumra* (new year), and Ranima and Jadonang's death anniversaries are marked within the Kelumki and participated in by the entire village. In this way, these rituals are a relatively communal affair, though people also have the choice to opt out of them. In the town (Haflong), it is more complicated. For instance, during *Jalua*, it is

Photograph 4.1 A Heraka Kelumki (prayer house)

sometimes not possible to observe all the prohibitions (see below) for the entire day if one is working in secular institutions. Indeed, the Heraka in the town still feel that to be a 'proper' Heraka one must go to the villages.

The Kelumki is separate from the rest of the village in the way it is conceived, as well as physically treated and respected. It is the most 'sacred' ground for the Heraka and every Heraka village must have one. It is usually built on the highest point of a village. They say it is an exact copy of the first temple built by Jadonang and Ranima, invoking tradition as a chain of memory for legitimation (Hervieu-Léger 2000). The caretaker of the Hsongle Kelumki explained the history behind it.

> The exact structure, as you see it, was given to Ranima in a dream. Every Kelumki must have a *naimik kakelum be bam* (sunrise prayer place) outside facing East. East is vital for two reasons: it signifies the direction of Bhuban cave, as well as that of the sunrise, which is of great importance during *Jalua* (full moon ritual). The sunrise prayer place must be elevated and is reached by three steps (symbolising life-death-life). There is a *kegeu* (veranda) before entering the Kelumki. The main entrance is called *muidi*; once inside there is another side entrance called *muicheiki* (small door) on the right, as it is strictly forbidden to place it on the left. If using the *muicheiki*, one must re-enter using the same door.
>
> Before entering the compound of the Kelumki, shoes must be removed. Inside, there are two sections: the right *hejet mbia* (for male) and the left for *heku mbia* (for female). On the left there is a bench facing the congregation for the Paileu[29] and on the right is reserved for the secretary, chairman, president, Paipeu and *tingkopau* (priest) of that village. Podiums are also present on both sides for those wanting to say a few words. On the podium is written 'Tingwang Hingde' and below that 'Sam Yi Besa Bam' (speak in truthfulness).
>
> At the front of the Kelumki is the altar, centrally placed and elevated. One must climb the three steps (life-death-life) to it, proceeding with the right leg, then left, and right. The altar is on two levels. On the first level (higher level), only fruits, vegetables and flowers can be placed while the second level (lower level) is for coins and paper money. This offering is accompanied by a prayer (personal and private). Once that is finished, one must turn anticlockwise (away from the right) and return to one's place. While one waits to reach the altar, a space must be kept between the right and the left for Tingwang to come and go in-between.

When one looks directly above from the altar, there is a small opening into a short wooden tower in which Jadonang allegedly kept the pythons with which he communicated. When the British destroyed the temple, they found two pythons inside the tower and shot them. Now, it is believed that when people pray in the Kelumki, Tingwang resides in this space (see Figure 4.1).

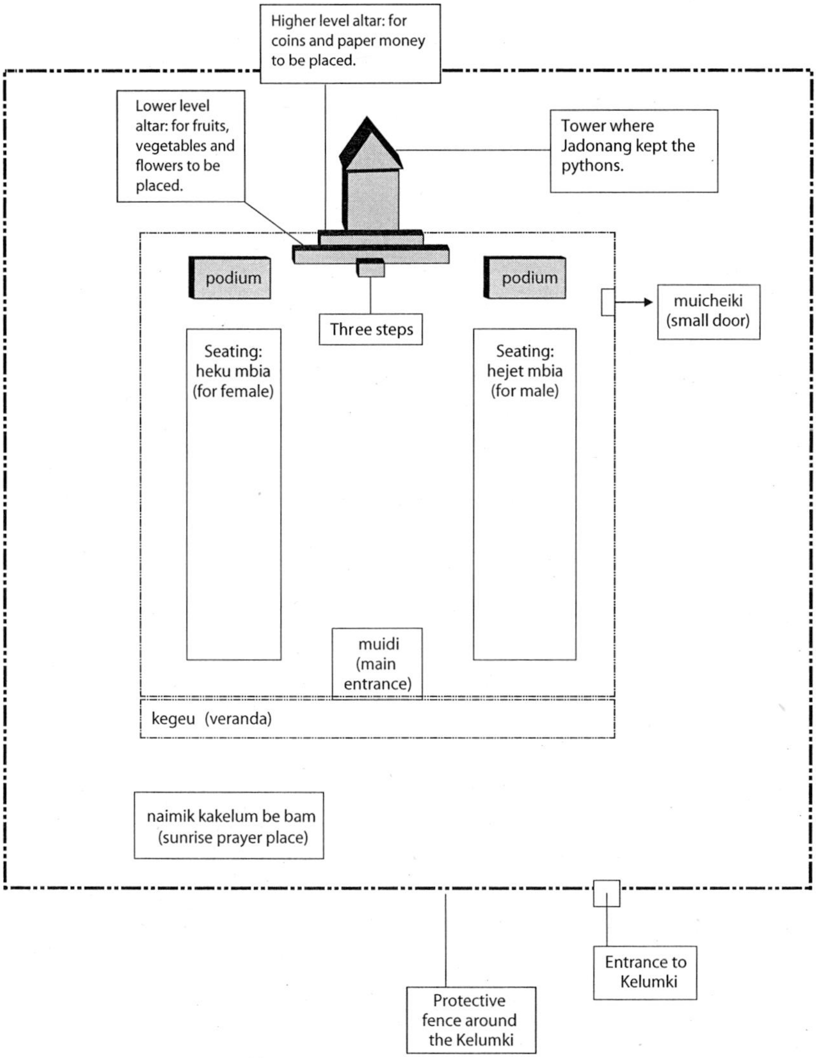

Figure 4.1 Kelumki

Analysis: Purity and Danger

With the establishment of the Kelumki, the sacralization of ritual space occurs. Kim Knott draws our attention to how, when seen from the perspective of 'spatial practice', 'ritual practice' incorporates 'religious meaning'. Religious meaning is performed in the context of 'space set apart as sacred and by an appropriate ritual practitioner'. In other words, sacralization of ritual space occurs when 'ritual, as sacred making behaviour, brings about "sacred" space' (Knott 2005: 43). This is certainly true of the Kelumki, for its specific ritual action generates 'religious meaning' demanded by all of its adherents. Failing this, it can be viewed as dangerous for the adherent and the community. But what do I mean by the 'sacred' in the context of the Kelumki?

The anthropologist Talal Asad points out that the word 'sacred' can be traced to the Roman Republic and their use of the word *sacer*, which referred to anything owned by a deity (Asad 2003: 30; Douglas 2003: 8). Freud finds similarity between the Roman notion of 'sacer' and the Polynesian 'taboo' (1983: 18), which, in the Polynesian sense, was contrasted with the 'common' or 'generally acceptable', hence meaning 'forbidden' (Freud 1983: 18). *Sacer* and taboo, in this regard, can also be associated with the Zeme understanding of '*neube*' (prohibition). There is a double meaning in the way I am using the term 'sacred' in the context of the Kelumki. The 'double sacred', Serge Tcherkézoff argues, can be seen from the perspective of the sacred or the profane where both planes have a pure and impure state from the position of the other (1987: 14; see also Knott 2005: 224).[30] The Kelumki can be seen in this perspective – that it has a 'double sacred in the relationship between the '*neube*' and the 'religious' aspect of the 'sacred' (Anttonen: 2000: 279; see also Eliade 1958: 14–15). First I will explain the *neube* aspect of the 'sacred'.

Blood sacrifices in Zeme Paupaise were followed by a *neube*; an occasion that was marked and set aside (certain foods must be avoided, sexual contact forbidden, and so on) for a set number of days. In this sense, any breaking of the prohibition was seen as a violation of the agreement between the God and humans, therefore rendering that sacrifice ineffective. In some respects, the Heraka have continued this notion of *neube* by similarly enforcing certain prohibitions and requiring its members to adhere to them inside the Kelumki and during *Jalua* (full moon day). For example, following the Kelumki service, during *Jalua*, certain *neubes* are announced. People are not allowed to husk rice, make handicrafts, hunt and fish, pluck green leaves and fruits, kill insects and birds, travel, indulge in any sexual activity, sell and buy, and wash clothes (P. Newme 2002: 11).

This period of restraint was considered the liminal period; the 'betwixt and between period' associated with great danger (Turner 1969). To avoid certain mixing of foods, to avoid going to the fields or to abstain from sexual activities was to protect the people from any untoward danger, as the spiritual power in the ritual was also associated with danger. In this sense, Mary Douglas, while examining notions of purity and danger, says,

> the universe is divided between things and actions which are subject to restriction and others which are not; among the restrictions some are intended to protect divinity from profanation, and others to protect the profane from the dangerous intrusion of divinity. Sacred rules are thus merely rules hedging divinity off, and uncleanness is the two-way danger of contact with divinity. (2003: 8)

There is also a sense that the Kelumki represents the 'religious' aspect of the Heraka Hingde. Daniéle Hervieu-Léger provides us with a way in which the 'religious' as a process emerges from two interacting and distinguishing factors. The process is evident in what she calls 'elective fraternities' who constitute 'a community of values and references which has developed through shared interests, experience and hardships'. Such a community becomes inherently 'religious' when it 'takes on permanence and, seeking to legitimate its existence beyond the inevitable routinization of the emotional experiences that led to the sense of forming a single heart, needs to call upon a common spirit that transcends its individual members' (2000: 150–2; cited in Knott 2005: 220). The Kelumki in a way highlights the position of the Heraka in terms of its transition from 'elective fraternities', evoking tradition, to memory which is inherently religious, and invokes beliefs (Knott 2005: 220). This can be seen in the way the right hand is associated with 'religious' elements while the left hand with the 'prohibitive' and hence 'elective' elements as discussed below.

Revolving Centre: The Right and Left of the Kelumki

The importance of the right and left in relation to one another is maintained in the Kelumki because it represents the balance between purity and impurity. For example, certain spatial considerations operate inside the Kelumki that mark these classifications. The side entrance, *muicheiki* (small door), is on the right as it is strictly forbidden on the left. The right side in this case is the point of exit and re-entry for those wanting to leave in case of emergency. On the other hand, any point of exit on the left is highly dangerous as it is considered inauspicious. The notion of life-death-life is connected with the steps taken by the foot, right-left-right. Similarly, once one leaves the altar one must turn away from the right, as this is where Tingwang's house is.[31]

The right side is associated with beliefs: in Tingwang (right), in rebirth (life-death-life: right-left-right), East (right) and in the Hingde (right). The writing of the Hingde Book, and the establishment of a Kelumki all suggest a specific 'religious system' mirroring Heraka Hingde. In a sense, this demonstrates the 'sacred' nature of the Kelumki as it embodies the concept of sacred rules, as Asad suggests, '"sacred" because of the source of their sanction, "rules" because of their impersonal and transcendent application' (2003: 250). This is done by making the group intrinsically 'religious' by adopting a framework of beliefs, and defining the corpus of the community as divinely mandated. On the other hand, the left side is associated with prohibitive elements in opposition to the right. Veikko Anttonen sums the relationship between the two:

> Menstruation, pregnancy, the post-parturition period and also the manipulation of corpses in mortuary rituals have almost universally been connected with the semantic field of the category of the sacred, in other words, with the idea of a boundary that sets socially impure members and elements apart from pure ones in the category systems of the community. The growth of things with social value (the 'religious' aspect of the sacred) is to be protected against the contagious impact of substances that are not confined within the socially defined boundaries of the human body, society and territory, and which have exhausted their capacity to produce growth for the benefit of society (the 'taboo' aspect of the sacred). (2000: 279)

From the argument so far, one obvious point is that the Heraka *mirase* intends to be viewed as a continuing tradition of the Paupaise, in order to legitimate Heraka rituals. Therefore, while abolishing the blood sacrifices, the prohibitions are still retained. There is a strong sense that the Heraka community, as represented by the Kelumki, intends to fraternize with 'tradition', in order to legitimize itself as traditional, while the 'religious' elements are very reformist. The paradox of the 'sacred' in a way reflects the position of the Heraka inside the Kelumki having a broader reach outside of it as well. This is best understood in relation to the two houses that encompass the organization of Heraka villages.

Relation of the Two Houses

While the Kelumki represents the enclosed space of ritual and personal communion with God, the Paiki represents almost the reverse. The Paiki is like any home in the village, the only specification is that it must have a door facing east towards the direction of Bhuban cave. The Kelumki, on the other hand, is specifically designed on the model of Jadonang's temple (one can draw parallels between churches and homes respectively). How does this connect with the organization of the Heraka village?

The Paipeu resides in the Paiki and is the single most important person in a Heraka village. The Paipeu and his household must have wealth, as his status requires him to entertain people or guests. The priest on the other hand is second to the Paipeu and is more of a symbolic figure. If the priest is absent the Paipeu can take over his role but not vice versa. This was of course not the case during Paupaise, that is, in the earlier pre-Heraka period. At that time, the priest was held in the utmost esteem. He was privileged in the village (the Paipeu did not exist then) and conducted all the rituals. In fact, the priest mediated between the visible and the less visible and maintained the cosmic balance. If the Heraka Kelumki is the sacralization of space what is its relation with the Paiki and thus the role of the priest and the Paipeu respectively?

One can draw several points from this. The reformers wanted to differentiate themselves from the Paupaise system, in particular they wished to avoid the symbol of the priest associated with the smaller gods and animal sacrifices, and instead replace it with someone, such as the Paipeu, who accommodated the message of the reform. In this sense, the role of the priest became redundant. Now, since the Kelumki has incorporated the 'religious' element of the reform, anyone can enter it, once purified and protected (by singing and praying). The relationship is now more personal, rather than mediated. But more importantly, the relationship between the Kelumki and Paiki is such that once the 'sacredness' of the Kelumki is dispersed among the people, the remnants of the activities conducted in the Kelumki are carried on to the Paiki, to the everyday world, to be embodied and dispersed again. The Paiki is also important because it was associated with Ranima and her time in the jungle. When Ranima and her followers went underground to avoid the Christian Naga nationalists, Ranima often communicated with God using *pai* (body cloths) as a *ki* (tent) (hence the name Paiki), pitched with wooden sticks. Here Ranima would receive all her instructions for her movement, from God. The Kelumki provides the 'essence' that has an effect of emanating spiritual power and danger. It is similar to the Paupaise symbol of lighting a fire at the *hezoa* (centre of the village) and carrying it to the homes as a sign of renewal – the point of dispersal is from the centre.[32] Therefore, the Paiki is the link between the Kelumki and the rest of everyday life. The Paiki is the cooling point, as it were, where the 'sacred' (when the danger has subsided) makes contact with the everyday world. Therefore, when proceeding from the Kelumki to the Paiki, songs are always sung to protect the people from any danger. It is also the place where the empty stomach is filled with the first cup of *zao*, symbolizing the breaking away from the danger of the sacredness of the Kelumki, to a place of security and conclusion (see Figure 4.2).

The symbol of the two houses also represents a metaphor for Heraka reform. The Heraka Hingde is exemplified in the *mirase* reforms and encapsulated in the Kelumki and the Hingde Book as encapsulating it. The Kelumki is thus highly ritualized, fixed and sacralized, and separated from the village by its boundaries. The Paiki, on the other hand, represents openness to the world and the intermingling of everything that is not possible in the Kelumki. Due to a *perceived* contrast of these two houses, there seems to be a noticeable demarcation between 'religious' associated with the Kelumki

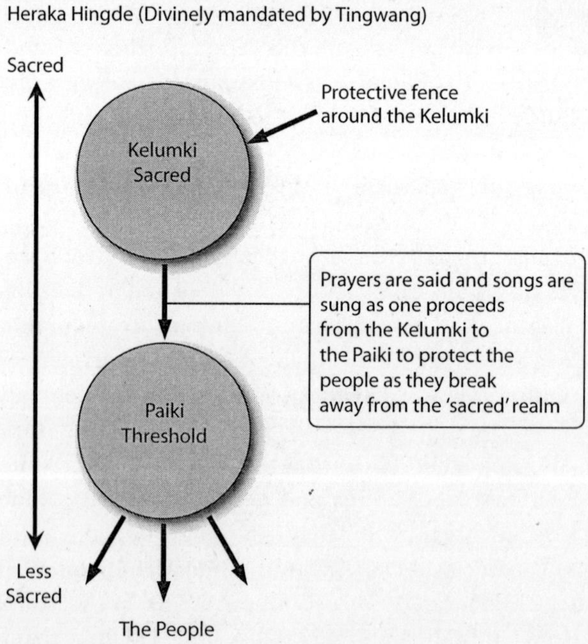

FIGURE 4.2 Kelumki and Paiki

and 'non-religious' associated with the Paiki. This relationship is visible during the *heliengi* festival in Hsongle.

Heliengi: The Harvest Festival

It was still dark as we left the hut around 4.30 in the morning. As we neared the Hsongle Paiki, a hint of light was piercing through the clouds and the stillness of the morning gave way to loud noises. A small crowd was hovering around the two *mithuns* bought for the festival. We waited for the young adults to start the process of killing and cutting the animal. It was around 5.30; still no sign of any of them. By this time the priest had become impatient and loudly reminded the group that the animal would have to be killed before the sunrise prayer to avoid it being a sacrifice. After his edict, we walked up to the Kelumki. On the way the *hangseoki* (male dormitory) was surprisingly full of adult men, drunk and accosting us to have a drink. According to Heraka *hingde* it is taboo for any Heraka to drink or eat before the Kelumki service. The religiously minded Heraka were complaining that these people are non-religious and that, since they are impure (due to the drinking), they should not be allowed in the Kelumki.

It was around 6.00 a.m.: still no sign of the Heraka youth to lead the sunrise prayer. We could hear distant drums from the neighbouring village; they had already begun their sunrise prayer. In *heliengi*, the Kelumki service follows the sunrise prayer. It is believed that for the sunrise prayer to be effective, traditional clothes must be worn as a mark of authenticity. Youths are required to lead the salute to the sun, but were conspicuously absent. Instead, after a lot of bickering and shouting by the priest, a hurriedly assembled group of young boys were given the part, albeit dressed in their trousers and shirts. By this time the sun had already risen and the auspiciousness dented by the delay. The timing of the prayer is supposed to coincide exactly with the sun's rise to its full glow. Another delay. The people responsible for killing the animal at the Paiki were late, and we had to wait for a further few minutes before we were given the word that the animal had been killed and the sunrise prayer could start. By this time, the priest and the elders were fuming. Once inside the Kelumki, the right side was bare with only four of us in attendance, while the left side was full – women and children. The priest hastily announced that the service would be cut short due to the delay. After the service, as we stepped outside, the priest told me that this incident was an anomaly; usually it was done properly.

As we proceeded to the Paiki for the official breaking of the bread, and the first cup of *zao* which is tasted before *heliengi*, throngs of men suddenly descended. The festival had officially begun. The example of the *heliengi* festival demonstrates the *perceived* differences between the two houses: whereas the men can drink *zao* in the Paiki, this would not be acceptable in the Kelumki. This is an example of the way the Heraka reform can incorporate choices by separating the 'religious' from the 'non-religious'. The festival also highlights the importance of what Asad referred to earlier: 'the changes in concepts articulate changes in practice' (2003: 25). This gives rise to the tension between Hingde and *mitulung*; 'rules' and 'action' evolve in relation to the reform and indeed the world itself.

Embodying Practice

Mitulung is very much embodied. In fact, *mitulung* literally means my-nature, which further incorporates actions of the world, its current trends, into 'a way of doing things', which through habit becomes my-nature. It can also be used as 'action'. The body becomes the metaphor by which meanings are communicated and predictable. The relationship between Hingde as divinely mandated 'rules' and the resultant 'actions', *mitulung*, that embody the 'rules', is centred around a shared way of life, divinely ordained. In other words, the Heraka community bound through a continuing tradition must reflect the divine 'rules' through 'actions'. The body, both kinaesthetically and emotionally, then, becomes the vehicle and repository of shared tradition. Hingde is therefore 'not merely a law whose authority resides in the supernatural realm, but the way for individuals to discipline their life together' as Heraka through *mitulung* (Asad 2003: 250).[33]

I now intend to clarify this argument, drawing on certain examples. Heraka Hingde is constantly in competition with other *hingde* through society's contact with the wider world. Heraka Hingde therefore tries to control actions by drawing up edicts and trying to mend 'bad action' with 'good action'. For example, when girls are having premarital sex, particularly with members of other communities, this threatens the purity of the group, and the reformers respond by drawing up 'Holy Marriage Certificates' (proof of the girl's virginity) as a way of curtailing sexual activities and maintaining purity. As a reaction, this is seen as 'good action' and praising virginity is now Heraka Hingde.[34] The same can be said about education.

Earlier millenarian expectations of the advent of a 'golden age', and the resulting reformers' indifference to education, cultivated such sceptical views about education that some people stopped going to schools. Now, education is seen as 'good action' and has become Heraka Hingde. Similarly, the reading of the Hingde Book, attending the Kelumki service, observing the *Jalua* and the prohibitions are all seen as 'good action'. In this manner, some aspects of *hingde* from the outside are made 'sacred' by Heraka Hingde while similarly some Heraka Hingde have become 'bad action' and 'out of Hingde'. This has happened, for example, with *zao*. *Zao* was a tradition that characterized Zeme culture; its use was widespread and ritualized. Therefore, *zao* for the Heraka was generally associated with tradition, prosperity and wealth. But, over the years, people started abusing *zao*, which caused innumerable burdens to families, affecting many areas of life. As a reaction to the problems caused by *zao* in Heraka society, excessive use of *zao* is therefore increasingly seen as 'bad action' and summarily condemned as 'out of Hingde'.

In this way, the Hingde for the Heraka is constantly evolving around *mitulung* (action): in subtle ways actions from outside *hingde* are incorporated into the Heraka Hingde. The Heraka negotiate with the wider world and police their boundaries. One of the consequences of the sacralization of the Kelumki, and its association with *mirase* reform, is the break between *mitulung* (actions) and *mirase* (god practice), and also with *mikise* (house rules). Because the actions within the Kelumki cannot be repeated outside it, the *mirase* associated with the Kelumki no longer relates in a substantial way to everyday actions (*mitulung*). Therefore, what was once a whole system of related activities has now become noticeable in its demarcations. It is difficult to say if any such marked separation of social elements will increase in the near future, but this difference has already yielded rules that are continuously defined and reformed according to the circumstances.

I therefore would argue that it is difficult to sustain, at least in Heraka society, the dichotomy between the 'sacred' as one fixed category and the secular or the profane as another. But with increasingly noticeable demarcation between the various spheres of life and the influence of urban life on the Heraka villagers, the social landscape of the Heraka will alter dramatically whereby such 'secular' elements will also become largely distinguishable from the 'religious'.[35] This is particularly evident in the way the 'sacred' is separated, creating a 'secular' sphere. The desacralization of *zao* from the Kelumki to the everyday world, for example, is a good case for the prominence of the latter. Another important related point is the way the separation of the Kelumki from everyday life creates a level playing field with the temple, mosque and church. It creates a vertical hierarchy, with the Kelumki on top, separated as sacred, while the other aspects, such as

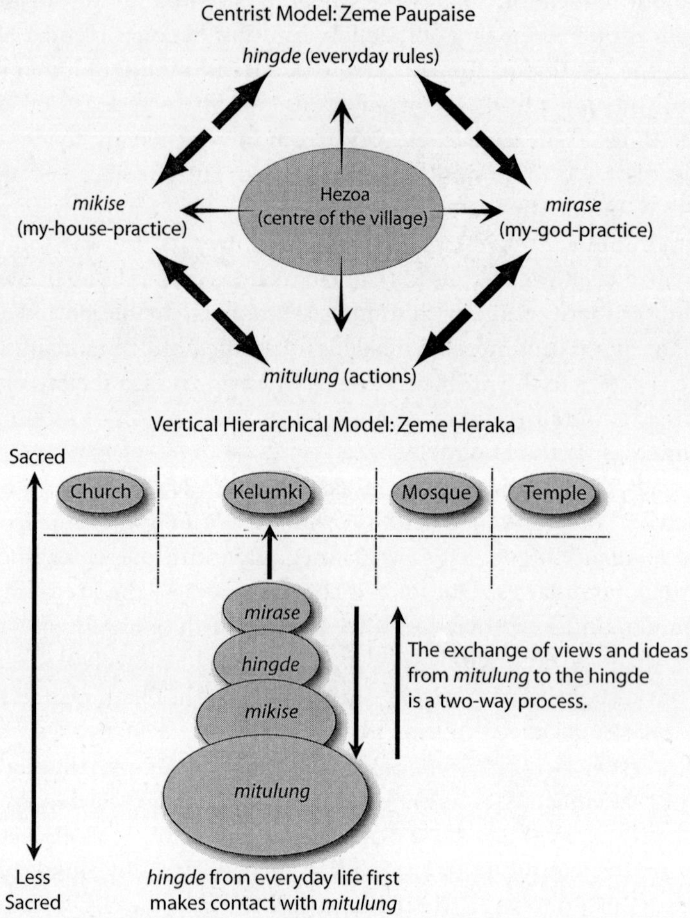

Figure 4.3 Centrist Model and Vertical Hierarchical Model

mirase, Hingde, *mikise* and *mitulung*, fall below. This is indicative for a reform that moves from a previously centrist model in the Paupaise era, to a more vertical and therefore hierarchical model in the Heraka (see Figure 4.3). This of course has vast implications for the way the reform has generated a religious system that copy dominant forms from other major religious traditions, particularly in how the 'sacred' is represented.

The creation of the 'sacred' has given rise to distinct practices, build around a 'religious system' for the Zeme Heraka. For what was once a tight knit Zeme community is now giving way to a situation where religious traditions create boundaries and separation.

Conclusion

This chapter has dealt with the nature of the Heraka reform. I have shown how the cosmology – in this instance the creation story – was reformed to reflect their current practices, while they also grounded any reform in traditional practices through maintaining the minor gods of the Paupaise. It is this grounding that legitimizes the reform. This has led to the distinct carving out of a religious system under the rubric of Heraka Hingde that, in contrast to the Paupaise, begins to make distinctions between religious, social, economic and political life. With the Paupaise tradition the 'communal' was the religious but this created tensions between the tradition and the modern world, which in contrast the Heraka reform could accommodate.

With the adoption of the healer Herakandingpeu and the rise of literacy in the form of the Hingde Book, the Heraka are also codifying their text and influencing behaviour, to an extent, particularly in the urban areas. People of the urban areas have begun to view education as necessary and as part of Heraka Hingde. The rural areas, in some cases, are still sceptical of such a project. Perhaps the most visible aspect of the reform is seen in the adoption of a Kelumki as 'sacred'.

By sacralizing this space, the Heraka makes the Kelumki the centre of the village, replacing the Paupaise *hezoa* (centre of the village). But while the *hezoa* was at times 'sacred' because of its placement, the Kelumki is a fixed 'sacred' entity. Moreover, the Kelumki represents the sacredness of the Heraka around which a 'sacred' community is continuously defined. The noticeable difference in the way people are seen either as 'religious' or 'non-religious' is evident in the *heliengi* festival and how the Paiki mediates between the two conceptions: the 'sacred' Kelumki and the 'non-sacred'. This is the case because the Heraka Hingde is primarily focused on the *mirase* reforms, the Kelumki and latterly the Hingde Book. Because the reform has emphasized primarily one aspect of Heraka life – the *mirase* – other aspects have almost been neglected. Due to this, Heraka Hingde has to retrospectively define Hingde, and thus, in turn, feed into 'action' (*mitulung*). This not only weakens the Heraka Hingde but, with the increase of Heraka contact with the wider world, there are more choices and more 'other hingde' to contend with.

In this chapter, my main argument has been that, with the introduction of a new religious system attempting to replace an older one, demarcations are established that lead the newer group, such as the Heraka, to integrate and systematize their world according to their 'rules'. The reform engages with the world and feeds it back into their practice and vice versa.

With the change of the cosmology and the way the Heraka religious system has produced demarcations since the beginning of the reform, the Heraka have, as I have recounted above, engaged with the world. In this sense, the place of Heraka in the Zeme landscape is contentious vis-à-vis the Christian population, other 'Naga groups' and the role of 'Hindu' organizations. Heraka identity and boundaries emerge through the interaction with these forces. Hence, not only are the Heraka trying to project a uniform religious system, but they also attempt to project themselves as the only true indigenous religious practice in the region. The next chapter will highlight some of these issues.

Chapter 5

Negotiating Boundaries

This chapter aims to provide us with an understanding of the dominant religious traditions of the region – Heraka, Christian and 'Hinduism'. By seeking to analyse relationships between the three, the aim here is to provide an analysis and assessment of religious boundaries in order to illuminate the logic of religious pluralism as it deepens and operates. This is also intimately connected with questions of identity. I argue that notions of identity are elucidated by closer examination of community and boundary: where does it begin, where does it end? Are these boundaries physical, symbolic, cognitive or psychological (Cohen 2003: 12)? Using historical data that marks the beginning of Christianity's effect on the Zeme, I examine how the relationship between Heraka and Christian are determined by socially constructed boundaries, and hope to shed some light on physical, symbolic and cognitive issues. Further, not only is this identity battle fought in the local scenarios of the villages, but identity is also exported and imported. These extraterritorial implications concern the role of Christianity, 'Hindu' organizations, like the RSS and the VHP, and the larger 'Naga' national question.

This enquiry into the politics of religious traditions is informed by my fieldwork in one Zeme village, Hsongle, as a way of understanding the general context in which 'religions' operate on a larger scale in most Zeme villages in North Cachar Hills. The first impression one gets of Hsongle village is of the rigid boundaries of 'colonies'. Each denomination of Christians, and the Heraka are boxed into a neat geometry of spatial order, each inhabiting its own garden of reason.

The Village

Hsongle village in North Cachar Hills, Assam, is the largest village east of Haflong. The river Jenam runs through Hsongle as it cuts the valley in half. On the other side of the hill lies Lozeihe village, the only Paupaise village.

The river provides fresh fish, a scenic view and features endless lines of people washing their clothes. It is located near the bazaar which has a weekly market day, attracting people from all the surrounding villages for purposes of trade. From the vantage point of the Heraka colony, the original village, the market-place lies at the bottom of the hill, just near the Jenam River. The market is conveniently located within reach of all the 'colonies' and is connected to the main road that leads to Hajaichak village in one direction and Ruham and then Haflong in the other. Hsongle roughly comprises 250 houses, with a population numbering 2,000 or so. It has 3 schools, 3 Churches and 2 Heraka Kelumki (prayer houses).

When Bower did fieldwork in the 1940s, Hsongle was primarily a Paupaise (ancestral practice) village. In her description, Hsongle consisted of 80 houses, 2 *hangseokis* (male dormitories), a rectangular mound of bare earth in the middle of the village called *hezoa* (the centre of the village, known as the heart of the village) and 2 huge wooden water-troughs for collecting water (Bower 1952: 48). The *hangseokis* and the houses remain while the *hezoa*, the water-troughs, and the Paupaise tradition which maintained them, have disappeared. The old Hsongle village is now basically the Heraka colony that sits on top of the hill as is traditional for Zeme villages. Hsongle expanded as new Christian converts formed pockets around the main village which became new colonies, at the entrance to the old village from the south, to the east of the Heraka colony, a cluster of loosely placed houses stands around a towering church, which gives the Presbyterian colony a sort of order. From the southern entry point of the Heraka village the muddy street leads to a steep ridge. Here the path forks and steadily drops towards the Baptist colony. Below the Baptist colony, after crossing the main tar road, is the Catholic colony, conveniently tucked away, at the edge of the hill and towards the river (see Figure 5.1).

Boundaries and Imagined Realities

The construction of these 'colonies' was a natural response to the growing population, but the ghetto-like expansion meant that these religious groups were somehow mutually exclusive and perhaps conceptually wary of the intermingling of different gods. These boundary areas (*heramrai*) have enabled the righteous to live in gilded cages of piety. The best way to establish boundaries is by separating themselves physically. As separate communities, they have too much invested in their 'sense of self' to become part of a larger unit (Cohen 2003: 108–10). Perhaps, also, by creating separation they find

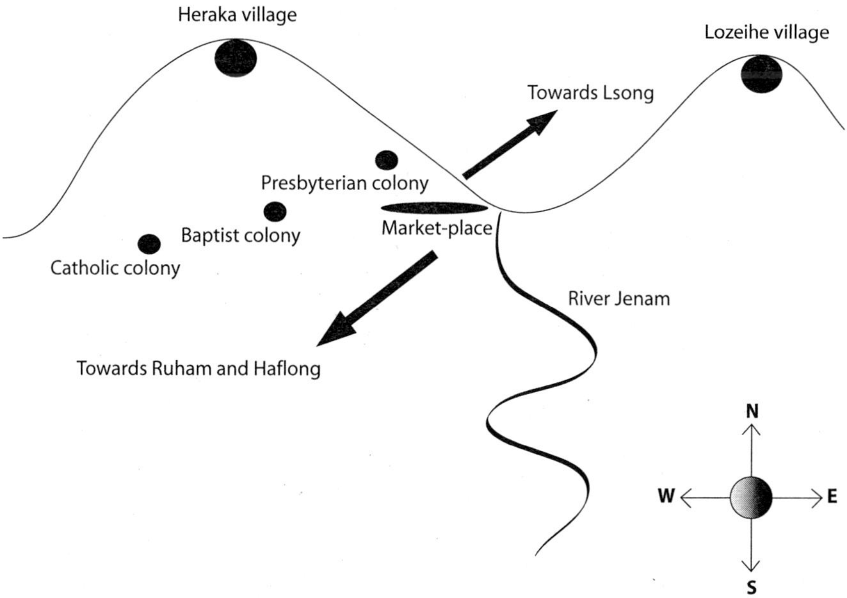

FIGURE 5.1 Hsongle village

it easier to deal with cognitive and spiritual issues among kin. That is, who is 'self' and who is 'other' – a division which applies equally to the divine.

One might ask the reason for this strong desire to identify oneself as Heraka, Christian or even Baptist, Presbyterian, or Catholic? Aren't all of them Zeme? At the root of this lies a bigger picture that is clarified by a closer analysis of boundaries and the identities they construct or vice versa. Religious boundaries are central to my inquiry and to be precise in its use, I propose the following definition from Fredrik Barth. Barth argues that the notion of boundary is used in general overlapping ways:

1. literally, boundaries divide territories 'on the ground';
2. more abstractly, they set limits that mark social groups off from each other;
3. and finally, they provide a template for that which separates distinct categories of the mind. (2000: 17)

As is clear from the discussion so far, the notion of marking one group off from the other is evident in the way 'colonies' are physically placed. In this case, this entails religious traditions marking themselves off from each other. The following example also reveals the pertinence of Barth's definition.

Tahulung, my co-worker, told me that his uncle of Lsong village, who happens to be the Presbyterian elder, started creating boundaries between the Christian and Heraka sections: any intermingling of gods could be threatening to the Christian habitat. He started to delineate boundaries – a certain tree was demarcated as the separating line between the two sections – sections that had never existed before. This is an example that demonstrates just how rigid the boundaries can be between the Heraka and the Christian. It is not enough that symbolic and conceptual boundaries are in place, but over the years physical ones have become necessary too. But how did the construction of these boundaries come about? Did the growth and spread of the Heraka and Christianity cause this rift?

Historical Niceties: Conquest of Reason and Faith

Asalu, a Zeme village, is an hour away from Hsongle in North Cachar Hills. The old colonial houses built by the British lie unused. Only the names of long gone lovers scrawled in black charcoal give a date to the buildings. The emptiness belies the vastness of the former British Empire, which grew steadily as new frontiers, beyond Bengal, provided new challenges, new heroes and new adventures.

Even though the British had some contact with North Cachar Hills from 1832, it was only in 1854 that an administrative subdivisional headquarters became operational in Asalu. The British presence in Asalu was largely a strategic entry point to the Naga Hills.[1] With the British presence in the region, Christian missionary movements also started making their presence felt. Some British administrators were wary of Christian missionaries penetrating into these 'native' populations, others, like the Chief Commissioner of Assam, David Scott, suggested the idea of introducing Christian missions among the hill tribes of Assam as early as 1825. In his view, Christianity would be a good humanitarian resource to tame the 'unruly' (Dena 1988: 20).

Following the Charter Act of 1813, which stipulated that the British administration must take more responsibility for the religious and moral improvement of the people of India (Chaube 1999: 53), William Carey of the Serampore mission sent his first convert, Krishna Chandra Pal, to work among the Khasis of Sylhet on the invitation of the British magistrate of Sylhet. Pal's mission yielded seven converts, all of whom were encouraged by the enthusiastic magistrate to be baptized immediately before instruction. Other missionaries were also operating from the Assam side into the Naga

Hills. F. W. Clark, another American Baptist Missionary, started his work from Assam in 1871 to penetrate the Ao Naga country (see Downs 1983; Dena 1988; Chaube 1999; Nuh 2006).

Subsequently, due to the interest in missions providing a humanitarian resource for the administrators, primarily in the field of education, the American Baptist Foreign Mission Society (ABFMS) was invited from Burma. They set up their office in Manipur in 1894, after an initial attempt in 1836 failed due to opposition from the local government, who had made Vaishnavite Hinduism the main religion by a royal edict in 1705 (Dena 1988: 31). This was followed by an autonomous mission society called Arthington Aboriginese Mission Society (AAMS) funded by a wealthy millionaire, Robert Arthington from Leeds, United Kingdom. Its minister, Rev. Pettigrew, was the first official missionary to receive full patronage from a British official (Mr A. Porteous, the Political Agent of Manipur) in the region.

Arthington's concept was based on the idea that 'every tribe in every land shall have the Gospel' (Dena 1988: 32). Pettigrew's intention was to penetrate the largely Vaishnavite Manipuri population. But the Manipuri people saw his intentions as imperialistic and connected with the British government policy. Due to this setback, he shifted his focus to the hill inhabitants, primarily the Nagas and Kukis.

The presence of the Christian missions in Assam and the Naga Hills slowly started yielding converts. The converts were mostly from the Naga and Kuki tribes of the hills. Medical facilities, and the establishing of a leper asylum, for example, outside Imphal, along with education, became focal points of attraction. However, this also started creating problems for the local traditions, which depended on collective observances of rituals to effect propitiation and remedy disease. But with a new Christian message and a positive collective response under the aegis of these church missions, tensions began surfacing. A confidential report written by a British administrator in 1927, says,

> To obviate friction between Animists who retain their aboriginal customs and Christians, who perhaps may display resentment or be tempted to dispute the authority of a local chief, the American Baptist Mission deliberately endeavours to arrange for a series of Christian villages, where the Christians live together apart from the Nagas and Kukis.[2]

Such tensions were not only a one-dimensional affair, affecting Christians and 'Animists', but also became a battleground between the Christian sects, with one accusing the other of encroaching on the boundary set by the British administration for mission activities. In one example of these tensions, in 1923, Rev. Pettigrew (in charge of the Aboriginese [*sic*] mission) complained to the Political Agent, saying that the

> Workers of the Thado-Kuki [part of the North-East General Mission] were proselytizing outside the allotted area, in parts of the hills where the American Baptist Mission had converts.[3]

These incidents of intramission rivalry became a major concern in many parts of the northeast region. In particular, the rivalry between the American Baptist Mission and the North East General Mission (NEGM; also known as North East India General Mission (NEIGM)), centred in Manipur, became a hot point of debate between the mission workers, the colonial administration, and the larger organizational units in Philadelphia and London with the functioning of the NEGM as the main issue. Some members of the administration accused Watkin Roberts, the alleged troublemaker of the NEGM, of usurping their authority by going into business ventures in Manipur, mismanaging mission funds and exaggerating church membership. The internal troubles were further aggravated when Watkin Roberts was forced to resign from the NEGM and started a new mission called Indo-Burma Pioneer Mission (Dena 1988: 58–61).

Other conflicts also arose between the Salvation Army and the Welsh Mission and between the former and the Roman Catholics in the Lushai Hills over denominational and doctrinal distinctions, and educational facilities. In one instance, when a French Canadian Catholic priest visited Aizwal in 1925, the Welsh mission was up in arms; it saw the Catholic presence as a threat to their doctrinal position. Since the Catholics had more financial resources to run schools, the Welsh mission saw it as their duty to stop this 'Roman Catholic menace'. In the American Baptist Mission conference in Guwahati, 1–6 December 1936, the conference came to the conclusion that, as part of a reorganization of the mission, churches must reorientate themselves according to the principles of the Protestant faith, while making Catholicism appear 'ungospel like and un-Christian' (Dena 1988: 66–9). It appeared that the age-old conflicts between the Roman Catholics and the Protestant faith were being rehashed in the far reaches of the world, where the 'native' inhabitants were the vehicles of the conversion war. The squabbling between the different churches is important because it further elucidates how notions of identity are formed through defining boundaries. Furthermore, these wars have spilled over to the different

Christian churches in North Cachar Hills. While many foreign missions were operating in the Naga Hills and Manipur, in North Cachar it was primarily the converts of these foreign missions who in turn made initial contact with the Zeme.

Zeme Christians

In the North Cachar Hills, the first recognizable outside 'religion' to come into contact with their world was Christianity, brought about by the Calvinistic Methodist Church of Wales (later known as the Presbyterian Church of Wales) missionary, J. Garlan Williams in 1904. Dituing Zeme of Kenareram village was the first Zeme convert through a Baite[4] missionary, Pu Haite of the Presbyterian Church of Wales in 1910.[5]

Christian conversion among the Zeme of North Cachar Hills was slow for various reasons: progress was actively opposed by the Heraka. Ranima allegedly said that 'Christians will be the greatest hindrance to the Heraka, but when the Heraka receives [*sic*] their freedom, Christians will be our slaves' (Pame 1996: 211). However, two revivals in 1948 and 1978 strengthened the growth of Christianity in the region. According to some estimates, the Zeme of North Cachar Hills has roughly around 40 per cent Christian, compared to 60 per cent Heraka (1996: 61–2).[6] The first Baptist mission penetrated the Zeme village from Manipur, in 1975–6, while the Roman Catholics have entered Zeme villages in the past 20 years or so.

The Baptist mission from Manipur had its first Zeme 'convert' from the Presbyterian Church (see also Jordan 1993: 285–6). In fact, during the ensuing years, most of its converts were from the Presbyterian churches. According to one witness the Presbyterians 'never adequately nurtured the word of God' (Pame 1996: 241). In their view, the Presbyterians were un-Christian because their leaders allegedly consumed *zao* (rice beer), chewed pan, smoked tobacco and did not 'live as servants of God' (1996: 241). Over the years, 21 Baptist churches have been established in North Cachar Hills. I would argue that the success of the Baptist church is grounded on two perceptions. First, for some Zeme, it provides for them a clear break from the Heraka and Presbyterians (the two are seen as similar due to the use of *zao*). Second, the Baptists are able to associate themselves with the other Nagas who are predominantly Baptists themselves, whereas the Naga Presbyterians are concentrated primarily among the Zeme of North Cachar Hills. This provides the Baptists of North Cachar Hills with a larger pan-ethnic movement and support. A feeling of being 'Naga' is reiterated by this bond.[7]

Reasons for Converting

When Christian missions first arrived and many local people started converting, the Christians emphasized the difference from traditional Zeme custom. Christianity became a distinct system with its particular form of worship, rituals and its insistence on altering certain notions of traditional life. For instance, in the Naga Hills, when Christian converts started emerging in the Ao area, to observe a 'day of rest' was highly controversial. It went against the rhythm and routine of Naga life that relied on communal participation for it to be efficacious (Eaton 1984: 7). Similarly, among the Zeme, new converts to Christianity were ousted from their villages and property confiscated. They eventually had to find another habitat; and thus new villages were founded. Slowly, converts started to accept the Christian message that discouraged headhunting,[8] and drinking the traditional *zao* (rice beer). Performing older religious rituals that involved appeasing local gods was condemned as idolatry, and animal sacrifices were also largely abandoned. These changes, as recounted by the early Zeme Christians, 'lightened our minds' and gave them the freedom to venture outside into towns (without having to conduct elaborate rituals when leaving the village), attend schools and seek government employment (see Chapter 3).

Heraka, similarly, was a strong force among the Zeme from the 1930s onwards. Unlike Christianity, it attempted to ban only large animal sacrifices, but over the years instituted a complete ban on animal sacrifice. As I have argued in Chapter 3, the impact of the scarcity of food in Zeme villages during the 1930s enabled the Heraka reformers to curtail animal sacrifices as a way of addressing this problem. Adopting one God and simplifying its mode of worship by instituting songs and prayers instead of the ritual sacrifice of animals, addressed this change. It is difficult to say if the negative response of the Paupaise towards the Heraka was spiteful or defiant. Some Paupaise now are simply indifferent, some are outright dismissive. The one Paupaise village left condemn Heraka as a foreign import, just like Christianity (see below). But Heraka was more popular than Christianity for two reasons. First, it was based on local reforms and gave the impression that it was not foreign. Second, Heraka retained much of traditional Zeme customs like the drinking of *zao*, preserving Zeme dances and clothes, and were more 'tradition friendly'. These issues are discussed further below. So, most of the Paupaise 'converted' to Christianity or became Heraka over the years, while some Heraka have converted to Christianity. Although reconversion rarely happens, there are some cases of it in Zeme villages.[9]

It must be noted that not all British administrators supported Christian missionaries. Some were clearly hostile towards the formation of Christian villages and the erection of churches. On one occasion, the village of Kaikao in Tamenglong, Manipur, complained to the authorities that the Christians were destroying the traditions of the village. The SDO of Tamenglong, Manipur, immediately asked the Christians to leave the village and fined them an amount of Rs. 4000 – a hefty amount at that time (Pame 1996: 50). The seemingly close relationship between the missions and the administrators which initially was sought, missions were generally seen as helping in humanitarian activities like education and health, became tinged with controversy. One incident that illustrates the disagreement was the adoption of Western clothing by the Ao Christian converts, approved and encouraged by the missionaries, which incensed the British official, J. P. Mills. He questioned this practice by 'charging that hot, baggy Western clothing not only exposed converts to new diseases and interfered with their field work, but had the adverse psychological effect of causing its wearers not to see themselves as Nagas, but in some way as foreigners' (cited in Eaton 1984: 14; see also Jean and John Comaroff 1986: 14).

Even though there were changes occurring in the social landscape of the Zeme, was there a clear break from past norms? Received knowledge tells us that conversion often provides the conceptual tools whereby a clear break is made possible. The acceptance of another point of view is said to enable a change of perception and attitude. However, recent studies have shown that the rigid boundaries between religious traditions, which are normally thought as the norm, are actually fluid and flexible in integrating or observing two or more religious systems (Cornille 2002; Hefner 1993). This is certainly true for the Heraka because boundaries are often fuzzy when it comes to issues like the drinking of *zao* that generally appear to be similar to Paupaise custom. In fact, the function may be different. In this sense, one can argue that the only contested boundary on the surface concerns animal sacrifice and therefore the separation between the Heraka and Paupaise. On the other hand, the strongest public boundary marker between the Christian and Heraka is that of *zao*. This boundary, though publicly advertised, examined and fought over, is by no means clear. It represents a superficial layering over which religious allegiances are fought. In the paragraphs below I demonstrate how religious traditions maintain boundaries between one and the other.

Food of the Gods: Boundary Makers

An important boundary marker is *zao* (rice beer). It is the one thing that differentiates (on the surface) between the Paupaise, Heraka, Baptist,

Catholic and Presbyterian. There are two assumptions that must be aired. The lines are drawn between those who consume alcohol and those who do not. One can argue that everybody consumes *zao*, but it is the manner in which this is done. Only the Paupaise and Heraka will publicly drink and make *zao* without constraints, either at home or for festivals. For them *zao* is tradition and must not be forgotten. Since the Presbyterians and Catholics do not brew *zao* or use it in public festivals, they provide income for the Heraka by buying from them. The Baptists, however, are a little more consistent. Their strict policy on avoiding *zao* is more determined, though some Baptist youths may slip out at night and join the Heraka in drinking *zao*. But why is *zao* such a huge boundary marker?

When the American Baptists first came in contact with the Nagas, their restrictions on drinking *zao* (or *zu* or *madhu*) were strictly observed. Those wanting to be baptized had to furnish evidence that they had not been drinking rice beer for more than three months. The missionaries' interpretation of alcohol, influenced by their mid-West prohibitionist sentiments, was enforced upon the Nagas without understanding the value of *zao* in Naga culture (Eaton 1984: 13). Thus almost randomly, the line between 'Christian' and 'animist/heathen' was drawn, creating misleading pigeonholes. By banning the use of *zao*, a value judgement was placed on Naga culture that refused to acknowledge the Naga universe as both religious and cultural, intertwined and imbedded. Many Baptist Christians hold this judgement over the use of *zao* even today: it has no religious or cultural use; it only hampers development (personal and social) as it makes the drinker lazy and incompetent. This view was perhaps based on the American Baptist arrogance connected with their 'civilizing mission'. Alcohol would bring about disorderly behaviour that went against the strict, regimented self the Christians were trying to shape (see Korieh 2003). This Baptist stance has gone on to shape the views of the Presbyterians and Catholics who are now officially against the public use of alcohol. In Nagaland, some also hold the view that the prohibition of alcohol is the right step forward towards a better society. This view has been taken up by the Heraka leaders who are discouraging the use of excessive *zao*, because they now feel that drinking affects the overall moral balance of the person and hinders development. But taking *zao* out of the equation is difficult for the Zeme in general and the Heraka in particular. J. P. Mills also observed that in the early parts of Christian influence in the Naga Hills

> one finds many men who have changed their faith as often as seven or eight times, or even more. A man will become a (nominal) Christian and

> be baptised. Then his soul yearns for 'madhu' [rice beer] and, since anyone who touches alcohol is expelled from the Baptist community, he often goes the whole hog and joins the non-Christians again. Later he may change his mind, give up his 'madhu' and heathen practices and be readmitted to the Baptist Church. (quoted in Eaton 1984: 15; also Mills 1926: 413–14)

Similarly, in Zeme villages, I have heard stories of people switching religious allegiances based on the use of *zao*. Another story, which most Baptists tell, is that 'if you want to become a Christian and still want to continue drinking *zao*, become a Catholic or Presbyterian.' Indeed, some people, wanting to accept Christianity because of educational facilities, join one of these churches due to its acceptance of *zao*. Presbyterians or Catholics have no strict rules regarding the use of *zao* at home; the main issue is that they are not allowed to brew it at home or drink publicly.

The *Zao* Story

The Heraka and Paupaise on the other hand see the use of *zao* as an important part of their tradition and the Heraka have gone to the extent of justifying its use by using the popular slogan 'loss of culture is loss of identity'. Most Heraka will state that slogan in a drunken stupor. When I first went to the Heraka village, I was given a cup of *zao* at five in the morning at one of the homes I was visiting. This first drink was surrounded by apprehension; the first suspicion about any outsider is that they are missionaries. By accepting the cup of *zao*, I was no longer a Christian missionary or a Baptist (since I am from Nagaland) in their minds. Crossing the boundary and coming over to their side, by accepting *zao*, was the first step towards acknowledging myself as one of them. If *zao* is rooted in their tradition and its importance is preserved, indeed marked, what are its roots and its use?

> Like most stories of origin, there is also one for the origin of *zao*.
>
> A couple decided to go to the jungle for jhum for three days. During those three nights they had sexual intercourse in the same spot, leaving behind their sexual fluids. After some time, at that very spot, a tree (*nduihi bang*) grew. One day, a group of people went to the jungle for jhum and rested under that very tree. They cut some of the top branches, but did not pull it down; the branches were left hanging. In the meantime, they left their rice bundles wrapped in a banana leaf under the branches and

went on with their jhum work. Liquid from the tree bark (*nduihi gei*) started dripping and fell on the banana leaf and mixed with the rice through a tiny hole in the leaf. When the workers came back to have their lunch, they got this wonderful smell. Upon opening the banana leaves, the smell exploded and overtook their senses. This, they looked upon as a gift, a gift from God. They soon discovered that it was the liquid from the tree bark that was making the rice ferment. Thus, began the making of *zao.*

Zao over the years has been used for many purposes. It has a medicinal purpose, helps relaxation after a tiring day in the fields, and is used on all ritual occasions. Once the liquid is filtered, the fermented rice was (and is) also used for many cures. It was the medicine (*reheu*) of their time.

Indeed, *zao* was used on most occasions. Libations were and are made to the spirit of the house and people believe that intoxication makes the person more prone to 'divine communication'. Jadonang, for example, could communicate with God only if he drank *zao* and was in an inebriated state. In his confession before the Civil Surgeon, for example, he says that 'I cannot dream unless I have *zu*, rice-beer'.[10] Further, he says 'I get Rs. 4/- for praying for the dead, a bottle of *zu* for interpreting dreams, and Rs. 3/- for treating the sick, when the patient recovers: if he does not, the money is returned.'[11] David Hardiman also shows how the adivasis in Gujarat considered alcohol as 'a food of the gods' and drunkenness during worship was seen 'as a form of intoxication by the divine spirit' (Hardiman 1987: 99). Alcohol is also used for rites of passage – birth, marriage and death – that brings people together and it is believed that alcohol brings people luck, fortune and many rewards (1987: 100). This is similar with the Zeme Heraka. Every public occasion is graced with *zao*; the lack of *zao* symbolizes the lack of hospitality. *Zao* is also drunk for itself, on quiet or more boisterous occasions. Red sticky rice beer is the most prized of them all.

But *zao* also had a social function for the Paupaise. It delineated age distinctions. Only older people are allowed to drink *duizao* (*zao* that uses an external fermenting agent from the bark of a tree), which is seen as stronger, and something that, because of its added punch and strength, could only be handled by a person of that age. *Duizao* is also taboo for non-elders because, the Paupaise say, 'it belongs to God' (*herazao* (god's *zao*)). *Tekuizao* (grain rice beer; less alcoholic) can be drunk by anyone and used on all ritual occasions, on the grounds that it is purer. Its purity is attributed to the exclusion of any fermenting agent; all the ingredients are from rice. *Klezao* (watered downed grain rice beer) is drunk particularly by children.

The Heraka and Christian, however, do not observe these age distinctions in relation to *zao*.

For the Heraka, *zao* also provides much economic wealth, both in villages and in towns. It is, for some families, the main source of income. Yet, *zao* has become an odd bedfellow for the Heraka. Many Heraka women complain that the men are addicted to *zao*, which causes a lot of hardships in the family home. This view was reiterated by one of the Heraka preachers (*hingde pame*) at a public gathering. Addressing the Heraka parents, he said, 'why don't you send your children to good schools? You have enough grain, food to eat, vegetables, and some have animals. Instead, you drink *zao* daily and live comfortably without sacrificing your money on education.' The preacher is referring to the broader question of education and how many Heraka families are lagging behind Christian families[12] because of the use of *zao*. In fact, this litany of accusations against the problem of *zao* affecting the youth in the town and villages went on for an hour. He targeted those who, instead of attending college, start making and selling *zao* at the market-place, bringing a 'bad name' to the Heraka.

During his exhortation, he raised an important point that is echoed by most recent converts to the Baptist church. The preacher said, 'when Heraka leaders ask you to stop drinking *zao*, why do you think that "Oh, I should then convert to Christianity": why do you think like that?' For the recent converts to the Baptist church, the story is somewhat similar. They wanted to stop drinking *zao* and to 'catch up' with Christian families, in terms of education, development, cleanliness of house and the future for their children. In becoming Baptist, there is a clear-cut boundary prohibiting *zao* and the Baptists are very determined about this. Hence, it should be noted that most of the recent converts from Heraka have joined the Baptist church, precisely because the Baptist church can offer clear boundaries when it comes to the use of *zao*, whereas the other churches seem to have flexible boundaries.

From the argument so far, it is clear that the advent of Christianity and the Heraka have had huge repercussions for Zeme life. The competing ideologies of these two religious groups are also visible in the realm of education, wealth and family position. Finally, they maintain boundaries between different 'colonies' that are conceptual as well as physical. The symbol of *zao* definitely provides them with boundaries, even if it is fuzzy at times. But what happens once this debate is taken to a national level? The answer involves 'Hindu' groups and the larger question of Naga nationalism in relation to the Heraka, and their status as belonging within India, or within a 'Naga fold' that is increasingly anti-Hindu and anti-Indian.

It must be mentioned that the position of the Heraka is amorphous at best. First, they want to be part of the 'Naga fold' and have publicly stated so, but historically the Heraka have had a tense relationship with the Naga Christians over proselytizing. Second, although the Heraka receive considerable support from 'Hindu organizations', they are wary to be seen as too close to them because then the Naga Christians will label them as 'Hindu' therefore jeopardizing their relationship with the larger Naga population. Moreover, it is tempting to suggest that the Heraka represent, for both 'Hindu' groups and the Christians, an ideological battlefield: one source of contention is the question of nation building of a modern, universal 'Hindu' India. On the other hand, the Christian Nagas question this project and are resisting larger hegemonic forces by espousing a decentralized federal India with individual rights over land, resources, culture and religion. It appears that 'religion' is the tool whereby the shift can occur both ways. In the following paragraphs, I address these questions in relation to how 'Hindu' organizations view the Heraka; how the Heraka and Christians exchange rhetoric over conversions; how the question of Naga nationalism affects the position of the Heraka; and finally, how the Heraka position themselves within the larger matrix of these systems.

Realm of the Naked

Received knowledge tells us that 'nakedness' represents a sort of primeval stage, lacking in sophistication and civilization. Ethnographers, missionaries and travellers portray this exaggerated image of the silent naked 'tribal', untouched by the modern world in their stories. Without these perceptions the image is somehow incomplete. When the British first made contact with the 'hill' people, recorded as 1832,[13] they borrowed the colloquial Assamese term 'Naga' to refer to those living in the hills. The area obviously was unknown to the British, but as they climbed each hill in order to bring these people into their colonial mapping and imagination, they conceived of a collective band of 'wild people' – the Nagas.[14]

The earliest Europeans to encounter the Nagas in Assam classified them into two groups: the 'pakka Nagas' in the north; the 'kachcha Nagas' in the south, near the Cachar borders. This arbitrary drawing of boundaries occurred in a terrain with hundreds of languages, customs and culture, all unintelligible to the explorers. It was therefore impossible, at least initially, to map them with any accuracy. Hence, some observers like J. H. Hutton used terms such as *pakka* and *kachcha* to loosely define the 'Nagas', and came to the conclusion that since the *pakka* Nagas were naked, they were the genuine Nagas (1965: 16). He says, 'The pakka or genuine Nagas in the north went naked, whereas the Kachcha tribes wearing a sort of short black "hobble" kilt were regarded on that account as "half baked" hence kachcha or "raw" . . . (1965: 16). Another view suggested that those Nagas in constant contact with the Assamese people were called *bori Noga* (tame Nagas) and those not known to them were called *abori* (untamed) (1965: 16).

Furthermore, Hutton suggests that a distinct group of people under the umbrella 'Nagas' make up the various people from the Assam Valley to the Hukong Valley in Burma. Hutton uses sources that point in this direction. For example, he says, Ptolemy, the great geographer of the second century CE, quotes the word *Nangalôg* spoken by the Hindus as the 'realm of the naked' and associates it with the region still occupied by the Nagas.[15] Ancient Sanskrit texts refer to the Kiratas, a golden-skinned people living near the Himalayas. This suggests that people similar to the Nagas were present in this region roughly 2000 years ago (Jacobs et al. 1998: 10). These anecdotes indicate the likelihood that the 'Nagas' were in contact with the rest of India and that their presence was recorded. This image is further reinstated by the notion of *vanvasi*, which means, 'jungle dweller'.

It must be noted that such words themselves are used in a manner that has developed from outside notions of what or who that community is. For example, the status accorded by the British to the Nagas must be viewed as a historical process in the current formation of 'Naga identity'. If we take into account how colonial powers 'invented "ethnic" differentiation as a feature of political administration' (Tsing 1993: 42) as the most viable way to divide administrative tasks, then it is most likely that the British created the 'Naga tribes' as relatively fixed (Jacobs et al. 1998: 17) with their own local language, customs, and so on, and with minimal or no interaction with the neighbouring tribes. It is possible that prior to colonial intervention, there was a constant economic and cultural traffic between the various people living in the hills as well as the surrounding valley. One example of this is that Ahom kings (from Assam) often employed Konyak Naga bodyguards and also took Konyak wives (von Fürer-Haimendorf 1946: 33). Such fluidity was arrested by the British, who wished to separate the people of the hill from the valley through the adoption of the 'excluded area' policy. Such separation, reinforced by the use of maps, census, administration and development along with the introduction of missionaries by some British administrators to 'civilize' the tribes, made the two into bounded subjects. This effectively established separate entities physically as well as conceptually and 'their stereotypes about each other – remained [the] powerful organiser of people's lives and thoughts' (Baruah 2002).[16]

Not surprisingly, in Nagaland, the use of 'tribe' is current and widely preferred over words that are rooted in Indic languages. The preference of tribe also presupposes a tangible fear that anything Indic affects the tone of a society that is now overwhelmingly Christian. This distinction is widely seen as oppositional: the Americans and British brought Christianity, so we prefer their language to Hindi or Sanskrit, as the latter is associated with methods of 'Sanskritization'. However, with groups such as the Zeme Nagas in North Cachar Hills, and primarily the Heraka, the word *vanvasi* (jungle dweller) is widely used as a representational tool by the 'Hindu' groups such as the RSS and the VHP, which are involved in their education and development. I address these issues in the following paragraphs.

Hindutva and Heraka: Marriage of Convenience?

When one hears of the RSS, we are immediately reminded of their staunch assertion of 'Hindu' identity and controversial right-wing politics in modern India. Although the RSS claims to be a cultural and not a political organization, it espouses a 'Hindu' identity and cultural heritage with political ramifications. This awareness is Hindutva, or 'Hinduness',[17] which attempts to define the 'Hindu' self, as representing the 'true, native nationalism' (Basu et al. 1993: viii, 4). But what is the 'Hindu' self? The 'Hindu' self is connected to the project of Hinduization that aims to construct a 'virile, masculine, aggressively communal self which is intolerant of other faiths, even of other conceptions of Hinduism' (Basu et al. 1993: ix). This is further linked with the catholicity of *adhikar-bheda*, which means that

> each level or group within the vast hierarchy that is Hinduism should legitimately have its own distinct rituals and beliefs, and thus enormous diversity could be reconciled within an overruling Hindu solidarity. (Basu et al. 1993: 7)

This definition of Hindutva and its goal of espousing a 'Hindu nation' has its roots in the way the word 'Hindu' has been constructed, and how 'Hinduism' evolved as a concept hand in hand with India's contact with European powers.

'Hinduism' as a unifying religious tradition and the distinctiveness of 'Hindu' culture as a bounded category was fashioned from the seventeenth century onwards due to interventions by colonial administrations, travellers, scholars and missionaries in the Indian subcontinent (Hansen 1999: 65). The word 'Hindu', associated with the land beyond the Indus or Sindhu river, that is, the Indian subcontinent (Thapar 1989: 222), soon became a common denominator for scholars, missionaries and colonial administrations, in order to wield together a disparate mass of people, languages and practices into one that was well ordered, resembling the Western epistemologies of the time (Hansen 1999: 65). The all-inclusive word 'Hindu' would have been bewildering to the people concerned because it included both *brahmanas* and the lower castes, which would have countered the precepts of Brahmanism (Thapar 1989: 223). Eventually, the formation of 'Hindu' identity was aided by intellectuals from the upper caste Western-educated social strata, who espoused a certain version of high-Hinduism, created a codification of 'Hindu' practices (Thapar 1989: 210–11). Thus, through the codification of the ancient body of text, the primacy of Sanskrit, common ritual practices, sacred geography and architecture and sites of pilgrimage, a vast religious diversity appeared to give rise to a single unified 'true culture', and eventually Indian nationalism (Hansen 1999: 66–7).

The current rise of 'Hindu' nationalism was advocated by V. D. Savarkar with the publication of *Who is a Hindu?*, a text that provided the ideology for the establishment of the RSS in 1925 by Dr K. B. Hedgewar. In the text V. D. Savarkar proclaimed a Hindu identity, or Hindutva, as not only a word, but also a history. Hindutva, he said, is 'not only the spiritual or religious history of our people as at times it is mistaken to be by being confounded with the other cognate term, Hinduism. Hinduism is only a derivative, a fraction, a part of Hindutva . . . Hindutva embraces all the departments of thought and activity of the whole being of our Hindu race' (Savarkar 1969: 3–4). Under this ideology, Muslims and Christians are not a part of the Indian nation. Their holy lands (*punyabhumi*) are located outside India, in Arabia and Palestine (Sumit Sarkar 2006: 274). But these trenchant views are modelled on, yet pitted against Semitic religions, which are seen as proselytizing religions. Everything must be done to preserve and protect the 'Hindu' nation and especially the *vanvasi* brothers from this fate. For instance, on the RSS website, the claim is made that Nagaland is threatening to carve out 'an independent Christian province' by engineering an armed insurrection.[18]

The project of Hindutva to include tribal cultures and its varied traditions into one overwhelming 'Hindu solidarity' is a strategy that has been part of the VHP[19] and RSS, since their inception. As early as 1978, an RSS worker told me, they started work with the Nagas under the organization Kalyan

Ashram (also Vanvasi Kalyan Ashram), meaning tribal welfare organization. By the late 1960s the VHP had already started work among the non-Christian Nagas, primarily the Heraka, and were defending them against Christian proselytizing. The VHP's aims are to organize a 'pluralistic Hindu society' throughout the entire Hindu world (Basu et al. 1993: 64, 57).

The ideology of the RSS and VHP has already seeped into Heraka rhetoric and their talk is often peppered with these nation-building bumper stickers. Phrases such as 'all religions have truth, compassion, and love and are like streams that go into the one ocean' or 'invasion of foreign religion and foreign culture will bring total destruction of Naga society. Beware of this danger' – are all too common. These phrases reflect neo-Hindu projection of self and tradition and constitute part of the mass programme of such unifying Hindu solidarity. Further, powerful symbols such as *om* and the *svastika* are commonly found in Heraka homes; images of Ram and Sita, distributed by VHP activists, find their way into these homes as well (see Photograph 5.1).[20] These visual materials are the new ways by which the 'Hindu' groups disseminate their ideology. By appropriating or encouraging the use of these 'civilizational symbols', the Heraka are immediately seen as assimilating, thus marking them off from the largely Christian population (Thapar 1989: 216). This assimilation is projected through the subtle deployment of 'sanatan dharma'[21] and the wider net of Hindu solidarity. The politics of 'sanatan dharma' are further clarified with the slippery notion of *vanvasi.*

Photograph 5.1 'Hindu' symbols on an altar inside a Heraka home

Vanvasi: Dweller in the Threshold

Vanvasi, literally means a person who lives in the jungle. But this has taken on an ideological dimension in relation to helping *vanvasi* preserve their 'eternal faith and culture (sanatan dharma)',[22] and appreciate the notion of 'Bharat', thus hopefully integrating them with the larger 'Indian society' (Dharmaraj 2004: 39). Organizations such as the Janjati Vikas Samiti (as registered in Nagaland) or Vanvasi Kalyan Ashram,[23] under the umbrella of Akhil Bharatiya Vanvasi Kalyan Ashram (ABVKA),[24] are active with the Heraka in developmental projects, education and also in providing organizational support. Integration with 'Bharat mata' (mother land)[25] is a huge financial and cultural investment, pursued by the Kalyan Ashram. For example, Kalyan Ashram has recognized Rani Gaidinliu and Haipou Jadonang as freedom fighters and has included these and other *vanvasi* leaders around India in a promotional poster that is pasted on almost all Heraka and Kalyan Ashram offices (see Photograph 5.2).[26] Attempts are

Photograph 5.2 A picture of Bharat Mata put up in some Heraka homes. The photographs surrounding Bharat Mata are those of 'tribal' leaders, including Rani Gaidinliu

also made to link *vanvasi* with the rest of 'Hindu' civilization. In an article, Stephen Knapp, a member of The Vedic Friends Association, writes: 'Why concern ourselves with the Northeast area of India? Because there are those who have been working for years to make it secede from India and make it into a separate Christian country. Yet it is a big part of the Vedic culture and tradition of India. For example, when we look back at the history of the region we find that Lord Krishna's friend Arjuna had married a Naga wife, Ulupi, in Nagaland.'[27] In another example, an article written by Krishna Sapre examines the Gaidinliu script[28] and its historical importance. He shows copies of it to Dr Wakankar, a renowned Indian archaeologist, and comments: 'In seeing the photocopies he [Dr Wakankar] said this is wonderful. The writings are in ancient Gupta Brahmi . . . which were in use through out India some 2,500 years back' (see Souvenir 1999: 26).

Obviously, the desirability of willing bedfellows is accentuated by the need to find some connection, as did scholars like Hutton, with the fabled and mysterious *Nangalôg*, thus making the notion of *vanvasi* all the more romantic and pristine. Instead of progressing with a sophisticated notion of 'tribal culture' and its place in Indian society, the notion of *vanvasi* reverts to an ideological pristine state that somehow can be preserved, though dependent on organizations like the Kalyan Ashram for its survival. It reverts to the old colonial policy of minimum interference in 'tribal life and customs' enshrined later in the NEFA (North Eastern Frontier Agency) philosophy of the post-colonial India of Verrier Elwin (1959) and Jawaharlal Nehru.

In the previous three sections I have drawn attention to the notion of *vanvasi* as projecting a sort of 'tribal identity' consonant with the way 'Hindu' groups represent and view the Heraka. From the mysterious *Nangalôg*, a fabled past has been created that links the 'Nagas' to the rest of India. This tenuous link is strengthened by the position of 'Hindu' organizations whose aim is to embellish and preserve such links. They are thus able to tie the notion of *vanvasi* into the larger notion of a 'Hindu' identity, espoused by stalwarts of the RSS and VHP, and viewed as encompassing the land of the 'Hindus'. Therefore, the Heraka are seen as preserving the sanatan dharma (eternal faith and culture), which is treated synonymously with traditional Hinduism. For the 'Hindu' groups the Heraka present a practice that is consonant with the rest of the 'Hindu' nation, according to the definition of Hindutva. These views were perhaps articulated best by one of the VHP workers I met in the Heraka School in Lsong village in North Cachar Hills.

Naked and Hindu: Reflections of a VHP Worker

A teacher from Guwahati (in Assam) associated with the VHP talked to me candidly about his isolation in such a far-out community, his avowed vegetarianism and his commitment to serve the Heraka. His notions of Heraka and what it means to be 'Hindu' are well reflected in his testimony.

> The Zeme Heraka don't know how to live properly, no cleanliness, don't know how to cook, bathe or clean. They don't know how to wear clothes, they are often naked. After the opening of the school they get a little education and they know a little about life. They are very religious minded: if they are ill, to overcome the situation, they will worship. On that day, they will abstain from work, stay at home and do only household work. They consume everything which is in the jungle, any animal they see they will eat. By giving them education, we want them to catch up with civilized societies. As a teacher I want to help the Heraka preserve their culture. Heraka is related to Hindu: if I believe in a tree, I worship, same with the Heraka. *Purnima* (full moon day) is also similar; they, like us, also worship the sun. Heraka are called *parampara*[29] before becoming Heraka. Heraka is an early form of *parampara* [*sic*].[30] The Hindus have no problem with accepting the Heraka in its fold, as it is also Hindu (religion of the soil).

These patronizing views are perhaps not uncommon among 'Hindu' groups, who often view the Heraka as helpless, and needing guidance. But the overall view is largely centred on the notion that the *vanvasi* population in general needs support to 'progress'. A comment attributed to the second RSS chief reads: 'It is a fact that Naga Vanvasi brothers take beef but for that not they but we are to repent because we have not treated them well and we have not enlightened them about civilisation and culture' (Souvenir 2003). In an attempt to integrate the 'vanvasi brothers' some sort of enlightenment needs to take place. The 'Hindu' organizations say that they are unwilling to associate themselves with the rhetoric of 'enlightenment', 'civilizing', and 'saving', which they consider a part of Christian mission ideology. However, they also often project this view unwittingly. But this 'enlightenment' project must come from sanatan dharma and not from the corrupt westernization that Christianity allegedly encourages.

Religious Boundaries: 'Loss of Culture is Loss of Identity'

Much ammunition has been collected to target Christians as the root cause of 'loss of culture and tradition' in the Zeme regions of North Cachar Hills. Most propaganda and even literature becomes oppositional in its rhetoric: it aims to discredit the church and its alleged conspiracy to make Northeast India a Christian nation. Christians' apparent closeness to 'Western culture', 'terrorism', and its association with Western forms of dancing, smoking, drinking and associating with the opposite sex, is alleged to make Naga society vulnerable and wanton.[31] But the main reason for this tirade of accusations is the question of conversion and the rhetoric of conversion (see also Barker 1993: 217–22).

The role of human agency[32] in conversion has become an important debate in recent years (Hefner 1993; Peter van der Veer 1996; Brown and Frykenberg 2002). While I agree with the notion that human agency must be acknowledged, it is often difficult to separate human agency, the 'strategy of identity', and, for potential converts, even divine will when it comes to conversion. Talal Asad has similarly pointed out that 'There was a time when conversion didn't need explaining. People converted because God has helped them to see the truth' (Asad 1996: 263). But as Asad and others (Jean and John Comaroff 1991; Hefner 1993; Viswanathan 1996; Karlsson 2002) explain, conversion is not a simple process. In some cases, as Jean Comaroff has pointed out with respect to the Tsidi of South Africa, it was not that people were forced to become Christians, but 'conversion' was not freely chosen either. It was more often a negotiation and maintenance of a 'coherent symbolic order' that Christianity provided (cited in Karlsson 2002: 138; also Jean Comaroff 1985: 253). Sometimes missionaries became a prized resource and were actively sought after, one tribe even preventing other tribes from acquiring their services (Jean and John Comaroff 1986: 3). Therefore, seeing conversion as something dependent solely on human agency is problematic: who defines this agency; what is the extent of this agency; who are the agents responsible to; can 'attributions of agency be successfully disowned'; 'can non-humans be agents' (Asad 1996: 272)?

The emphasis in the following conversion narratives is on situating the particular person in the context of 'their world'. But how is this world defined? The role of human agency as well as divine intervention, as I have found, is very important in situating conversion narratives. But I would argue that the role of human agency is not that simple. One is not in a clear position to choose between A and B as simple givens. The fact that the choices of potential converts depend on other circumstances must be taken into account. Here, the promise of education, upward mobility and pan-ethnic identity play a role. Therefore, whether conversion is divinely inspired, or attributable to human agency, it is neither forced upon the Zeme, nor is it freely chosen.[33] In light of this, I want to suggest that a combination of these perspectives is the best approach to deal with question of conversion.

These narratives, I have also found, are a response to the condition of potential converts. This generates an aspiration for something better with which the present religious group cannot provide them. Whether it is materially, socially or spiritually, the benefits are clearly expressed, sometimes as 'resources' that enable people to situate themselves in a new context with new possibilities (Brown 2002: 7; see also Karlsson 2002). But these narratives are also a way of denouncing the former group. By comparing the two they enforce a dichotomy between 'irrationality/backwardness' and 'rationality/development'. That is to say, becoming Christian immediately brings improvement 'not just in self-esteem but in health, education, and the prospect of social and economic advancement' (Brown 2002: 7) which the former (Heraka) did not. There is therefore intense competition between the Heraka and Christian to have control over these 'resources' (schools being the prime example), which is further intensified with evangelization on the part of the Christian church to convert the Heraka; while the Heraka work hard to maintain the status quo.

Conversion Stories

My first real experience of a conversion incident happened when I was in Haflong. A Baptist man came to Haflong from Hsongle (where I was based), and told me that they needed my Hsongle hut temporarily for a recent Baptist convert from Heraka. He told me that this 'convert' and his family had been disowned by his Heraka family and had been thrown out of his house and had nowhere to go. Since I had no family and few possessions, would I mind if they stayed for a week or so until the Baptist church found alternative arrangements? Of course, I agreed. The land where I was staying belonged to the Baptist church anyway, and I could easily extend my stay in Haflong.

When I did return to Hsongle, the family had not yet moved. Hasty arrangements for temporary accommodation were made for the family. The Baptist neighbours came and started to empty the hut of their belongings.

As I stood there watching, I felt slightly embarrassed and saddened by the whole episode. They had two young children; the mother was obviously distraught, while the father carried on with steely determination. I was witnessing a difficult displacement, not a massive mobilization of population from one place to another, but of one family, clutching on to their possessions of cooking utensils, clothes, furniture and animals, and photos of Rani Gaidinliu in frames and tiny lockets around the neck of the mother and daughter. I could not help but wonder if they would dispense with those images? With displacement, will they also transform from being without a home to belonging in one?

Later that evening the father, Heseu, came over to have a chat. When we started talking, he brought up the issue of conversion. He told me that he converted when he was browsing in the school library, where he works, and came across the Bible. He opened the Bible and came to John 3.16 and read the passage. He was immediately drawn to its words and decided then and there to convert. He continued, 'When Jesus said "I am the way", it made me think about life and its consequences. In the Heraka faith, people believe in rebirth, whereas now, in Christianity, we are like angels. We are happy and will never fall down again to earth.'

Heseu is from a well-known Heraka family in Hsongle. His older brother is the Secretary of the Heraka in the Nyanglo Longria region and his uncle on his wife's side is the General Secretary of the Heraka in the Northeast of India. The question at the back of my mind was why did he convert? According to his narration, he made an express decision to become Baptist; but was it solely due to human agency, and not a strategy of identity? The word 'conversion' sometimes invokes the notion of complete transformation: that converts will start talking about their faith and their 'Damascus road' experience; that they will start quoting passages from the Bible as if it was familiar. First, in Heseu's case the conversion experience was an 'event' and a process; although we cannot assess the nature of his acceptance of Christ, in an important sense if he says he has accepted Christ, he has! Second, Heseu's conversion reveals also a particular approach, a strategy, as evident in his conversations with me.

Heseu's case unravelled itself as he kept talking more about politics. For him Baptists are the true Christians, because they submerge their bodies fully, just like Jesus did. The Presbyterians and Catholics do not. Moreover, he openly remarked that for him becoming Christian meant getting further education. He said he wanted to study theology. His intention, as many people told me (Heraka and Christian) was to develop his interest in politics and that, as he said, 'becoming a Baptist would profit me, as Nagaland and most of the Nagas are Baptist and also the Baptists are the ones spearheading the movement for a Naga solution'. For Heseu, becoming Baptist speaks to his notion of a pan-Naga identity rooted in a particular understanding of Christianity. It is difficult to say what his own personal faith is or what his growing understanding of Christianity is, but clearly it is also to do with being associated with a powerful group. The Naga Baptists provide him with far-reaching support which may be beneficial for his long-term plan of taking part in finding a 'Naga solution'. The 'Naga solution' has a crucial role to play in the formation of identity in all the Naga inhabited areas. During my fieldwork, the yearning for a 'Naga solution' was at the forefront of many Zeme minds, and they kept referring to it in a very personal manner. Although the Zeme Heraka have endorsed their support for a 'Naga solution', they are in a difficult position, especially with relation to the Indian state (with the support of the RSS and VHP) on the one hand, and the relation with the majority Christian Nagas on the other. This ties in with the larger question of Naga nationalism and the politics it engenders in the region.

Naga Nationalism

The 'Naga insurgency', as it is known in the popular press in India, has haunted the subcontinent for over 50 years since India's independence.[34] The GOI is tight lipped about the ongoing peace process with various 'insurgent groups' in Nagaland and Naga inhabited areas.[35] Views of this 'insurgency' differ: is the 'insurgency' merely a law and order problem (which the GOI supports) or does it represent a larger political problem (which the GOI has been reluctant to accept)? The gap is widening and the problem becoming even more complex; worse still, it refuses to subside.[36]

When Indian independence was nearing, Zapuphizo, the President of the Naga National Council (NNC) and other Naga leaders met with Gandhi and Nehru to discuss the future of the 'Nagas' under the new India. These meetings took place roughly around July 1947. According to unsubstantiated accounts, Gandhi supported the 'Nagas' in their bid for an independent 'Naga area' while Nehru rejected the idea (Maxwell 1973: 8).[37] Dissatisfied with the hearings and finally realizing that the will of Nehru would be difficult to bend, the NNC declared independence on 14 August 1947. A telegraph message was supposedly sent to the GOI and the Secretary General of the United Nations, which, according to Mildred Archer's account, never got there because the Deputy Commissioner, Charles Pawsey, withheld the telegrams (cited in Jacobs et al. 1998: 158). It supposedly read: 'Southern Nagas including Manipur Hill Nagas and Cachar Nagas with Konyak Nagas declare independence today the fourteenth August 1947' (Maxwell 1973: 8).

Since this declaration, the NNC and the GOI have been engaged in important rounds of talks, most notably the 1948 '9 Point Agreement'. With no progress on the situation, 'overground leaders' under the Nagaland People's Convention (NPC) reached a compromise with the GOI with the creation of the state of Nagaland in 1963 and the signing of the '16 Point Agreement'.[38] The creation of statehood caused further divisions between the NNC and the GOI who saw the state as part of India.

Following various stalemates, political conniving and military operations in the region, the Peace Council of Nagaland, comprising eminent Naga figures, decided to try to bring the various parties to the peace table. The controversial 'Shillong Accord' was signed in Shillong on 11 November 1975 between the GOI and the NFG (the Naga Federal Government – the political wing of the NNC). This required the surrender and disarmament of the NNC. Zapuphizo, the President of the NNC, then in exile in London, was not consulted and learned about this only later (Steyn 2002: 156). It is often argued that the Shillong Accord marks the end of Zapuphizo's fight against the GOI. With this came the decline of the NNC and the rise of another group, the NSCN (Nationalist Socialist Council of Nagaland) under the leadership of Isak Swu, T. Muivah and S. S. Khaplang, who summarily rejected the 'Shillong Accord' as a sham and blamed the leadership for not standing up to it.

With the NNC waning, the NSCN began to gain ascendancy by attracting attention: skirmishes with the Indian army were common and so were its daring exploits expanding further into Burmese territory. Due to internal conflicts, and perhaps due to personality clashes, the northern Naga and Burmese Naga contingent split in 1988 to form the NSCN-K, under their leader Khaplang, who is from Burma. The remnant of the group came to be known as the NSCN-IM, after their leaders, Isak Swu and T. Muivah. The latter is the most powerful group in the region.

On 1 August 1997, a ceasefire was signed between the GOI and the NSCN-IM, and political negotiation at the highest level was to be held in a third country. So far the talks have included the main – but contentious – point of 'Greater Nagalim'. The aim of the NSCN-IM is that all Naga inhabited areas must be conjoined, if any viable settlement is to be reached through the talks. But what exactly are the Naga inhabited areas? According to the NSCN-IM website[39] the area is vast. Around 60 per cent of Manipur (mainly north Manipur, which is the most contentious part of their demands) is included, as are other smaller, but still substantial, chunks from Assam (mainly North Cachar District), Arunachal Pradesh (Tirap District) and regions bordering Nagaland in Burma are included in the map. Of course, there is huge opposition to these plans from the neighbouring states, and we are yet to find out what the final agreement will be between the GOI and the NSCN-IM.

The NSCN-IM has also been able to draw attention to their cause through international mediation and networking. Their machinery is quite impressive.[40] In the current situation, including the ongoing peace process, how do the various stances adopted by the different Naga groups and the response of the churches and NGOs affect the Zeme Heraka and their determination to maintain their religious identity? Aware of the various Naga movements, some Zeme are sceptical of the intentions of the NSCN-IM (they are the only ones operating in their region), in that they openly espouse a Christian ideology while suppressing other religious traditions such as the Heraka.

The Heraka say that the Naga claim for independence should be based solely on the common ethnic links and not on religious affiliations. A Zeme elder told me that when they went to meet the NSCN-IM leaders in camp Hebron (their headquarters), the leaders asked them if the Heraka still practised 'human sacrifice'. He laughed at the comment and assured them that this was a false accusation, a parody that was popular among Christian extremists who wanted to denounce the Heraka. While these stories are not unfounded, they also indicate the delicate relationship between the notion of 'Nagaland for Christ' and the Zeme Heraka quest for maintaining their religious identity. While there is a conscious revival among the Christians to promote the idea of 'Nagaland for Christ' extending to all Naga inhabited areas, the Zeme Heraka are responding with their own set of arguments. They suggest that first of all 'Nagaland for Christ' is touted only by fundamentalists, and second, that the notion of 'Zemehood' is intrinsically linked with the reform message of Heraka and therefore inseparable from who a Zeme Naga is. While these arguments find broader representation among the latter, it is clear that the religious element fostered by the nationalists and condemned by their enemies is relevant to this whole discussion of the Naga nationalism issue. But what is the position of the Zeme Heraka with regard to the larger question of Naga nationalism?

Nagas and India

Christianity played an important role in the relationship between the Nagas and India. The blame for fostering independence was squarely put on the Christian missionaries. Nehru reiterated these accusations: 'Some of the

Nagas were converted to Christianity and became educated to some extent. Because of this education they became the leaders of the Nagas. One of the last acts of the British was to encourage these Nagas to claim independence' (quoted in Steyn 2002: 74; see also Balwally 2003: 77–108).

Now some estimates say that 90 per cent of the Nagas are Christians.[41] The importance of Christianity has become imbedded in Naga identity not only as a religious tradition but as an act of cultural resistance to the largely 'Hindu' and 'Muslim' population of mainstream India (Baruah 2003: 329). The impact of Christianity played a crucial role in forging a Naga identity. For example, when the missionaries started translating the Bible into the local languages using the Roman alphabet, it meant that the people had to learn to read and write the Roman alphabet. The missions opened schools that taught in the medium of English. Since English was the language of the administrators and the educated, this appealed to the masses (see also Sumit Sarkar 2002: 231–2). English became attractive for upward mobility and government jobs; Nagas never really adopted Hindi as it was seen as the language of the 'Indian rulers'. In fact, the official language of Nagaland is now English.

Through these mission schools, different Naga groups could come together and for the first time communicate intelligibly in standard common languages, English and Nagamese (a pidgin of Assamese, Hindi and local dialects). With the reorganization of political structure and systems of governance by the British, the popularity of Christianity, and the ban on headhunting, young warriors no longer held traditional chiefs in the same esteem. It was these warriors who responded readily to Christian teachings (Eaton 2000: 256). It was mission activities and the reorganization of the social and political system that gave rise to a strong sense of a Naga nation as 'an imagined political community – and imagined as both inherently limited and sovereign' (Anderson 1991: 6). Christianity became the rallying point of this yearning. After Indian independence and during the troubled times before and after the creation of Nagaland statehood, a Christian revival took place that transformed the very nature of Naga identity. Traditional clothes, necklaces, beads, wood carvings, and so on were burnt publicly as a sign of shedding of 'old clothes' and taking on 'the new body of Christ'. This symbolic Christian imagery not only affirmed the religious solidarity of the Nagas but it also led to the overhauling and indeed the loss of traditional culture overnight. Their aim was to create a gulf, to sever the ties between their 'past' lives and the present and future promise.

While these activities were going on in many parts of Naga inhabited areas, others, like the Heraka, were consciously reforming their traditions to counter the threat of Christian missions; they were driven by the excesses of a certain form of Christianity with its emphasis on active evangelization among the Heraka. And, where better for such Christians to target their propaganda but against Rani Gaidinliu, by questioning her loyalty to the 'Nagas' and by making her an agent of 'Hindu' India? Rani Gaidinliu saw the Naga Christian vision of either/or as limiting and countered such accusations by stating her position that she was both Naga and Indian. In other words, she asserted that identity can be conceived in terms of both/and.

Rani Gaidinliu: Naga/Indian

When Rani Gaidinliu was released from prison in 1951 she was unhappy with the way the Zeliangrong people were being treated. She made contact with the President of India, Dr Rajendra Prasad, during his visit to Imphal and also met with Nehru to apprise them of the Zeliangrong situation. Her views are summed up thus:

> Till now the Government of Assam and the Government of Manipur had completely ignored the development of Zeliangrongs in Manipur, the North Kachar Hills and the Naga Hills. They were more stringently suppressed by the oppressive and repressive policy and measures than what was done to them during the period of the British rule, and they felt that they were treated as 'colonial and unwanted subjects' and that the authorities had desired to keep them illiterate, uncivilized, and backward, so that they might remain isolated from the mainstream of the Nagas and not pose a serious threat to the Government by not joining hands in the force of the Naga freedom movement led by Zapu Phizo, the President of the Naga National Council. (Yonuo 1982: 151–2)

Rani Gaidinliu was also of the view that the Naga movement, under the NNC, was imperialistic in its own way because it alienated many of her people due to its overt Christian message, coupled with the gospel of struggle for a Christian homeland. For her, freedom should be for all Nagas and proselytizing in any form must be discouraged. The elite Christians, on the other hand, saw Gaidinliu as representing all that was 'satanic', 'superstitious' – compared to the Christian gospel – in the indigenous religious traditions. In the Heraka view, she stood for all that was glorious about Naga culture, while the elite's embracing of Christianity constituted a violent rejection of all past religious beliefs and practices. Such Christians were taught, summarily, that everything 'traditional' must be deplored while everything Christian must be glorified. With extreme condemnation and isolation meted out by the Christians to these non-Christians, Rani Gaidinliu decided that she would fight for a separate Zeliangrong homeland (consisting of the Peren district of Nagaland, North Cachar Hills of Assam and Tamenglong district of Manipur), bringing the three kindred tribes into one administrative unit within the Indian Union, without any overt religious message. In 1960 she went underground with several thousand Zeliangrong fighters.

After six years of campaign, Rani Gaidinliu eventually surrendered to S. C. Dev, the then Deputy Commissioner of Kohima, on 20 January 1966. The meeting took place in Ranima's camp. As S. C. Dev recounts, Ranima greeted them with a garland and 'Jai Hind' (victory to India). During the meeting an unintentional query surfaced over her alleged blood sacrifices. Ranima, Dev continues, sternly replied:

> I am a simple illiterate woman, I please no spirit and worship none except Almighty God. Human blood is pious to me as to anybody else. My cause is simple and straight – the cause of my people – the Zeliang Nagas. I have fought for the independence of India along with Gandhi and Nehru. Our main aim was to drive away the British. I am an Indian, whatever may happen, I will live in the Union of India. For my people I want no State, no country, but only a district Zeliangrong within the State of the Indian Union. (1988: 76)[42]

In one of the rare interviews with Ranima, Dev recounts his conversation with her about her views on the Christians. Dev says,

> She had no ill-will against the faith of Christianity or any other faith. But she does hate the overzealous converts to Christianity who has [*sic*] abandoned the rich cultural heritage of the Nagas and is [*sic*] blindly copying the cheap aspects of western life. She said in an admirable simple manner: 'We are Nagas and we should live like Nagas. We have beautiful folklore and folk songs, colourful dress and culture. When I see these new converts copying the western way in a cheap manner it pains me.' (1988: 77)

Ranima did not hold back on her desire to lead and embody the notion of 'Indianness' while maintaining her 'Nagahood'. She readily accepted her role in defending India against the British, and her valour is already established through her alleged fighting alongside Gandhi and Nehru. This question of her strong 'Naganess' and 'Indianness' is augmented further in her conversation with S. C. Dev.

> For some, it was surprising when she said, 'If there is anybody who feels and thinks that he is or she is Naga – I am the one. Also, if there is anybody who feels or thinks that he or she is an Indian – it is me'. To her the Nagas and the rest of the Indians are not separate. They are one forming the great Indian Nation. Talking of their separation is nothing but madness.' (1988: 77)

To be or Not to be, That is the Answer?

All this puts the Heraka in a difficult position. Their numbers are largely concentrated around North Cachar Hills, and Heraka is practised mainly among the Zeme. Yet the majority of the Nagas are Christians. The Heraka are largely anti-Christian in their rhetoric because of conversion tactics employed by Christians in the past. Therefore, they try to distance themselves from Christian schools (in some cases) and instead rely on Government schools or schools started by the VHP like Saraswati Vidya Mandir, Vivekananda Vidyalaya and Kendriya Vidyalaya.

While these developmental trends continue with the aid of 'Hindu' organizations, there is clear opposition by the Christian majority who attempt to thwart their plans. In Hsongle, where the Christians form the majority in the village council, they have been able to influence the council vote against the running of a Heraka school because it is partnered with the VHP. The Paipui (female elder) of the Heraka community lambasted the hypocritical position of the Christians. 'Instead of loving their neighbours, they want us to suffer', she said. 'How else can the Heraka get education, if not from the VHP: If we rely on Christian schools then all they are interested in is converting our children.' 'They block our intentions because we are Heraka, it is discrimination.' These divisions occur, she says, because of religious boundaries that lead to conflict.

Yet on the flip side, the VHP-run school requires its students to say a pledge that indicates the difficult position the Heraka find themselves in. They constantly have to compromise on their identity. Who does one stay loyal to? In Saraswati Vidya Mandir, their morning pledge is:

> Bharat [India] is my motherland. All Bharatiyas are my brothers and sisters. I love my country. I am proud of her rich and varied heritage.

> I shall always strive to be worthy of it. I shall give respect to my parents, Acharyas [teachers], Classmates and all elders and treat everyone with courtesy. To my country and my People, I pledge my devotion. In their well being and prosperities alone lies my happiness. BHARAT MATA KI JOY.[43]

The strong integrationist ideology that is part of such a 'Hindu' organization places the Heraka in a difficult position and the old adage, 'to be or not to be', certainly reflects the ambivalent relation the Heraka have with both Christian and Hindu. For a start, these associations make the Heraka 'Hindu' in the eyes of Christians. The Heraka clearly try to distance themselves from any classification, partly because being close to 'Hindu' groups betrays the common sense ideology of the Naga being anti-India and therefore by default anti-Hindu (the church is often to blame for such extreme misrepresentation).[44] The Heraka understands the import of the term 'Hindu' and displays more sophistication in their exegesis of it than the Zeme Christian. A Heraka elder expressed his views in a jocular manner, that at first reading makes it obscure through contradictions, but many Heraka probably share his view. Affirming and denying propositions has little to do with what the Heraka are, but by juxtapositioning notions, they are able to assert their own identity as singular.

> Those who call us [Heraka] Hindu are mad! They don't know the process. The word 'Hindu' means a group gathering; the word 'du' in Hindi we don't quite know. But all those coming together mean 'du' in Zeme as in *pedui* (a small group). *Pedui* is group. That group is called Hindu – those who come together. *Ladu* is also round, isn't it, therefore 'du' is used. Yes, we accept that we are Hindu; if they [Christians] don't accept then it is also okay. But we are pure Heraka, not mix. Tingwang gave directly to Ranima and she gave it to us. Our *tingna* [period of ritual] is not formed by communicating through God (*hedachakpe* [as in *Paupaise*, or ancestral practice, which usually involved blood sacrifice]) nor by any knowledgeable person; our tingna is 'pure' in English and in Zeme *nchichiak*, not a mixture, we have not touched with any other. We agree we are Hindu, because we are also a group, but our 'dharm' is purely sent from the sky.

The Heraka rhetoric has been strategically constructed around the Christian and Hindu agendas that constantly evoke in them the need to adapt. So in a sense Heraka identity is formed along these distinct fault lines and, as a result, they are not seen as one or the other: in the eyes of 'Hindu' organizations they are anti-conversion and by default anti-church; and in the eyes of Christians they are 'Hindu', and therefore not 'Nagas'. Yet since they attempt to preserve traditional faith and culture, their belief is local. The amorphous relation suits the Heraka well, because by placing themselves in the middle and building a fence around, they are 'not touched with any other'. Such a purity complex is predictable in the case of the Heraka, because this is the only way they can find a place in this complex relation. This could suggest that their emphasis on purity is a reaction to the fact that they are anything but pure. They, like everyone around them, are also true hybrids.

As much as they are comfortable with their position, they also realize that being seen as Hindu is a difficult road to tread. For example, students who attend 'Hindu' institutions reflect on the exercise of worshipping 'Hindu' gods with a little apprehension.[45] A former Heraka pupil told me,

> for example, we have two *aarti* (prayers) in the evening: we pray to two to three gods: Lakshmi (wealth), Saraswati (knowledge), Ram/Sita (for us tribals, they are like our ancestors). Before we go to bed, we have two prayers: the first one is a mantra and we pray to Ishvaar (Bhagwan) to give us rest, then the Heraka have a prayer song, *Ndibantu Dinkuinin.* We don't pray to the statues, or idols, but we pray to our unseen God, Tingwang.

'We don't pray to the idols' is a strong monotheistic stance possibly of Christian provenance, that has been incorporated into the Heraka understanding. Such perceptions, of an opposition between 'idol worship' and 'praying to the unseen God', are reflected by the Pastor of Hsongle Baptist church, himself a recent convert from Heraka. He said,

> When I was Heraka, I visited the Hindu Mandir in Uttar Pradesh and got a picture of Ganeshji from that Mandir. I kept the photo of Ganeshji at the back of the house in a small locked box thinking that Ganesh was Tingwang. One day when I went to pray, the locked box where I kept the photo of Ganesh was missing. I thought that God himself ran away, for what reason I don't know? From next year, my family suffered. We were sick with fever and one of my sons also died. The houses where I prayed were all cured, except my house. Later when the Christians came to our house to pray, I refused to convert, until eventually when my wife was really sick, I relented. After that, my entire household was cured.

The Baptist pastor's conversion experience relies on the fact that 'God, Ganeshji, ran away': if such a God can be locked inside a box, then God is limiting. As the pastor later told me, the notion of God being portrayed in pictures seems to suggest 'idol worship' to the Baptist Christians, from which the Heraka are also trying to distance themselves. For the Christian and also to some extent the Heraka, monotheism implies a form of worship, which is anti-Hindu. God is in the sky, limitless, and accessible wherever one is. No earthly images, as with the 'Hindus', can portray such a powerful being. It is difficult to say if the Heraka are anti-Hindu here or just trying to beat the Baptist Christians at their own game.

The rhetoric of conversion or the perceived threat of conversion is littered with playful and sometimes well organized diatribes that make certain assumptions about what tribal people, such as the Heraka, are. These also reveal how they represent, for the larger 'Hindu' and Christian groups, a battlefield of ideas and practice. In December 2006, a major Janajati Youth Convention was held in Guwahati organized by the Janajati Faith and Culture Protection Forum that works with the tribals of Northeast India and Nepal. In what was a right-wing Hindu ideological speech, the Chairman of the Forum, Bikram Bahadur Jamatia, exclaimed that the collective tribal people's view could be summed up thus:

> Our Bharatvarsa [land of Bharat] is devabhoomi [abode of the gods], poonyabhoomi [holy land] and karmabhoomi [field of action], but Bharatvarsa in the Northeast is more so due to the variety of human race, divine beauty of mother nature, the mighty Brahmaputra and other rivers, colour culture and sanatan dharma practised in different forms, and purity and piety in human behaviour. If our sanatan dharma is protected, our culture, language and history are automatically protected. The enemy forces describe us as non-Hindus and non-Christians. What is this? When I refer to our dharma as sanatan dharma, I mean the eternal or primordial religion practised by our forefathers through the ages. That is nothing but nature-worship. The fissiparous and divisive forces, which have extraterritorial loyalty, describe our evolution as danger to our identity. Our constitution has described that all the sanatan dharmas (eternal religions of all the janajatis) fall under the category of Hinduism. By describing us as non-Hindus, the Christian missionaries are trying to segregate and isolate us from the rest of the country so that we remain weak and vulnerable for Christian conversion.[46]

The rhetoric above is cluttered with such images of 'holy land', 'Bharat' – they represent the world-view of 'Hindu' neo-traditionalists. Their romantic notion of nationhood can be found in various websites and in materials churned out by their propaganda machine.[47] The similar rhetoric of a homeland based on religious belief has also been taken up by the Heraka to project a unifying ideology, not solely based on ethnicity but on indigenous religious practice as determining one's ethnicity. In this sense, the Heraka advocate a religious practice that is limitless and accessible to all but one that prizes indigenous practice as legitimating their religious tradition as well.

Ethnicity and Religious Belief

One of the ways the Heraka are able to improve their marginal status is by playing the modern ethnic card. Being rooted in an indigenous religious tradition is an assertion of their identity as Zeme. Therefore, by saying that the true ethnic link from the past to the present is maintained and practised by the Heraka, they are able to assert an authentic self. By appealing to nativist traditions, they are able to draw the distinction between the Heraka and Christians as a yardstick against which the latter can be condemned as foreign. These sentiments are based on primordial attachments. Clifford Geertz, while examining such primordial attachments among new states from around the world, asserts that these attachments are based on 'givens' or 'assumed givens'. This, he says, is expressed by 'immediate contiguity and kin connection mainly, but beyond them the givenness that stems from being born into a particular religious community, speaking a particular language, or even a dialect of a language, and following particular social practices' (1973: 259). These bonds are reiterated by 'some unaccountable absolute import attributed to the tie itself' (1973: 259). Clifford Geertz further observes that people who become either Christian or Muslim from the Balinese religion

> would be tantamount, in their eyes, to ceasing to be Balinese, and, indeed, an occasional individual who is converted is still considered, even by the most tolerant and sophisticated, to have abandoned not just Balinese religion but Bali, and perhaps reason, itself. (Geertz 1973: 181–2)

Similarly, for the Zeme Heraka, this tie is bound up with their religious tradition, which is summarily explained in terms of its indigeneity as opposed to its foreignness. This distinction or separation of local identity is rooted in their religious practice. But what exactly is local is coloured by their views on what the other is. In a typical Zeme logic, if one is not of a particular religious group, one is a foreigner. The Paupaise, the ancestral way of life, often do not understand why the Heraka and Christian quibble; in Paupaise eyes, they are the same (as in foreign), in that Christianity is started by Jesus Christ and Heraka by Ranima. As an example, a Paupaise woman replied:

> I heard from others that Heraka is still practising Zeme song and dance. But the practice of song, dance, and wearing of ornaments alone is not complete Zemese and not complete Zeme. To be a complete Zeme and Zemese [Zeme practice], they should follow the rituals as we are doing, because they are original, from our ancestors. So Heraka are half-Zeme. What they are practising is empty (*perua*).

The strong case of Paupaise's association with being a Zeme, is something the Paupaise are able to maintain by arguing that Zemese is being Zeme. Forsaking Zeme identity, by adopting foreign religions, is akin to denouncing their identity (see also Kammerer 1990: 281). The Heraka would respond by saying, 'the Paupaise generation is the *kemeume* generation (prophecy generation) and it is over. Now is the generation of the Heraka, as every people has generations that they live under according to the situation and context.[48] By doing this they similarly cut off the Paupaise and regard them as *perua*, empty. However, the most carefully constructed critique is between the Heraka and Christians. A well-known Heraka preacher, in a public event, said this:

> Christians say, there is no place for Heraka in heaven; but there is no heaven in the universe. When Jesus died, he was buried in the earth; no one saw Jesus going to heaven, above the sky. Christian worship is not Indian; the British came and wrote about the story of Jesus Christ, so they [those Christians] follow the British form of worship. So those who have converted to Christianity don't forget your local religious practice, because in the time of death your body will not be sent to the British country, so it is better to preserve our own.

While the theme of conversion is intertwined with the above rhetoric, the interesting thing is the response. The Heraka are trying to find links with the local. By rejecting a global religious practice, such as Christianity, they ground their identity in the reality of home (see, for example, Kammerer 1990). Burial is a vital part of Zeme tradition; the wish to be buried in one's home is tantamount to gaining ascendance into *heruimeram* (soul village).

This feeling is maintained to some extent by those who have converted as well. To be buried in one's home is in a sense proclaiming one's tie with the *kelua* (village) and the people (*Zemena*). In effect, the Heraka construct a viable rhetoric of indigenizing their faith while proclaiming Christianity as foreign – and by evoking powerful Zeme symbols, such as death, they are able to cement this bond and encourage their members to hang on to their practice.

The Christian response is more scathing. Although they appreciate the Heraka for their strong sense of preserving 'traditional faith and culture', they also regard them as having 'no everlasting or eternal life' (John 3.16). In a lighter response the Baptist Pastor in Hsongle told me:

> Heraka is temporary. For example, if your mother and someone go to the forest and the other person returns first, you ask her 'where is my mother?' And the person says, 'here play with this lollipop till your mother comes back.' So playing with the lollipop is Heraka, it is only temporary, or merely a passing of time.

Categories of the Mind: Beer and Baptism

Returning to Barth's definition of boundary as divisions 'on the ground', marking groups 'off from each other', and as that which separates 'distinct categories of the mind' (2000: 17), the following summary explicates this definition. There are clearly two broad camps: Heraka and Christian. The Heraka are a relatively single group, while the Christians are again divided into Presbyterian, Baptist and Catholic. The Christians can also be categorized on the surface into (1) infant baptism and beer drinking group and (2) adult baptism and beer rejecting group. The key concept here is infant and adult. Many people wanting to stop drinking beer become Baptists. When accepting the Baptist faith through *adult* baptism their belonging within that tradition is made *explicit*. Those who continue drinking beer (Presbyterians and Catholics) believe that since baptism has occurred as an *infant*, one is already within the grace of God and the Church; their belonging within that tradition is *implicit*. The range of these issues within the same ethnic group itself delineates the distinct categories on the ground, from one another, and in the mind.

These distinctions are further made on the level of the relationship of religious affiliation determining ethnicity. These conclusions are made based on how external agents are perceived in relation to the group.

The Heraka are hence categorized as 'Hindu' or Christians as 'foreign or Western'. Even among the Christians themselves similar perceptions are evident. The Baptist Pastor told me that the

> Catholics are not proper Christians, they are Roman. They pray what is written in the Prayer Book, nothing much. And they say only Father, Son and Holy Spirit while eating, sleeping, and so on . . . But Presbyterians and Baptists are the same because we pray and ask a lot. Catholics are not Nagas. For example, if we ask them, 'pray for the nation's workers', they say, 'without the consent of the Father, we cannot pray'. They are Roman, they take orders from the Father, and not Nagas.

Even though these descriptions are used at the level of ideas and rhetoric, the feeling is that no one religious group has a monopoly over Zeme culture after all many share it. Everyone has a stake in what Zeme culture is and an idea about what constitutes 'original' or 'complete' Zeme identity. The issue is not about what one is – for all are Zeme – but how authentic one is perceived to be. While all these arguments are pertinent in how one's identity is constructed within the larger ethnicity of a group, religious affiliations are primary in shaping the ongoing debate.

Conclusion

Tribal groups like the Zeme demonstrate very specific ways to deal with the question of religious boundaries and their own version of ethnicity in relation to these. The contention becomes oppositional in its character: between the tribal and the non-tribal, between Heraka and Christian, between Hindu and Christian, and even between Christian groups themselves. Therefore, where tribal identities are vital in this interlocking genre of religious affiliation, the need to find some rapprochement is accepted.

Notions of identity formed by closer examination of community and boundary are important for the Zeme in the different religious traditions. Although one can say that such boundaries are fluid, the need to maintain them, on the surface at least, is explicit. Such is the case, specifically between the Heraka and Christian communities and to some extent between the different Christian communities. These dynamics were very evident and centred around one Zeme village. But how are these parameters framed when the Heraka are positioned in the larger society of national politics and regional identifying?

I have shown that the closeness the Heraka have with Hindu organizations, in the eyes of Christians, not only betrays their seeming allegiance to a sense of pan-Nagahood, but it also constructs religious boundaries. The Christians constantly jibe at the insecurities of the Heraka by questioning if their feathers have been smudged by 'Hindu' incense. The Hindu organizations, on the other hand, seem to assert a sense of historicity by linking the *vanvasi* to 'Bharat Mata'. By doing this, they aspire to put the Heraka Zeme back into the jungle where their 'sanatan dharma' is untainted by the process of modernization and the effects of westernization (that most Christians seem to undergo at breakneck speed). Such rhetoric is doubly situated in the context of India, where such groups like VHP and RSS represent integration with 'Bharat Mata' and oppose westernization (connected with Christianity) while encouraging them to preserve their traditional faith and culture in the comfortable confines of their 'jungles'. An RSS worker told me, perhaps rightly, 'change has to be done by the local people, according to their need and own wisdom. The reforms which are taking place in America or United Kingdom cannot be copied nor can they be helpful for us here in India.'

The difficulty of finding a comfortable identity for the Heraka is also connected with the larger question of Naga nationalism and the politics it engenders. For the Naga Christians, the GOI is not trustworthy. Its politics of nation building is a source of historical suspicion. In fact, the position of Rani Gaidinliu and the expression of her 'Indianness' as well as her 'Naganess' is something the Heraka does not want to draw attention to, due to the present political sensitivities. Naturally, the Heraka do not wish to commit to any single group or ideology in this system. Due to their ambiguous position, one gets the impression that the Heraka have to oscillate between these two powerful groups they have to confront and live with everyday. The Heraka are trying to broaden the indigenous, to accommodate to modernity but also to ape (while rejecting) powerful religious groups. But they too want to transcend local power and elevate the indigenous so that it can compete with 'world religions'.

These questions are pertinent for the Heraka as they find a niche of their own within Naga society, and their larger position and place in India. Within the slippery realm of 'religion' and identity, the Heraka seem to slide between various positions. Could they eventually blend in with Christianity or are they a way of understanding the process of how one becomes a 'Hindu' or how one was a 'Hindu' in its nascent form? It is in this regard the Heraka represent for both the 'Hindu' organizations and the Christian Nagas an ideological battle in terms of the larger Naga identity or an Indian (or Hindu) identity. For the Heraka, difference is a strategy that suits them well. And, in an obvious way, their relation with both the Christian and 'Hindu' organizations helps define Heraka identity.

The forging of Heraka identity against such religious groups as the Christians and the Hindus is pivotal in the way they define a particular sense of belonging. This belonging is centred on the construction of community. The next chapter deals with the internal differences in ideology in relation to the formation of community and the future of the Heraka community. In the previous chapters, we have seen the process of agrarian reform, the religious reform, and how the forces of history have given way to the precarious position of the Heraka vis-à-vis the Christians and 'Hindus'. The forces of history have also given rise to a particular way the Heraka perceive themselves and dissenting voices. The next chapter attempts to place this dialogue in the construction of *heguangram* (free community) and the promised return of the *heguang* (agent of that freedom).

Chapter 6

Community Imaginings and the Ideal of Heguangram

For the Zeme Heraka people, the ideal of *heguangram* (free community) embodies life, hope and freedom. One could even say that this is etched on the body of the Heraka people. The foundations of the modern state are wrapped up in the flesh of a *heguang* (one who brings freedom), projecting a notion of cosmological unity over its social order. This is a social order that attempts to construct a community across tribal boundaries and effect a resurgence, in the hope that the Heraka will become the central and single religious body for the entire Zeliangrong people. This concept of *heguangram* clearly relates to notions of millenarianism; that is, a chosen person who will eventually redeem the people from oppression and create an atmosphere where there is harmony, joy and abundance for all (Burridge 1969: 3–14). In the Heraka context, these notions are held mainly by the rural population, and opposed by the urban population, making it all the more contested.

This chapter will examine the above points by considering a series of linear events. The construction of this community begins at Hangrum and the Hangrum war in 1932. The Hangrum war represents the historical point from which the notion of the *heguangram* emerged. The narrative surrounding *heguangram* is realized in the coming of a *heguang*. The different interpretations and ideas concerning the nature of the *heguangram* and *heguang* is the central focus of this chapter. My attempt is not to resolve the tension inherent in these notions, but to present the different arguments and help the reader understand some of the central tenets, discrepancies and conclusions. Local knowledge, historical materials, textual reading and narrative – all these contribute to our understanding of the notion of community and its implications.

This chapter is therefore twofold in its imagination and technique. It is a narrative dialogue between 'concept' and 'evidence'. These above symbols of *heguang* and *heguangram* attempt to envision a community encapsulated in the narrative tradition of the past, its text, and its future significance (Dube 1999: 121–2). This community, I argue, is symbolized by the construction of the concept of *heguangram.*

Heguang and Heguangram: Some Conceptual Tools

The word *heguang* can be used in two ways. It can either mean a state of rest/freedom or one who is the agent of this freedom. Most Zeme Heraka associate this with a king (*heguangpeu*), a single head representing a hierarchical and centralized rule. However, I want to suggest that the word *heguang* is too limited if we apply it only to a king, because the word is neutral in gender. I therefore want to examine the possibility of *heguang* being both male and female. *Heguangram* on the other hand has territorial connotations of the *ram* (village) or community (see below) where such freedom will exist or be exercised by the agent. However, careful consideration will also be given to the concept of king and kingdom. These nuances will become clearer as the chapter proceeds.

My first attempt to envisage *heguangram* is by seeking to 'capture members' experience of it'. In this sense, the question we should be asking, according to Anthony Cohen, is 'What does it [community] appear to mean to its members?' (Cohen 2003: 20). In his book, *The Symbolic Construction of Community*, Cohen goes on to explore this notion. He concludes that overall a community is symbolically constructed and contrasted by its boundaries and the members' awareness of it. This awareness 'hinges crucially on consciousness' of its members and depends on shared 'repositories of meaning' rather than a set of automated linkages. The community is experienced in the way people think about it rather than consisting in 'social structure or "the doing" of social behaviour' (2003: 98). Put simply, community exists in the minds of its people and is connected through symbols that hold and perpetuate its meaning for its members. Moreover, Cohen says that the community must be regarded as an '*agg*regating device' rather than an '*in*tegrating mechanism' because community need not be uniform. In other words, a community can sustain commonality and difference because it values identities not based solely on individual qualities but includes additional references (Cohen 2003: 109). Similarly with the Heraka, the earlier *ram* or village with its gates and boundaries has given rise to 'community' as a reference to larger identities. Therefore I use *ram* to mean community rather than village. The 'aggregating device' Cohen suggests can be a helpful way of looking at the Heraka community in its varied nuances.

Therefore, within the larger notion of community, it might also be useful to examine *heguangram* as an idea aimed at bringing about a cosmological, intertribal solidarity (the Zeliangrong), and a 'higher-level integration' (Tambiah 1976: 74). This idea is also common within the symbolism of kingship: representing 'a mythical system through which people can experience the world as a totality' (Yamaguchi 1977: 151).[1] It also strives, by association with a particular place and its history, to find a central idea in locating an 'exemplary centre' – that which encompasses epochs and collapses them into one single space-time continuum. This idea is represented in Hangrum, the establishment of a king's court (see below) and the rituals that accompany such formality, as the symbol of the 'exemplary centre'. Geertz, while examining the 'theatre state', Negara, says,

> . . . the court-and-capital is at once a microcosm of the supernatural order – 'an image of . . . the universe on a smaller scale' – and the material embodiment of political order . . . The equation of the seat of rule with the dominion of rule . . . is more than an accidental metaphor; it is the statement of a controlling political idea – namely, that by the mere act of providing a model, a paragon, a faultless image of civilized existence, the court shapes the world around it into at least a rough approximation of its own excellence. The ritual life of the courts, and in fact the life of the court generally, is thus paradigmatic, not merely reflective, of social order. (1980: 13)

On another level, the *heguangram* could have been envisaged as nascent nationalism in an organization that attempted to draw people from across borders and establish a larger political unit, or pan-tribalism. This constituted a unit that was internally purified, more unified and, perhaps, better equipped to function against other dominant groups such as Christians, other Naga groups or even the state government (Brown 1991: 403; Worsley 1970). Burridge has argued that when millenarian movements spring up, old symbols are destroyed and with it cyclic time. Due to this there is a period of anomie, then a desire to start afresh, to recreate history, and linear time is established: 'the events of the millennialism become mythologized, qualifying or even displaying the traditional mythology' (Burridge 1985: 228). I do not totally disagree with Burridge's analysis, but it is difficult to comprehend what he means by anomie; a period perhaps akin to Victor Turner's liminality (1969), where there is anti-structure and a feeling of disorientation before being reintegrated into society? Rather, as I will show, the rhetoric of the *heguangram* in a way concerns the recreation of history, but not at the expense of 'traditional mythology'. Rather, there appears to be a fluid transition from one to the other, and not a clear, marked, distinction. This fluid transition is what confers verisimilitude on the imagined community. According to Benedict Anderson, this is akin to state managing or nation making that 'is an imagined political community – and imagined as both inherently limited and sovereign'. Yet, such communities are imagined not only because of their 'falsity/genuineness, but by the style in which they are imagined' (Anderson 1991: 6). It is this style of imagination in which I am interested. This imagined community begins in Hangrum.

Sacred Geography

Hangrum is one of the biggest Zeme villages in North Cachar Hills, Assam. Its beauty and difficult terrain, Ursula Graham Bower says, make Hangrum a

> dramatic setting on a knife-edged ridge; range after range of the Manipur hills looming blue and green out of the cloud on one side of it, razor-backed spurs sweeping down to the Jenam on the other, the forbidding mass of Hemeolowa blocking the outlook to the south; its smoke stained houses a study in shades of brown and tan and darker brown, like a sepia drawing. (Bower 1952: 52)

The dangerous terrain makes communication difficult; it was not until recently that a motorable road was functioning, and that only sporadically. In the monsoon season, due to the landslides, the road is blocked for several months. This leads to water shortages and inadequate food supply. But, as a military site, it has benefits, including a vantage point that overlooks the valley below when the morning mist has lifted, and easy escape routes along the smaller ridges leading to the Manipur border. Such escape routes were utilized by Rani Gaidinliu during the Hangrum war of 1932. This war was, for the Heraka, the starting-place for the *heguangram.*

Fugitives and Gods: The Hangrum War 1932

An elder of Hangrum village narrated the story to me of the Hangrum war fought in 1932. He said:

> We look after Hangrum camp because when Ranima fought with the British Army – on that day – only Hangrum men fought. When the British

> army fired the first shots, only water came out, as Ranima had used her magic (*kiantau*). After that Ranima changed the magic, the bullet came and could not enter her body and she collected the bullets in her shirt. The third time, they [the British] brought new guns from Baladhan, Longma. So before Ranima could start her magic, the British soldiers fired with the new guns. On the first round three of her followers died and four were seriously injured. On that day Tingwang and Banglawang [Zeliangrong gods] also came and were very sad after seeing the blood of our people. At that time Tingwang told them that 'Hangrum is the place for the starting place of Zeliangrong *heguangram*'. Even if Hangrum is a rocky place, it is Tingwang's chosen place; therefore it cannot be a plain area. So that's why we still protect and preserve Hangrum camp. Every night we pray, not only for the Heraka, but also for the whole world.

While the above is a narration of events according to the local elder, the British archives provide a different account.

By the time Jadonang was imprisoned, in 1931, Gaidinliu along with some of the followers escaped to the nearby villages. The British government by now was quite incensed by the unfolding events. J. P. Mills, the Deputy Commissioner of the Naga Hills, commented as follows:

> The real danger of the movement is the spirit of defiance now abroad. Nagas who are ordinarily truthful and friendly, have been taught that officials are to be lied to and deprived of information. These lessons will not be quickly forgotten. (quoted in Reid [1942] 1997: 170)

Unable to track down Gaidinliu and frustrated in his attempt to wean information out of people, these events bothered Mills. He clearly wanted a willing native to submit to authority rather than the defiance shown by Gaidinliu and her 'cult'. A reward of Rs. 200 was placed on Gaidinliu's capture and arrest by the Manipur state. This was later increased to Rs. 500, with remission of house tax for 10 years as well. This was to be given to any individual who provided information on Gaidinliu's whereabouts (Singh 2002: 132). For a while nothing came of this. Gaidinliu remained at large, due to the cleverly organized movement that was forming under her commander, Masang of Kepelo, and its network of spies. Their methods were to utilize both the myth and aura of Gaidinliu and for her soldiers to employ deception in order to trick the British. Gaidinliu would come and go like a ghost, rumoured to be dressed in white and escorted by girls; people would whisper that her presence was felt only in spirit, and the maze of connections that they created in the villages concealed her movements. A network of tunnels, back entrances and secret hideouts made her inconspicuous to the British but very visible to the people. Their confidence and faith in her strengthened. Rumours of her exploits – turning bullets into water and foiling assailants of her party by her magic (*kiantau*) – spread like wild fire (see also Bower 1952: 43).

On 18 March 1932, about 50 to 60 fighters from the village of Hangrum rushed down a slope and attacked the sepoys who were positioned below in their post. The vantage point of the soldiers below could not have been better. Those rushing down the slope were easy targets for those with guns; spears and arrows were no match. Bower ponders why 3 times the number were not killed (only 6 deaths have been recorded) (1952: 43). It is still a mystery why the attack took place or why it occurred on a column of soldiers in broad daylight. One account from administrative reports suggests that Gaidinliu held a 'puja' (worship) the night before and promised the men that 'she was God', and no harm would come to them if they attacked the sepoys. When the attempt failed through the power of British guns, the village gave up. As a punishment the SDO burnt the village down. The villagers swore a 'new oath of allegiance to the British Raj, breaking their previous oath to Gaidiliu'.[2] Gaidinliu managed to slip away to Pulomi where a last stand would be staged with the British.

By the time they reached Pulomi, energy and morale were low. Gaidinliu apparently instructed the people to build a huge fortress that would accommodate her and her warriors. It was a palisade copied from the Hangrum fort, according to those who witnessed the construction. Gaidinliu herself was blockaded inside with her followers. Administrative reports suggest that the Pulomi villagers worked like slaves and even used up their own supply of firewood from the jungle to build the 18-feet-high stockades. To inspire the people inside she purportedly told them that 'she [Gaidinliu] would strike the Sahibs dead with magic and her supporters were then to use daos [a hacking knife] only, for they would be enough'. When Captain Macdonald, the commanding officer sent to capture Gaidinliu, ordered the attack, Gaidinliu's army melted away and there was no magic. There was no provocation from the people inside or a single bullet fired. The village, it reports, was clearly relieved when the sepoys dragged out 'the biting, scratching girl for whom they [the village] had uselessly worked so hard and killed so many cattle'. In her confessions, Gaidinliu naturally denied all the claims made by her captors. She had no part in the construction of the palisade, she said, nor was she responsible in any way for the attack on the Hangrum post.[3]

Mirroring the Divine: The Anthropologist and Gods

With the capture of Gaidinliu and the wide-scale revolt hanging in the balance, pockets of resistance erupted proclaiming similar agendas against the *sarkar* (government). These resurgences proclaimed Jadonang and Gaidinliu as their inspiration in refusing to pay taxes to the government. Ceremonies in commemoration of Jadonang and Gaidinliu continued unabated with prophets touring villages and proclaiming 'magical powers to cure illnesses'.[4] The government adopted precautionary measures by arresting the remnants of the Jadonang and Gaidinliu cult and particularly those involved in the murder of a Kuki family in Lakema. The ethnic tensions with the Kukis were already simmering. One, Ramjo of Bopungwemi, was arrested for leading the party that committed the murders. The British Army tracked down another man, Gomhei, allegedly responsible for instigating the above murders. He remained elusive for a while but suddenly reappeared, stepping into the shoes of Jadonang and accompanied by a girl, Areliu, with divine powers, taking on Gaidinliu's role. They toured villages, cured diseases and preached the coming of the 'Kacha Naga Empire and their own apotheosis'. Hutton, a British administrator, comments, 'it may be pointed out that a tour of this kind brings a considerable amount of money to the touring medicine man in the form of fees and presents.' With the help of the Kachari and the Kukis, they were finally caught in North Cachar Hills.[5] Pockets of resistance continued to surface, and increasing desire for a 'prophet' who would bring some hope for the Zeme did not fade with time. Ursula Graham Bower recounts an experience, in which she is taken to be Gaidinliu's incarnation, in a kind of apotheosis.

While administrators were kept at a distance, anthropologists seem to have been treated with more respect. For example, Bower's time with the Zeme of North Cachar Hills during the Second World War gained her much respect. In fact it is still remembered. Her role in the 'V' force that organized Zeme scouts for the Watch and Ward section during the Japanese invasion acquired her the British nickname 'Naga Queen' (1952: 214). It is a strange coincidence that Bower and Gaidinliu shared the same adjective 'Queen'. Both were admired for their daring exploits: Bower for her role with the 'V' force, Gaidinliu for her role in resisting the British (the title of 'Ranee' was given to her by Nehru in his eloquent rendering of events in the Naga Hills).[6] Bower, however, was familiar with and critical of Gaidinliu and her movement (see Chapter 3). It is perhaps not so strange that Bower was mistaken for Gaidinliu. In a rather surreal passage, part an expression of exasperation, Bower records her conversation with Gaidinliu's disciple and right-hand man Masang, now a part of Bower's entourage:

> But before Gaidiliu was arrested she had told Masang and the rest that even if she were caught it would not matter; the Government would imprison only her simulacrum and her real and divine self would be safe elsewhere, to return in the course of time in such a shape that her enemies would never know her and only the faithful could recognize her. Masang had not forgotten. After all those years he was still looking for her reincarnation.
>
> I didn't know it at the time, but he found it in me. (1952: 45)

This reincarnation of Gaidinliu in Bower is narrated by the latter, in the context of her visit to the village of Hangrum where Gaidinliu fought the British forces in 1932. The notion that Bower represented hope, or even perhaps, inspired faint messianic moments among the villagers is reminiscent of the conversations I have had with the Heraka people. It is said the next *heguang* will come from the East, and Hangrum is the most likely place for this. In Bower's own words,

> The villagers, men and women, swarmed on me like bees. Cup on cup of rice-beer was forced into my hands. They caught hold of me, pulled me by the wrist, tugged at my clothes, and even prised my hand open to make me accept, in person, the gifts they offered. In fact they behaved as I had never known a Naga village do before, with raving insanity. I hadn't a second's privacy the whole time I was there. No matter what I was doing, sleeping, eating, resting, or even bathing, the hut was invaded regardless by somebody crying parrot-phrases: 'O my Mother! O Queen, O Goddess! You are our mother, you are a goddess, there is none greater, there is none better than you!' (1952: 53)

Her vexed response provides us with some insights into events, especially the enormous importance of the idea of the *heguang* and also the fact that not all Naga villages shared this ideal. Where the Zeme are concerned, Bower was either the return of Gaidinliu, or a random 'stranger' taking on the spirit of Gaidinliu. The account reveals Bower's refusal to see Gaidinliu or the Gaidinliu cult as anything substantive. She maintains her previous position that it was a money-making racket. When honoured by another village, Guilong, her frustration clearly shows. She calls the subsequent dance in her honour a 'three-ring circus – a performance of stark, staring, undiluted anarchy' (Bower 1952: 54).

It also reveals the difficult position of the British and their response to the Jadonang and Gaidinliu uprising: on the one hand the British believed it to be exploiting the economic malaise in the region in its promise of future wealth and prosperity from a divine source (see Chapter 3). Bower, along with all British officials, embraces this extreme position. On the other hand, the Zeme considered the uprising an act of defiance: the people hang on to Gaidinliu and all that she embodied. Maybe they did see something in Bower that signalled their longing for a promised 'saviour': maybe her gender, her assertiveness, her independence, emitted appropriate signs? Both Gaidinliu and Bower, as autonomous women, were seen as an anomaly in that era. Bower's status with colonial powers, and her work with the people emitted powerful symbolism to the Zeme, which facilitates a relationship with the gods who are both like and unlike us. This event reveals the deep ambiguity of the Zeme who are fighting the British and yet divinizing a British woman. Bower's divine status gives rise to the larger question of hope in the face of helplessness that reverberates within the Heraka in different ways. Could it be that the continuing poor economic conditions of the Zeme in their villages creates a greater desire for the *heguangram*? It has been asserted over the years that someone will return in Gaidinliu's stead and that the making of the *heguang* will herald a new era for the Heraka.

Articulation of a Vision: Heguangram and Its Critics

Hangrum represents an articulation of resistance within the rhetoric of an overpowering mythic narrative as expressed above by the local elder.[7] My concern here is not with the categories of myth and history as separate entities. Rather I treat them as implicit practices (Comaroff 1985: 125) grounded in everyday life. Most of how the Zeme narrate the past is referred to as *rasam* (story) which they differentiate solely in terms of time: 'in the past so and so happened'. All of it is seen as history in the sense that it is about the past and is true (Tonkin 1995) or as myth as a naturalization of meaning (Barthes 1993). There is no particular concern to differentiate between history and myth, for it is only stories they tell.

This articulation is structured around the ritual of the *heguangram* called 'Sunrise Prayer' and 'Hangrum Parade' that exhibits some order, even if only of an imagined kind (see below). The lofty, white colour 'Martyrs Column' commemorating the dead in the Hangrum war is also a reminder of some collective 'national' identity soaked in the blood of these martyrs. These rituals and symbols are a way of remembering and transforming historical memories into tangible realities for the Heraka as they struggle with the conflicting systems brought about by modernity. These rituals serve 'increasingly as a symbol of a lost world of order and control' (Comaroff 1985: 119).

As much as the *heguangram* is the articulation of this vision and a viable alternative for some, for others it is simply the remnants of a past tradition, a symbol of lost millenarian glory. They say it is an emotive and naïve ideal espoused by certain people to find absolution for their problems, primarily economic woes. They proclaim the 'end of the world' as a remedy for their problems. For instance, a consideration of the history of the Heraka movement shows that stopping work or ceasing to farm in the face of the millennial event was widespread. The assumption was that a world filled with freedom, surplus food and leisure was imminent. Grain would fall from the sky; no education was necessary as the *heguangram* was at hand; work should be abandoned and one should spend freely and live lavishly. These slogans were like mules that carried a message of hope along with their physical burdens for the villagers reeling under the dire constraints of poverty, near famines and failed colonial policies. These proclamations gained currency and became the norm, because they provided hope, inspired elation; many responded with eagerness. Some took the message to the extreme, spurred on by erratic and passionate preachers, who asserted that it was only a matter of time before 'some *heguangram*' would usher in a state of absolute bliss. Ranima herself, I was told, never proclaimed such an extreme reversal of fortune. It was her followers who, in their eagerness for the new system, exaggerated her words. Their emotive appeal to people and their promise of freedom and leisure, were perhaps also ways of providing an attractive option to the growing Christian missionary activities taking place in the region.

The movement did little to assuage the feelings of the people for the promise of an instant outcome failed; eventually the millenarian feeling faded and gave rise to a more 'progressive' approach – the Heraka as founded in 1974. That Heraka movement seemed to some very elitist and biased towards urban people. It did little to speak to the needs of the rural population. The difference between the urban and the rural population is apparent here: while the latter still regard the promised millennial event as probability, the former consider these views with suspicion, and rejected altogether such superstitions. On the one hand, the notion of *heguangram* is rooted in the ideals and religious promises of the Heraka people. It constitutes a form of redemption, a time when the Heraka will be free, and no longer marginalized by 'outside forces' such as Christianity and Hinduism.

On the other hand, this idealism is precisely what others decry – they assert that succumbing to these 'superstitions' and suprahuman feats and events is what makes the Heraka lag behind when compared to 'outside forces'. These narratives, I was told, ensnare the rural population and put them in a bind of superstitions that the urban population see as their duty to dismiss. It will be recalled that the Heraka have changed through the years and are increasingly adopting a modern approach. In fact, they trace their history back to 1974, and use Gaidinliu's image as both 'woman' and 'modern' to support their ideals. In a sense, this period is seen as the watershed event when the movement adopted a more 'do it yourself' position rather than the 'helpless peasant' attitude, dependent on external forces. Due to the circumstances in the villages, the latter view appears more attractive to the rural population than the former which the urban people have inculcated into their practices, enhanced by their world-view.

These views can be illustrated by using Hegel's dictum: 'Seek for food and clothing first, then the Kingdom of God shall be added unto you', which may be equated with the 'rational' view, in this context (Benjamin 1999: 246). The symbol of Hangrum encourages the inverse: Seek for the Kingdom of God first, then the food and clothing shall be added unto you. The situation in the villages, it might be argued, necessitates such a response. However, it is not possible to imagine the growth of the Heraka movement solely within these dynamics, without reference to other factors. In other words, to appreciate the growth and articulation of the Heraka vision, the Christian element is also important. The Christians provided the contrast, the competition and sometimes the model for such a community to be formed, in direct opposition to their own.

Historical Context and Seeds of Discontent: Heraka and Christian

What happens when a system of living inhabited by spirits, gods, animal sacrifices, *gennas*, taboos, and so on is suddenly overhauled and replaced by Christianity and the Heraka? One effect of this is that the prominence of chiefs and priests, privileged under Paupaise diminishes as do their roles (see Chapter 3). They quickly fade into the background and are symbolically rendered inane and ineffectual. To replace them, the Christians found a way of organizing themselves under various synods and church organizations that met annually, celebrated common festivals according to the Christian calendar, and also agreed on religious teachings propounded by the Bible. In a sense, the Christians were more interested first in setting up their particular church and second in the immediate prospects of mobilizing the population by taking advantage of the education system and the prospects it promised. The Heraka movement, on the other hand, paused to think about the repercussions of these alternative trajectories. Already, differences emerging through the introduction of colonizing religious ideologies bore the seeds of discontent and malice.

Unlike the Christians, who were extralocal (as their networks extended to other regions), the Heraka movement was locally limited. So what happens when the reverence for priests wanes and the leadership of the chiefs is eroded? Was there another system to take their place? Clearly for the Heraka this was not the government or the churches. Obviously, the local system of governance, at least for the Heraka movement, still depended on some sort of traditional order: landowner and priest, and the body of elders. With the old authorities discredited by the Heraka movement itself, and the slow response by the government to this change, alternative authorities had to be found. This was vital if they were to be able to unite the people under one religious tradition and also maintain the intertribal solidarity. Alongside the wider Heraka agenda, the desire for a *heguangram* constituted an alternative to the idea of government itself (see also Gorst 1959: 39–53).

Narrative and Story

So far I have covered a range of issues concerning the historical context in which the notion of *heguangram* was being articulated. Historically, for the Heraka, the Hangrum war represents the landmark event for the construction of the *heguangram.* By evoking this event even now some of them manage to hold on to a vision of unity and inspire a higher level of integration, enhanced by various cosmological and divine factors. However, it should be noted that not all Heraka people hold this view.

In this section, I want to examine my own discovery of this Heraka vision and how certain insights enabled me to understand the notion of *heguangram* and *heguang* more clearly. My point of entry into the importance of *heguang* and *heguangram* is located in the narrative of the Heraka itself.

When I first encountered these notions, I was struck by the limits of constructing a viable history with such a paucity of information in written records. These notions were developed relatively recently (in the past 60 years or so) and hence not much secondary material has been generated. Archival sources regarding the particularities of *heguang* and *heguangram* are non-existent, nor are there any Heraka written materials on this subject. This highlights the power differential between the elite and the subaltern. It also reflects on those who attempt to manage the rhetoric of Heraka, and who, in controlling the means of production, present and establish the official version of Heraka history. Despite some sketchy references to kings and kingdoms, in Zeme narratives there are no traditions of divine kings or kingship among the Zeme. Indeed, in the story of Asa and Munserung, two popular folk heroes, Asa is often referred to as a 'king'. There are other references to specific kingdoms, for example, in the popular story of Amang the orphan. Amang was a poor orphan who became wealthy, gained immortality by marrying a god, and showed his wealth by sharing it with others. It was during this time that the land was plentiful, abundant and full of joy (see also Pame 1996: 103). However, he is best known for the feasts he gave; indeed he was the first feast giver. It was during one of his feasts that the deities, humans and animals received their kingdoms (see also Soppitt [1885] 1969: 433–4). These stories are remembered nostalgically, because the story of Amang represents a lost social order, in which animals and humans communicated and lived in harmony. These stories in themselves say little about the organization or role of a kingdom, but in the Zeme tradition the notion of *heguang* signifies the possibility of a rule that might bring about a unified social order.

I had to find alternative methods of narrative solutions that could alleviate the feeling of incompleteness on a topic so important for the Heraka. This required going into the field and collecting materials within the community. Even after fieldwork, the vague conceptual understanding of *heguang*, and *heguangram*, along with the importance of Hangrum with its myriad symbolic interpretations, left me in a quandary. For instance, people talked about *heguangram* all the time, but explanations of it varied considerably in degree and detail. Perhaps *heguangram* was tailored to people's particular frustrations? Or was its engine for survival the speculative magic of divine providence?

It was much later that I received a curious typewritten text (through divine providence?) in Zeme, the biography of Rani Gaidinliu. This typescript was on tracing paper with tiny burn marks at the edges. I realized that the text was published only in Hindi (under the title Rani Maa) and not in Zeme; and that most of the Heraka public were unaware of the work.[8] The Hindi version was translated by the head of the Saraswati Vidyamandir in Haflong, based on the Zeme transcript and assisted by the original biographer, Ramkhui Newme. I am using both versions of the text. Although the Zeme text is primary, I sometimes use the Hindi translation to supplement the Zeme source. The two texts are close except in some places; I will attempt to highlight some such discrepancies in the following paragraphs. The Zeme text has no title, while the Hindi title is Rani Maa Gaidinliu (1990). The Hindi version is more polished with didactic undertones, and the attempts to 'Hinduize' certain sections, in comparison to the Zeme version, are quite visible.[9] Along with fieldwork materials, the text helped form an alternative narrative for the notions of *heguangram* and *heguang*. Here I use narrative in the Barthian sense, as it corresponds well with the Zeme understanding of *rasam* (story).

> [N]arrative is a hierarchy of instances. To understand a narrative is not merely to follow the unfolding of the story, it is also to recognize its construction in 'storeys', to project the horizontal concatenations to the narrative 'thread' on to an implicitly vertical axis; to read (to listen to) a narrative is not merely to move from one word to the next, it is also to move from one level to the next. (Barthes 1977: 87)

The Text

The text is important for several reasons. First, it is the only biography of Ranima; it captures her childhood and religious activities during the 1930s. Second, it helps us in finding some answers regarding Ranima and her possible status as a *heguang* with respect to Jadonang. Finally, while clarifying the second point, it also points to the role of the text as a form of resistance against the patriarchical social order. It further elucidates how Ranima sees herself vis-à-vis the Heraka society and her larger position within India itself.

The text consists of a narrative *bricolage*, constructed from a diverse range of sources. Levi-Strauss argues that myths, like *bricolage*, 'take to pieces and reconstruct sets of events (on a physical, socio-historical or technical plane) and use them as so many indestructible pieces for structural patterns in which they serve alternatively as ends or means' (1974: 33). This piecing together is similar to Barthes' notions of constructing 'storeys' with the narrative moving from one level to the next. Thus creating vertical and horizontal planes of meaning reflecting a variety of angles for different audiences and for particular purposes (see Goffman 1959).

The text utilizes a repertoire of Zeliangrong myths, most of them about gods, tradition and symbols that are part of the ongoing Zeme oral tradition. It therefore is a mystery why this biography was not available to the Zeme

Heraka and instead published only for a Hindi-speaking audience. In a sense, the leaders appear to control the image of Gaidinliu and her message by preventing the spread of her message of *heguang* and *heguangram.* It is possible that for the Zeme the notion of a Goddess (in the text) was too difficult to handle, whereas this would be unproblematic for a 'Hindu' readership, due to the common occurrence of goddesses in the 'Hindu' tradition. Also, the threat of Christian criticism (that the text is too 'Hinduized') could have provided another reason for not publishing it in Zeme. It was clearly an attempt to acquaint certain Hindu populations with Ranima; this could perhaps generate more interest and even more financial aid for the Heraka. This patronage is clearly aimed at essentializing the Heraka as marginal but at the same time it is helpful in projecting a form of nationalism from the margins. This links the struggles of the Heraka with the larger scheme of what it means to be in Bharat (India). This ideological battle is not only locally situated, but has repercussions all over the Northeast of India (this is described in Chapter 5).

I would also like to suggest that the text itself represents a form of resistance, articulated in the idiom of local symbols. It attempts to relocate issues of gender, leadership and divine choice within a wider framework of reformation. Could this be the reason that it was not published in Zeme? Could the implied criticisms in the text against patriachical succession be too much for the patriarchy to handle? The following examines these issues beginning with the dismantling of Jadonang's succession in Ranima's narrative.[10]

An Exposition of the Text[11]

Jadonang, it is said by administrators and local scholars, was the promised saviour of the Zeliangrong people. That is, according to administrative reports, he is the king whom 'tradition' said would come. But he is subsumed under so many other categories such as 'messiah', 'healer', 'shaman', 'king' and 'priest', that it is difficult to ascertain the exact nature of his status or how others saw him.

According to Gangmumei Kamei, during the 1930s Jadonang supposedly proclaimed the establishment of *Makam Gwangdi*[12] which the British interpreted as 'Naga Raj' (loosely Naga kingdom). The same author claims that the reforms initiated by Jadonang were religious in nature and that his aim was also to unite the various Zeliangrong people scattered around in different administrative areas. Using religious reform as the platform for this unity,

Jadonang proclaimed that: '*Makammeiru Gwang Tupuni*' (*Makam* people will be rulers, king) (Kamei 2004: 150). Jadonang proclaimed that 'our days have come. Our powerful weapons are kept hidden by god at Zeilad. We shall pray and worship God. With his grace we can become kings' (Kamei 2002a: 32). Kamei also mentions that Jadonang prayed to God Bishnu in Bhuban cave to grant him the kingdom over which he wanted to preside (2002a: 33). This vision of the kingdom, as Kamei explains, '[was] for religious purification, cultural resurgence and social integration, his political dream of a kingdom was a natural response to the British colonialism which was always resisted and never compromised by him, nor by his people in the past' (2002a: 30).

Jadonang's short-lived prophetic life witnessed its own measure of success and failure. In Ranima's own account, Jadonang failed in his quest to please Tingwang. She reveals the tension between her and Jadonang when they go on their final pilgrimage to Bhuban cave on January 1931. In Gaidinliu's account, Jadonang is denied entry into the cave because Tingwang, in the form of a python, blocks his entrance. Tingwang tells Gaidinliu and Jadonang, 'due to Jadonang's negligence [referring to his drunkenness and his arriving late at the cave] Tingwang in the form of a python is sitting behind the door'. Jadonang immediately takes out his frustration on Gaidinliu and blames her for causing his downfall. She consoles him and assures him that 'he is the backbone of the movement' and the 'father' while she is merely his follower. Further, Tingwang warns Jadonang that 'he will not have time to eat this year's harvest', meaning that, he would die before the harvest. The prediction comes true as Jadonang, upon returning from the pilgrimage, is caught, tried and hanged by the British for allegedly murdering some traders and sacrificing them to his gods.

The above incident reveals the simmering tension between Jadonang and Gaidinliu. Gaidinliu portrays herself in a favourable light and highlights the 'divine choice' in her favour, as a way of taking over the role of Jadonang. In her account, Jadonang is asked by Tingwang to hand over everything to Gaidinliu, who is affectionately known as *Cherachamdinliu*. According to Heraka narrative *Cherachamdinliu* is the daughter of Bhuban god who is sent by Tingwang to guide the Zeliangrong people. *Cherachamdinliu*, it is said, enters the womb of Gaidinliu's mother and is born as Gaidinliu on 26 January 1915. Throughout her life an unseen friend, Namginai, another daughter of Bhuban god, guides Gaidinliu. Gaidinliu also refers to her as Goddess. Through Namginai, Gaidinliu meets Tingwang in Bhuban cave. Bhuban cave becomes an important place of pilgrimage for Gaidinliu as well as Jadonang and it is here that they receive religious training and instructions for the reforms they must carry out (see Chapter 2). According to Gaidinliu's account, they receive instructions about the construction of temples, arrangement of flowers on the altar, initiatory rites, song and dance arrangements, New Year festivals, organization of villages, and how to reduce animal sacrifices. These instructions become an important part of the Heraka practice over the years. Here I want to focus on how the notion of *heguang* evolved within the space of Bhuban cave and to examine the symbols associated with such a proclamation.

There is an incident inside the Bhuban cave that Gaidinliu recounts. On the third religious journey, 26 January 1930, Gaidinliu's birthday, Gaidinliu and her followers reach the cave. Other people from around the area have also come to the cave for prayers. But Gaidinliu's followers could hear only her voice as she prayed; the other voices were muffled. It was quiet, when suddenly a lightning like effect flashed near the entrance of the cave. A strange light illuminated the cave. There in front of them, the goddess suddenly appeared; she was visible only to those whose faith in the goddess was strong. Elated by the incident they started singing praise songs. The voice of the goddess was then heard loud and clear telling them that she had hidden a gun for them and that they should start looking for it. After searching the cave, Lingtuang from Langkao finds it. It was 5 feet in length and red in colour. The gun was extremely heavy, and while carrying it, it was as if they could not see the path ahead, nor were they visible to others.

When they reached the village, Gaidinliu went to tell Jadonang about the incident. That night both of them had a dream where Tingwang instructs Jadonang to shoot at the *Hebuibang* (Semal tree?) and Gaidinliu at *Njingchibang* (a fruit-bearing tree). The next morning, in Jadonang's backyard, Jadonang takes the gun and fires at the *Hebuibang*. Before shooting he says, 'if I destroy the *Hebuibang* with one bullet, I will be a *heguang* and rule over the earth like the sun.' The bullet hits the stem of the tree but there is no sound from the gun or the bullet hitting the tree, one can only hear *chiyi-chiyi* (possibly the sound made by the bullet whizzing through the air). Gaidinliu then utters the same words as Jadonang and fires at the *Njingchibang*. The bullet hits the middle of the tree, goes through it and up towards the sky and then comes back towards the tree again. It enters the tree: the tree and its roots are blasted into pieces. Thus, in the eyes of the elders Gaidinliu becomes the clear winner. Her name spreads around the region and she is celebrated as their leader and even referred to as goddess. She starts healing, prophesizing and preaching about the new religious teachings received from Tingwang in the cave. Her activities are also legitimized by the curious arrival of Goddess Namginai who comes riding on a lion pushed by the wind of God. The Goddess arrives at Gaidinliu's house and drinks water from the pond and rides away to Nsimbutlua Mountain. The people were surprised and somewhat frightened of these powers and regarded Gaidinliu as the incarnation of the Goddess.

The question of leadership and the position of the *heguang* for the Heraka become clearer in the fourth and last religious journey to Bhuban cave on January 1931. As already mentioned, Jadonang is denied entry because of his negligence, but his status is also clearly mapped out in Gaidinliu's account when God asks him if he still wants to be *heguang*. His silence is interpreted by God as a weakness and he is instructed by God to 'hand over all things to *Cherachamdinliu* [Gaidinliu]'. Gaidinliu, from here on, is clearly the next leader. But is she the *heguang*? The manner of choosing a *heguang* is very specific and her account attempts to provide this link. In Zeme tradition, a python usually chooses a *heguang*. The capture of a python is associated with prosperity and popularity. It is said that a person does not capture the python, but the python chooses the person. The *heguang* is someone who has perfected themselves with all rituals and must be without a scar or injury, which is considered unclean. They must be wealthy and well respected in the village. Gaidinliu recounts that the Goddess came to her and told her to bring a python, to test Gaidinliu's faithfulness. The Goddess directs Gaidinliu to the exact location of the python: 'The python will be found inside the tree covered in betel leaves.' The villagers think that Gaidinliu is insane. In any case the idea of following a 12-year-old girl is madder still. Gaidinliu assures them that these instructions are according to the Goddess' wishes. She offers a prayer and the villagers bring the python. The villagers then address the python: 'if you are God go and locate the *heguang*.' The python immediately goes to Gaidinliu's house and curls up under Gaidinliu's bed. Zailad god, or the python god, appears to Gaidinliu and tells her that he will come back after nine days to take away the python and not to harm it. On the ninth day a ritual is performed for the python and the python suddenly disappears. Then the Goddess appears and tells Gaidinliu that Zailad god was very pleased with Gaidinliu's devotion to the python and that she was reaching the state of perfection.

From her account, Gaidinliu is chosen as a *heguang* through the ritual associated with the python, but how is this connected to the *heguangram* that the people envisaged? To connect these two, one must return to the story of Asa and Munserung, popular folk heroes for the Zeliangrong. Popular because of their selfless deeds, they are often portrayed as mischievous and playful. They are also portrayed in different guises: warriors, blacksmiths, jokers, kings, and so on. According to this story, Asa and Munserung meet on the banks on Zailad Lake and start making iron. The python king inside the lake is irritated with the constant banging and instructs his minions to go and stop this noise. Seeing the pythons, Asa and Munserung immediately catch them, roast their flesh and eat them. With none of the pythons left, and the noise still unabated, the python king surfaces in anger. He swallows Munserung and returns deep inside the lake. Asa then devises a plan to drain the lake of water and rescue Munserung. He toils for days until the lake is drained out and the python king is visible. Asa threatens to eat the python if Munserung is not freed. Munserung is immediately freed and out of fear the python king also gives two gifts to Asa and Munserung: a magic sword that kills any living being if employed along with the word *hingpeubila* (this is an ancient untranslatable word) and a magic spear that also kills anything with the help of the word *di* (also untranslatable) (see also Miri 1991: 53–64). (According to the Heraka, there is a magical rope called *pipereu* kept in Zailad Lake along with the gun Gaidinliu found in Bhuban cave). The python king keeps all these weapons for safekeeping; they will be given to the *heguang* who will establish a *heguangram.*[13] It is interesting to note that *heguang* is at a mythical level of the community, while other symbols such as Bhuban cave are on the level of the individual. This could indicate a more individual, personal, and perhaps even a private progression of religiosity for the Heraka in contrast to the communal level of the traditional past. The symbol of the *heguang* and Bhuban cave highlights the tension.

Judging from these accounts and the local stories used to legitimize and establish her role within the Heraka understanding of *heguang* and *heguangram,* one can say that Gaidinliu is the *heguang.* But this claim is lost in much of the current rhetoric of the Heraka and has become sketchy and vague. The Heraka *heguangram* was connected with the divine and prophetic Ranima. With her death and the current position of the Heraka, some of the Heraka are questioning this claim. Why haven't we yet received our *heguangram*? One interpretation, told, for example, by a current self-proclaimed 'heguang',[14] is that if the Heraka do not receive their *heguangram* within 1,000 years, the universe will come to an end. Other, more sceptical, views see the *heguangram* as a progression. They associate *heguang* with freedom, development, economic wealth and education – these together will bring about the peace and fulfilment of the *heguangram.* This notion is more to do with achievement rather than a gift. Along with these views, other pertinent debates persist: when will the *heguangram* come? Will it arrive suddenly? Should we abandon education, agriculture turning to song and dance to usher in the *heguangram*?

Blood and Weakness: Gender Issues

Before returning to the theme of the *heguangram*, I want to examine the text of Ranima's biography as a possible site of resistance against the patriarchical social order.[15]

If Ranima portrays herself as the *heguang* according to her biography, the issue of gender is clearly significant. The narrative attempts to reposition certain assumptions and draws attention to themes of resistance and victory, by elevating marginal elements. The text is typical in its narrative flow and its repertoire of symbols and folk heroes. People often equate Ranima's activities in the continuing tradition of a *herakapui*, a traditional female shaman; one who communicates with god only for healing sickness. It was easy for her to slip into such a role, since there was a precedent. But it was more difficult to be viewed as a leader or chief – as that was only accessible to men. So an important question is: why is Ranima of such great importance when the society is primarily patriarchical? In the following paragraphs, I will consider this question.

The primary weakness women possess, according to Zeme men, is perceived in women's bleeding: the 'hole that bleeds' (referring to the vagina). Blood for the Heraka remains a strong marker for purity and pollution: menstruating women are not allowed to pray or enter the *Kelumki*, prayer house (see Chapter 4). They must stay at home. Other markers are also evident: women are relegated to the left while men are to the right, since the left is seen as weaker (see also Tsing 1993: 184–6). These markers are ritually maintained in both the Heraka and Christian communities. Therefore, Ranima would not attend prayers when menstruating and she could not lead certain prayers publicly, because of her gender.[16] In fact, she is also known as *heguangpui* (queen) and four-eared woman, while her army commander Irangkeung, a male, was known as *heguangpeu* (king) and eight-eared man. These symbols refer to the traditional notion that the world consists of eight corners: men can access all eight corners while women can access only half of them.[17] Yet, in the text Ranima is portrayed as the 'chosen one' over Jadonang and even seen as the perfect embodiment of a *heguang*. Why is the narrative of the text explicit in its resistance, while the public display of dissent was absent in Ranima? She was of course operating largely under Zeme culture that was structured according to patriarchical principles. In order to succeed, she had to adapt. Was the text a way of voicing her resistance? The following paragraphs attempt to answer the question by examining the text as a source of resistance, and the many ways in which Ranima sees herself as the symbol of empowerment.

Gender as Embodiment

When I would ask people how they remembered Ranima, men would often respond that she was tall and beautiful – a stereotypical answer – and not susceptible to illness (a trait associated with men who are considered strong). Women would be more personal and direct. Someone said Ranima had the strong features of a man, but dressed in woman's clothing, while another told me that she loved eating meat – a trait again associated with men. This androgynous image is presumably a middle way, a rapprochement between two sexes regulated in rigid social structures. It could also be an echo of androgynous 'Hindu' deities. It is therefore possible that Ranima could have been seen as both male and female to encompass the stereotypical male/female dichotomy within Zeme society.

Here, I am reminded of Julia Kristeva's work on gender, which focuses not on the differences among 'men and women as subjects', but the 'construction of masculinity and femininity' (Kristeva 1982: 92; cited in Tsing 1993: 180) as ways to place this argument in the context of Ranima's biography. Could we assume that Ranima transgressed the male/female dichotomy as a social construction, as a 'strategy of identity' (Kristeva 1982: 92)? Kristeva's argument helps us understand how Ranima's position could affect perceptions of her, and how she projected her identity in a patriarchical society. In the text, she comes across as 'tomboyish' and in certain respects dominating the men around her. On the other hand, she maintained the boundaries of womanhood herself (not performing certain rituals when menstruating). The traits of a *heguang* are exemplified primarily in men; women would not even figure in many of the stories. Why then does Ranima figure prominently within the tradition of *heguang* and why is the divine choice ultimately in her favour?

Could we also see Ranima's narrative as a woman's narrative, which 'when read in relation to history . . . [is] a forbidden story that exists within and threatens to disrupt the social order' (Susan Friedman 1989: 144)? Could it be that this is the reason why it is not translated into Zeme, because it would openly convert the promise of the *heguang* into a real presence in the world of everyday life? Or is this writing a form of resistance as an 'insistent record – a trace, a web, a palimpsest, a rune, a disguise – or what has not or cannot be spoken of directly because of the external and internalized censors of patriarchal social order' (1989: 142)? Instead, I would argue that the Ranima narrative is an honest revelation to the reader. What is pertinent here is that Ranima is not narrating against 'internalized censors of patriarchal social order'. Instead the text appears to question such constructed gender roles; it resists by not playing the gender role of the 'return of the repressed' (1989: 142).[18] In effect, her reported voice exists freely in the text; but the physical text itself is hidden – locked in the vaults of men. But the broader question that can be asked with regard to narrative and its function is 'how relevant is it for social mobilization?' What 'role' does the narrative play in the realm of collective identities (Hart 1992: 633–4)? First, the problem with this particular narrative is that it has not been diffused to the general Zeme Heraka public sufficiently for there to be any debate concerning these issues. Second, the transition from narrative to text, at the moment, is largely about the 'individual' because it has not engaged with the outside world, outside the text. One can suggest, therefore, that any 'mobilization narrative' (1992: 635) of the question of *heguang* with regard to the larger Zeme Heraka society is attenuated. Having said this, much of the content of the text had earlier been dispersed through oral narratives by Ranima and her followers. It appears that oral narratives are by definition more fluid, while the texts are fixed and meanings are hierarchized, generating commentaries (see also Chapter 4).

Divine Liturgy: Ranima as Durga

For Ranima to get her message across, she had to embed it in local narratives and effect continuities in people's imagination, using idiomatic language. For example, the use of narratives that link symbols (such as the weapons) to Asa and Munserung is dialectic and instantly recognizable for the Zeme. Similarly, the use of trees as a metaphor enhancing Ranima's ascendancy appeals to folk imagination. Claire Russell, in a fascinating article, makes reference to a fruit tree as the oldest form of '*heritable* fixed property' which must be cared for to 'certify kinship succession' (1981: 56; italics in original). Ranima's shooting of the *Njingchibang*, a fruit-bearing tree, can convey two meanings. First, by destroying the tree Ranima is expressing a new lineage, a new succession, that will follow her. Second, by being given the *Njingchibang* tree by Tingwang, Ranima succeeds to the status of the *heguang*, continuing that tradition.

Other symbols of the *heguang* again embed the narrative within the social matrix. The twist in the text, or rather the narrative jigsaw, that, I think, makes the text vulnerable and contestable is the question of 'divine choice'. This is compounded by Ranima's alleged divine lineage (she is *Cherachamdinliu*: daughter of Bhuban god) and her association with Namginai (daughter of Bhuban) that establishes her above, and over, Jadonang. The date that

Gaidinliu recounts in her narrative – 26 January – links the pilgrimage to Bhuban cave with her own birthday. This is significant because it attempts to establish connection with her receiving divine instructions in Bhuban cave and her birth – that, symbolically, she is returning to her father (Bhuban god) every year on that day as a reminder of her 'divine status'. The Bhuban cave could symbolize rebirth as one enters the cave and returns to the world, similarly it may signify Ranima's rebirth too.

I would also like to suggest that Ranima saw herself as a symbol of empowerment in the image of Durga. This can be related to Goddess Namginai who comes to Ranima's house riding on a lion and then retreats to *Nsimbutlua* Mountain (Durga also is depicted as riding on a lion and residing in Mount *Meru*). People there are reportedly amazed and view Ranima as the incarnation of the Goddess. Is Ranima seeing Durga as herself, or as a model for expressing her 'supreme female divinity' (Pintchman 1994: 118)? The classic example of Durga is in the Mahabharata, where she is associated with both Siva and Krishna and sometimes equated with Sarasvati and Savitri. She is also seen as an expression of *Devi-Mahatmya* (Great Goddess) who

> is lauded as the supreme female divinity of whom all other goddesses are partial manifestations, or else the existence of a single female reality is affirmed as the unique source of all goddesses – and often nondivine female beings, such as human women, as well – who are described as her portions. (Pintchman 1994: 119)

In the *Devi-Mahatmya,* the most revered text among *Saktas* (worshippers of the divine feminine) Durga takes the destructive form (Kinsley 1978: 490). Durga is famously seen as destroyer of demons, particularly Mahisa; she protects and preserves the cosmos by restoring order (Pintchman 1994: 198). Thus, Durga as the goddess of victory is associated with warriors and soldiers in South India and used as a claim to power in a South Orissan jungle kingdom (Harle 1963; Schnepel 1995). Durga is also seen as the *sakti* (energy/power) of Siva, the goddess of fertility, ruler of the vegetable world with power over infectious diseases (Santiko 1997: 213). There are many other images of Durga.

The image of Durga as goddess in relation to Ranima also conjures up the possibility of Ranima being seen as Queen Mother (*Apui Rani*). The Queen Mother imagery is perhaps best used in the context of uniting groups of far-flung people. In an interesting study by Ronald Cohen on the Queen Mother in Africa, the King is installed along with his mother because 'the Queen Mother is present both among the people who emphasize patri- and among others who use matri-lines for succession and descent' (1977: 14). Besides her specific role, she is also seen generally as that which 'symbolizes the value of continuity, wholeness, and integration, as opposed to conflict and the breakup of the polity into like units that remain small, weak, and politically independent'. Like the dual monarchy model of the King and the mother in African society, the dual representation, one can say, of the Heraka organization of *heguangpeu* and *heguangpui*, seem to have common linkages, although the *heguangpui* is generally the wife rather than the mother. 'Linking groups through women, especially the Queen Mother, obviates the conflict, competition, and ultimate splitting associated with linkages through men in lineage-based politics' (Cohen 1977: 23, 26).

One can take this further and apply it to the notion of Bharat Mata (Mother India) (Mckean 1996).[19] This idea is taken from Bankimchandra's celebrated hymn of his motherland. Indeed, in the song, the Mother is imagined as Durga with her ten weapons of war. The song *Bande Mataram* (salutation to the mother) became the patriotic slogan for mass nationalism in the early 1920s and later became the rallying cry of right-wing nationalist movements like the RSS (Tanika Sarkar 2001: 163–90; Mckean 1996). Under her aegis, right-wing movements formed a coalition that attempted to construct a Hindu nation through the formation of the ideology of Hinduness (*hindutva*), a concept elaborated by V. D. Savarkar in 1922. He said *hindutva* 'is compatible with any conceivable expansion of our Hindu people . . . The only geographical limit of Hindutva is the limit of our earth' (quoted in Mckean 1996: 255). Thus, their vision of a united India with an integrationist attitude towards disparate groups such as the Heraka became something of a reality (see also Chapter 4). The imagery of Ranima as Mother Goddess could coalesce with Bharat Mata; the idea that strands of the Mother Goddess could be partially manifested in humans like Gaidinliu, would not be out of place in a 'Hindu' context (see Figures 6.1 and 6.2).

In the narrative, Ranima portrays herself as the great unifier – selfless, humane, compassionate and above all divinely chosen for her people. She plays with themes common to the Zeliangrong people, combining them to some extent with symbols uncommon among them. The adoption of powerful symbols like Durga, indigenized within the tribal system (Schnepel 1995), as in this text, is not uncommon for those seeking to gain ascendancy. Such mobilization of pantheons may garner power and authority. By embodying such symbols, Gaidinliu also speaks the rhetoric of empowerment. Durga is the great, victorious goddess who kills the great demon Mahisa and proclaims victory. And, as mentioned above, Durga is also associated with

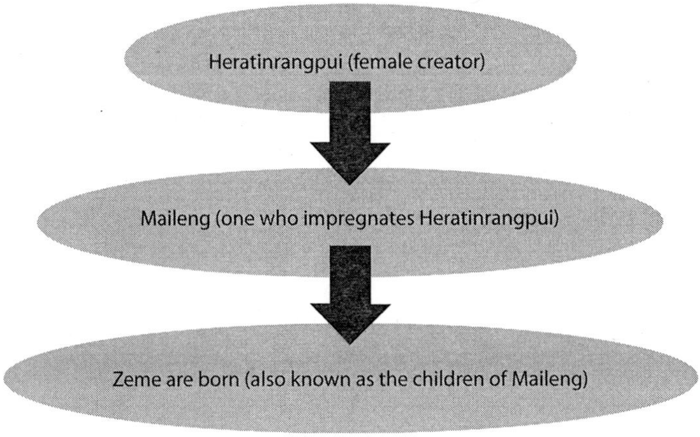

FIGURE 6.1 Alternative Zeme Heraka + Paupaise version

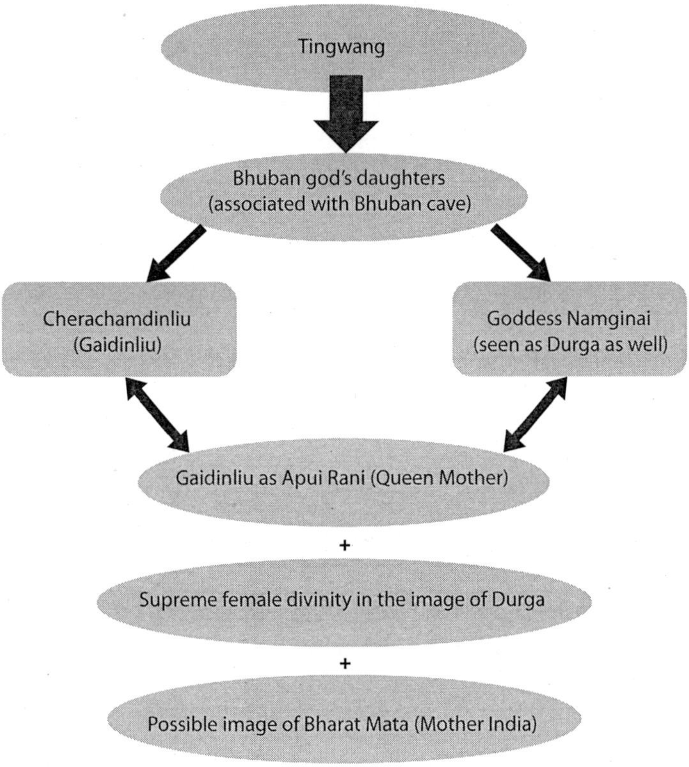

FIGURE 6.2 Rani Gaidinliu's pantheon

Bharat Mata who was constituted in the twentieth century as a territorial deity presiding over India (Ramaswamy 2001: 103). In Ranima's quest to unite disparate ethnic groups over boundaries, she resembles the Queen Mother who chaffs at the petty politics of men and unites them in an imagined community. This defies attempts to make it fade away, like the text locked up in a vault. As Durga, Ranima is herself akin to a manifestation or embodiment of power (*sakti*).

After the death of Ranima, there has been no one yet to fill her place. Some say that Ranima will return to Hangrum, others are tired of this idea and of waiting. However, there is a person proclaiming himself to be the 'heguang' in Hangrum: Is he the promised *heguang*, replacing Ranima?

The next section recounts ethnographic examples from my stay in Hangrum camp. It attempts to place the poetics of resistance articulated in the body of the self-proclaimed 'heguang', and argues that they represent an alternative vision within the Heraka community. My account highlights the dialogue between the rural and urban aspects of Heraka. In the course of my stay, my conversation with the current 'heguang' focused on his construction of the *heguangram*, as he interrogated notions of history, selfhood, status and sacred authority. It was in a remote, marginalized setting; only a few go there.

Hangrum Camp

I am on the edge of one hill, overlooking the deep gorge as it splits the land in half. On the other side stands another hill looming large behind the cover of mist. It is dark, stupendous in its aura and awkward in its rise, as it stands towering over the smaller hill on which I am standing. This hill is 'Hemeutum, the commander of God's army. Some say that in God's language it is called Mehutia'. People tell me Hemeutum guards Hangrum, and protects the spiritual aura of Rani Gaidinliu Inspirational Home (in English), otherwise known as Hangrum Camp.

The Rani Gaidinliu Inspirational Home is not spectacular in the least. It is a difficult place to like, due to the scarcity of water and its cold and wet weather conditions. But for the Heraka, Hangrum Camp is the spiritual centre – it represents the symbolic centre of the world. It is from here that prayers emanate to all corners of the world. Like the eight corners of the world, I was told, each letter of Tingwang (T-I-N-G-W-A-N-G), represents one of the eight corners.

Rani Gaidinliu Inspirational Home is consecrated as sacred ground and separated from mundane space by a boundary wall. As a mark of purity, no human waste may enter this consecrated space. It is also sacred because of the historic 'Hangrum war' fought with the British, and because the promise by Ranima that the *heguangram* will start from Hangrum.

I now want to examine how rituals give substance to the idea of the *heguangram* and its overall effects on how people envision this state. Following Hocart, I suggest that ritual precedes the formation of government or kingdom. I propose to use Hocart's conception to make the link between the organization of ritual, which will eventually make way for a government, and the coming of the *heguang*.[20] Hocart, in his classic study, *Kings and Councillors*, says,

> There is, so to speak, a governing body before there is any governing to do. If a man is needed to regulate the lives of the people, to be the supreme arbiter of right and wrong, there is such a person prepared to assume the responsibility: it is the king. (1970: 31)

But what is the government doing before any governing? The answer, he says, is in the organization of ritual. For Hocart, ritual is like the umbilical cord that ties life (the mother) to society (the foetus). And, 'ritual organization is vastly older than government, for it exists where there is no government and where none is needed' (Hocart 1970: 35). This can be understood in the ritual itself, as Hocart further explains:

> To understand how a dead man can reign we have to go back to our principles of ritual. We insisted again and again that the principal need not be man, or even a living being: it may be a stone, an image, the corpse of a whale; it may even be, as with our philosophers, an idea. (Hocart 1970: 135)

This 'idea' can be further explained in the ritual that imagines it splendidly through its enactment and its embodiment in song (see below).

The King is the Sun[21]

When Jadonang made his promise to Tingwang, he said, 'if I destroy the *Hebuibang* (Semal tree) with one bullet, I will be a *heguang* and rule over the earth like the sun.' Gaidinliu makes a similar promise. In the ritual instituted by Ranima, this is precisely what they remind themselves of, and they mark their boundary accordingly. The ritual is called *naimik kakelum*, sunrise prayer. The sun is akin to the king of all the stars because of its heat and energy (*sakti*); the vitalization that occurs on every level is depicted by the salute to the sun. Three young boys dressed up in traditional Zeme attire, stand in a row and perform a kind of a military salute just when the sun is rising. The people behind them sing a song, *Cheham Rani*[22] three times before finishing. These songs are highly coded and consist of praises to all the gods of the eight corners of the earth and sky, and are therefore, I was told, difficult to translate. These songs are also a way of keeping away the evil gods, as they are also praised. This is connected with the abandonment of animal sacrifices. Now songs are used as a medium to control, induce, praise and mystify the workings of the universe.

The traditional clothes, I was told, symbolize their unique identity that only God can recognize. They also signify a resistance to the modern materialism rampant in towns; the view is generally held that trousers and shirts represent a form of incompleteness in the eyes of Tingwang. It is better to wear the appropriate dress and ornaments to identify oneself as Zeme, as a way also of preserving tradition, when requesting anything from Tingwang. This makes prayers complete. *Cheham Rani* was the song that Ranima received in Bhuban cave. There is a narrative that in Ranima's first journey to Bhuban cave, she encountered a guard with a gun at the entrance of the cave who asked her, 'have you come here to live or to die?' Gaidinliu replied, 'you have called me here and so I have come to live'. This conversation, Ranima said, was the theme of the song *Cheham Rani*:

When will God let us be free?
Even if others trouble us
I'll live free like a *heguang*
If other people dominate us
We can also dominate them
We can't overcome them by ourselves
But by the blessing of Herawang [king of gods] from the beginning
Now you are victorious
But when the day comes from Herawang, we'll be victors
Everybody calls on God
They call on Ram and we call on Herawang
And we can't stop calling Herawang
To rid us of a bad god, we can't stop praying to Herawang

The song is clearly about resistance and victory. The theme of freedom and life is common in Heraka songs. Freedom is not living among other religious groups, but with the Heraka themselves. The songs also speak of continuity, of a certain direction, as their history comes through their voices and songs. This history is embedded in the 'Hangrum Parade', a nostalgic reminder of the time when Ranima and her soldiers hid from the British and later the Indian army and other Naga Christian nationalists, who saw her movement as conniving with the devil. Her resistance, her embodiment of the cultural traditions of her people became the rallying point of their dissent, particularly when the Christians went on readily destroying symbols of the past. For that reason Ranima always wore her traditional clothing, her beads, and necklaces, as a reminder to the Christians that she embodied traditional identity and that the politics of power were etched all over her body.

The 'Hangrum Parade' is also a reminder of a nascent nationalism imagined through the sheer force of their emotions and their latent power. These, with promised weapons from Zailad Lake, enhanced their religious fervour. A person who served in her army told me that during those days they witnessed miracles everyday. They were guided by a spirit called *haideurang* (one-ear man), who communicated with Ranima. Sometimes another woman, Rangngailakle, would interpret the language *haideurang* spoke: it sounded like Zeme but sometimes it appeared to be of an unknown tongue. It was also difficult to tell the gender as the voice would sometimes seem thin like a female's but at other times deep like that of a male. *Haideurang* would also join them for meals, but a cloth would be placed around his food and they could not see him. The mystery of *haideurang* is such that no one questioned his reality, and all believed in the power of this spirit. People who served under Ranima during this time tell of the miracles witnessed. Mihuibe, a stalwart of the jungle movement with Ranima, said:

> On our way to Nagaland, we reached Kacha hill and Ranima told us to rest here. But we told her, how can we rest, where there is no water here nor nearby? Ranima seemed unperturbed and told them to make a hearth with fire. Then, she took us to a spot and suddenly water flowed. We felt as if a dried up river had come to life. When we took what was needed, the river immediately dried up again, just like that. Our amazement was all too much for Ranima to bear so she told us: 'God gave us this water'!

It was during this time that they would perform the sunrise prayer every morning and the Hangrum parade. It is believed that Jadonang created this 'parade for the kingdom', resembling the modern day national parade. At the beginning of the parade they would all stand horizontally facing east

Photograph 6.1 Volunteers performing the Hangrum Parade

towards Bhuban cave. A list of commands would be uttered by the leader for the drill to begin as they are still (see Photograph 6.1):

Stand straight, attention!
Fall in (repeat twice), bend down and touch the ground with your right hand
Hold your right ear with your right hand
Let go of the ear and spread your legs
Join your legs again
Bend sideways!

(Immediately following this, a song, *Ntarata Rani*, is sung)

Now we will start communicating with God
God's door will open
Listen! Do you obey and live with your mother and father?
Do you want to live in the jungle? Or do you want to live in the village?
If other 'religions' come, will you listen to them? [A reference to proselytizing by Christians].
Also their words?
Will you listen to the good words at all?
That which has been spoken to you, don't neglect it
Be fair, work with truthfulness!
Don't live with change
God's spoken word will never cease.

(After the song the following sayings are pronounced three times, each symbolizing the cycle of life-death-life).

Rani Gaidinliu, the greatest
Jadonang, the highest
Heraka, the best
Heguang, it is
Zeliangrong, long live

These rituals establish the primacy of Hangrum and the promise of the *heguang*. They are enacted by the sunrise prayer, the singing of songs and the final parade, as an act of remembrance. In fact, the boys who perform at the parade are usually selected from the villages. They must be sincere, honest and model youths – a paragon for the *heguangram*. Just as Hangrum is preserved in the eternal memory of Ranima, people tell me, so she is present everywhere, overseeing and hoping for the *heguangram*. Indeed, what makes these rituals great and significant 'is the encounter with an earlier life' (Benjamin 1999: 178).

But these views are not shared by all the Heraka. I was told by a Hangrum elder that some leaders from the town have attempted to shift all of Ranima's belongings (kept in Hangrum) to Haflong for safekeeping and to close the place altogether. This elder cautioned the leaders and told them that since Ranima chose Hangrum as her home, it should remain so until eternity. He was equally angry with some leaders who have taken things belonging to Ranima to Langkao (her birth place), Kohima (where she was stationed for some time) and to Haflong (the organizational headquarters for the Heraka) without proper discussion. He told me that according to Ranima her things must be kept in Hangrum 'until the next King or Queen comes'. When Ranima left Hangrum, she reportedly said to the elder, 'keep this place until I return'. There is a veil of uncertainty as to what Ranima meant by this statement. It could have meant until 'I return from Kohima' or until 'I return spiritually or have taken on another body'. 'Who knows' said the elder, 'all I know is that someday she will return'.

This debate was pointed out to me in a carefully managed interview the current 'heguang' gave me. He is a controversial figure within the Heraka movement. Many believe that he envisions something that is unpractical and unreal and even that he is out of his mind. But his elevation to this position does have some importance in the overall articulation of not only the validity of Hangrum but also the promise of a *heguang* who will start the *heguangram* from Hangrum. But the important question is still unanswered, is he the *heguang*? People are afraid to commit to this view because the notion of *heguangram* is discouraged by the urban leaders. But the 'heguang' flaunts his status and wants people to believe that he is the *heguang*. This tension is clearly visible in the interview described below.

The Event: Meeting the King

I was more than elated when we were on our way to Hangrum, the last Zeme village I was to visit. Hangrum always held a sense of mystery and spiritual aura associated with the history of the village and the close ties it has with Ranima. I was told many times that I should meet Kanriakle, who was known as the second Rani because she was closest to Ranima until her death. Unfortunately, Kanriakle passed away before I arrived. The recent death of someone so close to Ranima (whom I have come to know and admire through my fieldwork) evoked in me a strong sense of loss: perhaps her closeness to Ranima would have helped me learn more about Ranima.

I heard of a 'prophet' in Hangrum,[23] who was causing a stir within the Heraka movement. What intrigued me about him was the fact that he was openly espousing the idea of *heguangram*, which in many quarters was 'old hat'. What disturbed me further was the hesitancy of Tahulung, my co-worker, to go there. Tahulung is Heraka and judging by his comments and behaviour he did not subscribe to the prophet in Hangrum. He felt that going there would only aid in legitimizing his authority, in some crude manner. Anyway, it was arranged for us to go along with the ex-caretaker of the camp and the youths associated with the 'Hangrum parade'.

Earlier, I was listening to the song about the *heguang*, *Heguang Samdin Wang*, as a way of familiarizing myself with its content and its vision. It goes as follows:

> *Heguang*! Waiting for your coming with hopes
> To bring all good things in our village
> With the songs and the words, we are enjoying
> Waiting for your coming
> Waiting for you with hopes, when you come.

The day we reached Hangrum, we were immediately introduced to the 'prophet' whose name is Namteuding Nriame. Perhaps it is fitting to capture the moment in detail, as I recorded the event in my diary.

The King's Court: Symbology of Power

The hill (*Hemeutum*) behind keeps a firm eye on the 'Inspirational Home'; it appears as if the eye keeps shifting as the fog moves from one end of the camp to the other. It is a treacherous battle fought between the stationary and the moving. We enter the hut to the commingling of voices; two disciples sit hunched beside the 'prophet' as he chants away in a feeble voice, interrupted only by the rolling of his tobacco. I was already giddy through excessive consumption of local tobacco by the time he signalled for us to come for the interview. He insisted on a public interview, though the request was for a private one. A Heraka preacher present there immediately left the hut, as if to say 'I wash my hands of this; I have no part in it'. That note reverberated and I could feel the nervousness of Tahulung. The disciples fixed their eyes on their master with rapt attention. Youths gathered, shuffling their feet nervously. Before I could open my mouth, he instructed me not to ask useless questions of the past: 'I will answer only questions about the present generation', he stated in his feeble voice. My first nervous question was 'some call you a prophet, what would you say to them?' I was nudging Tahulung to translate, but instead he stared at me with a blank expression. I could see the unwillingness on his part to utter the sacred word of 'prophet'. There have been no prophets in the few years since Ranima's death and she did warn against false prophets; and I wondered if this was the reason for the stricken look. Perhaps he did not wish to legitimize a crazy person? The interviewee replied,

> Let them say I am a prophet, I am not angry with them. *Kemeume* [prophecy] cannot teach Hingde and they [prophets] cannot transcribe and translate the songs of Heraka. They don't know the specific dance and song combination and the prophet can only understand during sickness and can then communicate with God. In a job, for example, many scientists are there for a specific purpose, some for space, earth, and so on. Like that, my role is different to that of a prophet. Let them call me a prophet, as they are ignorant about what my authority is. So my authority is to arrange the Heraka Hingde [rules governing everyday life][24] and songs. which Ranima has not arranged [according to their respective rituals]. Ranima did not arrange the Hingde, she just taught the songs and Hingde. It is up to me to arrange the Hingde and songs.

My question was actually different. I mean 'prophet' in the sense of a 'seer' of the future. His interpretation was different. The Heraka, including this man, believe that the *kemeume* (prophecy) generation is over; it is often associated with Paupaise, an ancestral practice. 'Prophet' in Zeme usually refers to a shaman of the *kemeume* generation, that is, the past (signifying blood sacrifices), while *heguang* is associated with the future (signifying purity). The reason he denies his link with *kemeume* is perhaps evident in his use of the word Hingde, because that implies different contexts, present and future according to different generations (see Chapter 4). Once one knows the Hingde (as in Heraka Hingde) then one is able to translate the songs and arrange the sequence of song and dance (remembering that songs are sacred and hence untranslatable), and also arrange the Hingde and songs. The latter, the 'heguang' believes has not been done by Ranima (she only taught the songs and Hingde separately). So what does this mean? Once one has translated the songs according to the Hingde, then, the laws are rewritten, history is recreated – and only one person can do this. Once these are translated, he achieves divine status, perhaps akin to a *heguang*, the promised *heguang*?

He continued as follows:

> In the universe, the time has come for the Zeliangrong people. He [Tingwang] sent Ranima to reform the Heraka Hingde. Now we, the loving sons of Ranima, follow according to her Hingde.
>
> I was born in 1968, 6th June, Thursday evening, in Puateujam village. From 1968 to 1996, I was living, as you are, a boy of his village. I received authority from Tingwang on 30th July 1996, Jalua day [full moon day; holy for the Heraka]. And, I took a promise from Tingwang on that day. Before the 30th of July, I thought, 'what should I do?' And I had 39 points of promise. I read out the 39 points in front of my village and I showed an example to the villagers with pebbles. I asked the boys to collect the pebbles and I gave one pebble each to the mature boys and girls (those wearing a kilt), married women and men, and not to the younger ones. After I distributed 39 pebbles to 39 people, I started to read my 39 points. After I read it out, I said again, 'we are making a promise not for bad works, but for good works'. With these words I believe that I am still working with righteousness, with power and authority from God. At that time, it was very difficult for me to read my agreement with Tingwang because of my weak voice. So I asked Sri Duajeing [his friend] to help me.
>
> Duajeing's father was the *gaonbora* [village elder] and *tingkopau* [priest]. So Duajeing's father gave an opening speech for the meeting and the opening song was *Gungtupuihang*. During the meeting I decided to sing three special songs together with the villagers, but they criticised me and

ignored me, so we sang only two songs. The second song called *Cheriupuina* was sung at the conclusion of the meeting. From that day onward I did not feel well in my body because most of my villagers criticised me. I have become weak because of this *hemui* [this can happen to a person if he is either praised or criticised too much; traditionally, to alleviate the burden one must sacrifice an animal to a god].[25] I often thought, 'oh, I don't want to live on this earth' [because of the weakness]. My body was weak up to January 1997. On the night of 2nd of January 1997, I couldn't sleep because my body was hot, as if it was burned by fire. I didn't sleep the whole night. On the 3rd of January, I had no alternative so I asked my brother Sri Riakeung Nriame to pray for me. At that time I wanted to go to God [die], but because of the people I couldn't go and I couldn't live with the people either. Tingwang scolded me, 'why do you stay with them?' With this problem I couldn't sleep for 4 to 5 months (January–August).

I started feeling better on the 28th of August 1997. After that day, we observed Jadonang's martyrs' day. From that day, I decided to visit each village, but couldn't go out. On the 3rd of October 1997, I went down to Lodi [near Haflong] and some people agreed to come with me as followers but the leaders rebuked them and they stopped. The followers were from Nchubonglo, Guilong and Michidiu. In 1998 I decided to live out in Hangrum camp, but at that time no one wanted to visit me. So from 1999–2002, I kept quiet and stayed in my village.

In the year 2003, I started going around the villages again. In 2003, I got my good followers (Sri Heujiabe Newme and Zinkaulang Nriame) from Kipelua [also Kepelo] to come with me. So the three of us would go preaching from village to village in *Nianglo Longria* [NL] [name of a Zeme region]. After my preaching, my name became popular in the NL area. So the NL leaders asked me to rearrange and preach the Hingde in my home; and I said 'no, my home is a family house that's why I cannot.' So the leader sent me to Hangrum. I told them, 'if I stay at my house, my prayers have no meaning, as everyday my house is not holy.' So I asked all the leaders of NL, 'what time can I come to Hangrum? You make the programme and come to my house and I will come along with you.' So on the 8th of July 2003, I went to Hangrum with the leaders of NL. On that day I told all the leaders: 'you observe if I am doing good works or not?' So from that day until now, I am always doing my work well. I also met Kanriakle [the previous caretaker of the Hangrum camp] the successor to Ranima [affectionately known as the second Rani]. On her death, I arranged the funeral programme. She died on the 20th December 2004. Before her death, Kanriakle told me everything she faced in her life, the sadness as well as happiness. After the death of Kanriakle some leaders of

> NL decided to abandon Hangrum camp, but some leaders and I said that 'it is not right to leave this place, we must continue our prayer service which was done during Ranima's time as well.' *Ndibaungtu* and *Ragwang Damtuang* are sung every night and the sunrise prayer is done every morning. So nowadays we continue what Ranima did in her time as well. *Kelum* [thank you or can be used as a blessing].

This 'heguangs' devotion to this ideal is singular in its vision. His narrative is also replete with significant signs, symbols and dates like Jadonang's martyr day, and Heraka songs. His recognition of Hangrum as holy, and his closeness with Kanriakle (the second Rani) – have an effect of legitimizing his activity and status (though no one knows his 39 points). Some do admit that he is gifted, in that he has translated a few songs and is arranging the Hingde, parts of which Ranima could not complete. I was told that some people in the village call him *heguangpeu* (king); and preachers and leaders came to Hangrum to ask him to stop preaching that he is a *heguang*. (There is a story that he once came to Haflong in 1997 proclaiming that he was Jadonang reincarnated and gathered some followers of his. However, he was beaten and thrown out of Lodiram (the colony he was staying in), because some thought he was crazy and that his claims were completely unfounded.) But those who espouse more moderate views told me that 'some of his words have come true. But we are yet to believe that he is *heguangpeu*. Moreover, Ranima prophesized that someone special will come from the East. He goes from village to village and the old people usually believe him as they hang on to Ranima's words – that one day a *heguang* will come from the East.'

However fleeting the notion of *heguangram* seems to those who criticize it, those who subscribe to the idea wholeheartedly keep the hope of it alive. The so-called heguang said 'if we get the *heguangram*, it will be one king rule. The king will be that person who knows the story of the Zeliangrong people from the beginning. Educated persons cannot be king, as they don't know the history of the Zeliangrong people.' Education and development are crucial to this understanding of *heguangram*. Those who oppose *heguangram* are of the view that only the uneducated are drawn to this idea. The resistance expressed in the above view has become something of a dichotomy between those who want *heguangram* and those who do not. If education is the measure of success and the reason for the abandonment of the idea of *heguangram*, then the so-called heguang says, to hell with you – we do not want you and your education. Indeed, this view is carried forward by his view that 'Rani Gaidinliu Inspiration Home' should be changed to 'Zeliangrong Heraka Heguangse Rambeki' (Zeliangrong Heraka King's court). Is he, then, the king, the *heguang*?

By asking that question, I want to finish this chapter. He definitely thinks so, but many around him do not. It is only a matter of time, they say, whether he turns out to be the promised one or not. There is one song in which I am interested here that plays on the theme of this chapter and also contextualizes the imagery of Ranima's visits to Bhuban cave in a provocative way. *Ailiangrine* is the song the Heraka sing when they visit Bhuban cave, at the entrance of the cave.

> Turn around again Bhuban God who is good
> Give us victory in everything
> Your figure is good and your name is also good
> Bhuban God is good
> Give me the power to be victorious in everything

Here is the same song the current 'heguang' translated for me when I met him.

> Who is to be the *heguang*? His spirit has reached his house [Bhuban cave]
> His choice of *heguang* will never fade away
> Like the discipline of God, who is to be the *heguang* should also be disciplined
> Bhuban God is good
> Every work will be completed without fear

This totally different translation indicates the problems of a definitive meaning. This ambiguity can fulfil different agendas, as it does here.

I now want to return to the argument laid out in the beginning with regard to community. The Heraka movement is evolving into a community that hinges 'crucially on consciousness'. The Heraka are aware of their boundaries, and the identities they inhabit through the processes of reform and interaction with the wider world. Not only do they forge identities due to external pressure but internal differences persist and the various interpretations of narratives within the Heraka, following Cohen's definition of community, seek to 'capture members' experience[s] of it'. Within the community, the notions of *heguangram* and *heguang* sustain the 'aggregating device' variously in the image of the Queen Mother, the symbol of Hangrum, and the claim to be *heguang*. These symbols perpetuate meaning at a emotional level, reminding people of their past history. However, the ongoing debate, particularly concerning the promise of a *heguang*, is still contentious to the extent that 'camps' have formed on either side. This is not to suggest that a breakup of the Heraka community is imminent. Instead, what this discussion requires is that we remember 'the gloss of commonality which it paints over its diverse components gives to each of them an additional referent for their identities' (Cohen 2003: 109).

Conclusion

The last song perhaps eloquently sums up the chapter. The current 'heguang' and his proclamation as king through the song help us understand the very nature of Heraka reforms and the historical precedents that have made the Heraka what it is now. The question therefore is implicit throughout this chapter. What direction does the Heraka take now? The symbol of Hangrum is a reminder that there are two different understandings of Heraka history and its predicaments. Although, there are urban and rural divides regarding the issue of Hangrum, any blatant denial of the position of Hangrum might lead to further fissures between the rural and urban Heraka population. Furthermore, by understanding Hangrum and its place in Heraka ideology, we can also get a glimpse of Heraka in its more millenarian, mystical and perhaps emotional stage. These millenarian attitudes are clearly embodied in the *heguang* and the promised *heguangram* for some people. Evidently, a state of freedom, joy and abundance is more real for those who are under dire circumstances in the villages than for those in the urban centres who tend to view millenarian ideals as superstition.

In this chapter, I have shown that *heguangram* is an important part of the Heraka practice, at least in the villages. At a conceptual level *heguangram* represents high-level integration and cosmological unity by articulating a vision centred on the *heguang*. Based in Hangrum, the Battle of Hangrum is the starting-place of heroism, bloodshed and the promise of the *heguangram*. While the notion of *heguangram* and *heguang* is sketchy, Ranima's biography sheds some light on this issue. This helps us appreciate the nuances of the *heguangram* and *heguang*. From her biography we are drawn to investigate, 'was the *heguang* Ranima?' It is clear in the text that Ranima comes across as the *heguang*, representing not only herself in that esteemed position, but also through the image of Durga. She thus becomes the Mother for the Heraka and also the Zeliangrong. As much as Hangrum represents the imagined community, it is also a reminder of a particular kind of community that has resisted the 'progressive' ideals of urbanized Heraka and, by its very existence, defies the establishment and challenges the internal organization of the Heraka itself. The tension is not visceral to the extent that a breakup is imminent, but the tension is evident enough for there to be a debate. So far, Hangrum represents the poesies of resistance.

Chapter 7

Conclusion

In this book, I have focused on the Heraka, a religious reform movement and its impact on the Zeme, a 'Naga tribe', in the North Cachar Hills of Assam, India. This book outlines the formation of the movement in 1974 from scattered groups beginning in the 1930s through to its present state. A pivotal examination is the evolution of Heraka identity, and its emergence into the arena of competing and often contested ideologies of 'religion' and 'ethnicity' in Northeast India. The ways by which the movement has evolved, exhibiting the contextualization of an indigenous identity, grounded in custom and tradition, are examined. These factors, along with complex relationships with a traditional group Paupaise, 'neo-Hindu' organizations such as the RSS and the VHP, Zeme Christians, and the larger 'Naga' Christian groups, have shaped pronounced yet fluctuating Heraka identities. This book demonstrates the difficult transition the Heraka movement faces as it shifts from the local to the regional and even the national.

I began this book by evoking the imagery of the pilgrimage to Bhuban cave taken by a group of Zeme Heraka during the month of January 2005. The more time I spent with the pilgrims, both young and old, during the journey there and at the cave, the more I realized the magnetic pull of the cave for the pilgrims, and its significance in the evolution of the Heraka. As they recounted their stories of visions, images, miracles, of finding joy and hope, or the emotional upheaval that some felt during the 'sunrise prayer' at the mouth of the cave, I understood the symbolic efficacy of the cave in the everyday lives of people and its relation to the reform movement. The Heraka believe the reform originated in Bhuban cave. Their pilgrimage reveals both the emotional depth and intuitive quality of individual and communal journeys as they map their paths, familiarize themselves with history, and seek answers to the many questions that haunt them. Will the promises of their leader, Gaidinliu – that she would return and all Heraka would live in paradise – come to fruition?

The symbol of Bhuban cave gains prominence in Gaidinliu's biography of her numerous journeys there. Her biography enhances her position as the *heguang* (a leader who will usher in a free community) due to her being seen as the daughter of Bhuban god, *Cherachamdinliu*. As is evident in Chapter 6, this notion is central to the future of the Heraka in the symbol of *heguang* and *heguangram* (free community). Is the promised *heguang* Gaidinliu? Chapter 6 discussed the validity of Rani Gaidinliu's biography with reference to her use of tradition and adoption of powerful symbols from 'Hinduism'. This brought out contested material, both in her role as a 'woman' that challenges patriarchical notions of gender construction, and in her projected role as *heguang* and Durga, a 'Hindu' Goddess, as 'divine'. This highlights questions of legitimation for the Heraka. The pan-Hindu idea of 'Bharat Mata' (Mother India) as a territorial deity correlates with the image of a 'mother', in Heraka contexts, and 'Goddess' in Gaidinliu's biography. It portrays an imagery as uniting and including disparate groups in India, such as the Heraka, under the wings of 'Bharat Mata'.

Yet this notion of *heguang* persists to the extent that the people are still waiting. This longing is symbolized by Hangrum village, the alleged place for *heguangram* and where the *heguang* will appear. The future of Hangrum is central for Heraka reform. If the rural population has its way and Hangrum with its ideology becomes the pivot for the Heraka reform, then the millenarian ideas would take an important lead in determining the direction for the Heraka. Therefore, if the 'king's court' with its millenarian vision succeeds, further thought is required to ponder the significance of *heguang* and the role of the current self-proclaimed 'heguang'. This brings our focus to the question of how 'traditional' or how 'progressive' the Heraka have become, supported by the 'rural' and 'urban' population respectively. These ideas give us a glimpse, on the one hand, into the protracted socio-economic malaise in the villages, particularly reflected in the poor functioning of schools, in contrast to the towns where the population is generally sustained by modern comforts and advantages. These are questions that liberate and haunt the Heraka in equal measure.

While Bhuban cave is vital for the Heraka, it also represents a familiar sacredness which other religious traditions relate to. As pointed out in Chapter 2, the terrain of symbols is vast and contested during the pilgrimage and within the cave rituals, with the Poupei Chapriak (a form of traditional Rongmei practice) and the Heraka both vying over notions of 'primordiality' and 'authenticity'. Yet, a common ethnic identity, Zeliangrong, has been adopted by the Zeme, Liangmai and Rongmei to symbolize a heritage, unified by elaborating on their point of origin in a mythical place known as Makuilongdi. However, such unity of common ethnic identity is contested in Bhuban cave, signifying how religious traditions challenge such unity below the surface. While clear religious categories are maintained in superficial rhetoric, some of the Heraka adherents profess multiple belongings, utilizing and, indeed, borrowing from Poupei Chapriak (and vice versa) spiritual and cultural emblems that could enhance their profile. This, for example, is evident in the symbol of the 'sadhu' who is regarded as 'holy', for reverence is paid to him regardless of religious categories imposed by the Heraka and Poupei Chapriak.

The ideological terrain marked by the Poupei Chapriak and the Heraka requires further investigation with regard to the fluid notion of Zeliangrong representing an ethnic unity. The way both traditions are placed within the context of the Bhuban pilgrimage, its symbolisms, and the larger quest for 'authenticity', could elucidate interesting correlations with the present study on the Heraka and further ramifications with regard to other neo-traditional groups in the region. It could also indicate further research possibilities in the Cachar region with respect to Poupei Chapriak and in the Manipur region, with other neo-traditional groups such as the Tingkao Ragwang Chapriak, an offshoot of the Heraka. While the limitations of the present work is obvious in its focus on the Zeme Heraka, an investigation of the links with these different religious traditions will provide a base for future research in the region.

In many ways the cave embodies the tension for the Heraka of the necessity to be both 'traditional' and 'modern'. Traditional in the way that establishes their ancestry, their credibility, and the fact that they are 'original'; and modern in their ability to adapt to the changing world. One of the pilgrims reminded me that just as the visions inside Bhuban cave vary from year to year, so do humans in the way they relate to the world, and the cave. He was conveying the point that the Heraka are not trapped in stringent traditions that refuse to change but are able to participate in the changing world. The tension between tradition and modernity is nevertheless evident in the way the reform has been generated over the years, with the beginnings in the 1930s, and as we have seen, such tension is vital for the growth and organization of the Heraka.

In Chapter 3 I examine the process whereby the reforms instigated major restructuring and organization of the village, developing the identity and increasing the popularity of the then 'Gaidinliu movement'. Kuki immigration, failed agricultural experimentation that led to near-famines and the inadequate response of the colonial government in trying to deal with these issues led to the Heraka reform having a practical appeal to the people – following Heraka brought better health and improved economic status. Initially, these attitudes were associated with millenarian ideas. This is clearly illustrated in the emotive appeal projecting a 'golden age' that the 'Gaidinliu movement' was able to generate in its followers. It connected the notion of a land of plenty and freedom for all with popular Zeme folk heroes and important landscapes, imaginings spread through popular mediums such as songs and the mobilization of itinerant preachers.

These mediums were persuasive in conveying the message of the reform. 'Old' systems of village organization also needed rethinking to construct the 'new' system which could then reflect the social and divine relationship in a meaningful way. Thus the cleaning of the village and its renewal according to Heraka principles was aimed at ushering in a 'new way' of doing things, by deliberately undermining the past traditions of Paupaise as 'dirty', 'unhygienic' and 'evil'. The reform and the growing need for the accommodation of economic change are thus further exemplified in the symbol of the Paipeu. The Paipeu, who now acts as the Heraka village head, is the symbol for the changing economic scenario and the prestige associated with the mobile, efficient, and expedient market economy, rather than the archaic and stagnant agricultural economy. This is reflected in the way the Heraka perceive 'superstitious' beliefs that rely on 'divine gifts' as the way to prosperity, beliefs that are inherently connected to the continuous propitiation of deities for maximum benefit, rather than the 'do it yourself' attitude introduced by the modern way of thinking. This modern attitude, according to Max Weber, accords with the 'rational mode' of thinking exemplified by the Puritans who relied on a healthy connection between heavenly rewards and a good work ethic. In a way, the Paipeu embodies the trait of rationality routinized, embedded in a 'life of good works' as theorized by Weber.

Therefore the Heraka song, 'The World has Changed', not only acts as a metaphor for practical changes, but also invokes meaning on a higher level – cosmological change. As we have seen, the Heraka brought this cosmological change about by encouraging the abandonment of sacrifices to the smaller gods. Reform also lifted prohibitive barriers – both in belief and economic status – to mobility in terms of education and outside employment, and was an active response to near-famines. Indeed, the cosmology was reconstituted, with the abolition of various gods, reduction in sacrifices and the establishment of a monotheistic god. This enabled the Heraka to change in a way that was demonstratively beneficial, aiding adaptation to a changing world that the existing ancestral religion, Paupaise, could not. The evolution of the Paupaise is also interesting within the Zeme system. Paupaise is a self-conscious identity, a neo-traditional group that defines itself against a reformist, a new movement. Thus, a distinct Paupaise identity is carved out and is representative of all that is 'traditional', in contrast to all that is 'new' or 'reformist'.

While the historical materials are adequate for an analysis of the conditions of the Heraka stimulated by the evolving situation in the North Cachar Hills, changes in the Naga Hills, particularly in the Peren district of Nagaland, were different. Although an in-depth study has not been conducted in Peren district, notions of sacrifice differ in the two regions. In Peren sacrifice is widespread, supported by Ranima's alleged view that sacrifice should continue, while in North Cachar it is largely abolished, which also incidentally was based on Ranima's teachings. But why this difference? It is tempting to speculate that economic repercussions for sacrifice were not as widespread in the Naga Hills as in North Cachar Hills in the early part of the twentieth century, where they were further compounded by pressures of Kuki immigrants and their usurping of Zeme land. These factors could have had minimal effect in the Peren region of the Naga Hills. The difference surrounding the notion of sacrifice in the two regions, however, could provide interesting insights into corresponding cosmologies, their tie with village organization, and the overall practice of the Heraka in Nagaland, compared to those of North Cachar Hills. As has been discussed, at least in North Cachar Hills, these changes were drastic.

Chapter 4 demonstrated how these changes, both practical and cosmological, led to the formation of a movement and the evolution of the Heraka as it is today. I examined the study by Robin Horton (1975) on how cosmologies reflect the functioning of social relations. Although Richard Eaton (1984, 2000) has made valuable contributions to an understanding of Christian conversion in relation to Naga cosmologies, similar to Robin Horton's model, there is scope for further studies on this matter especially with regard to the impact of American missionaries and the Nagas. As Jean and John Comaroff (1991) commented, in their study of African Christianity, conversion is a two-way process: the picture is enlarged only when the study is taken to include both the missionary culture at the time (in the West) and those they are 'missionizing'. These correlations could throw light on numerous issues concerning the self, morality, economic background, religious upbringing, political views and how these notions have been modified in present contexts.

Robin Horton's model is particularly pertinent to the way the Heraka use the creation story to reflect social relations. The creation story is not only a viable way to aspire to a unified and elegant rendering of the cosmos by reconstituting scattered accounts, but it also manages to influence the way the Heraka perceive themselves by grounding changes within different generations. Each generation within Heraka rhetoric has a prescribed Hingde or divine rules, given to the people at a particular time. Hence, the Heraka Hingde encompasses the current generation's practices while the older *hingde*, Paupaise, has become outdated. By utilizing these generations the Heraka are able to make the connection between how the change in generation requires a change in practice. This change is legitimated by invoking a time when 'no sacrifices' were needed and therefore envisioned as 'pure', embodied in the story of a famous healer, Herakandingpeu. The Heraka are convinced that theirs is the age that mirrors the generation of Herakandingpeu, grounding the message of reform powerfully in the familiarity of local symbols.

While these stories are powerful reminders which take the listeners to a higher level, they have been utilized by dissenting voices within the Heraka itself. The current self-proclaimed 'heguang' manages his image as the chosen saviour by telling his followers that the time for the Heraka has come with his birth, his mission from Tingwang and his inevitable position in Hangrum as the seat of the *heguang*. His wish to alter the 'Rani Gaidinliu Inspirational Home' to 'Zeliangrong Heraka King's Court' has a powerful effect on Hangrum as a symbol and the associated prophetic reading of history, especially for marginalized voices in Heraka villages. These factors could generate challenging but important features in the evolution of the Heraka in the next few years. For example, the rural population in particular have to adapt to the way their leaders are making uncomfortable choices for them; the closeness to 'Hindu' organizations is something they are suspicious of. They also feel that their leaders do nothing about the growing threat of Christian proselytization through the control of important resources such as schools. The problems take on a third dimension as negotiations with traditional groups lead to conflict over 'tradition' and 'change'.

In particular, I discussed the Heraka's identity in relation to the Paupaise and the growing Christian population. The increasing influence of Christianity, with its monotheism, and the threat of proselytization gave rise to intense competition. This demonstrated that the need for a unified religious system to compete with the Christians, and to some extent the 'Hindus', gives rise to differentiated forms of social life. It also marked the creation of a 'sacred' community. This began the evolution of a 'religion' and 'the sacred' within a culture where previously, in Paupaise, there was no separation of the sacred from the mundane. Economic, political, judicial and religious aspects were all embedded in what a Zeme was, a human (*zemena*); there was no distinction between everyday actions and 'religious' practice.

The establishment of the Kelumki (prayer house) embodied this distinction. The Kelumki is the 'sacred' centre of the village which encapsulates the *mirase* (my-god-practice) reforms as both 'elective fraternities' (Hervieu-Léger 2000: 150–2) maintaining the Paupaise tradition of prohibitions, evoked by the symbolism of the left; and 'religious elements' and therefore reformist, symbolized by the right. In other words, the 'left' is symbolized as preserving tradition, while the 'right' is symbolized as projecting the reforms. The Kelumki elicits powerful symbolism in relation to how the 'sacred' is conceived as separate and demarcated by the physical as well as the spiritual fence protecting it from defilement. Its imagery establishes parallels with the Temple, Church and Mosque, as that which is 'set apart' from mundane space. This not only enables the Heraka to envisage a proper 'religious' system, but it also binds them into a particular religious community, aware of its boundaries formed by categories both physical and cognitive.

In this regard, Chapter 5 delineates aspects of boundary formation and the position of the Heraka vis-à-vis Christian and 'Hindu' groups that not only have a direct relation to the larger 'Naga' population but also to India itself. Taking on the widely debated issue of Christian conversion in India and its ramifications, I look at conversion not as a simple given, but as a process that interrogates notions of choice, divine will and the strategy of utilizing resources, in some cases, for increased political profile. However, what is interesting is that becoming Heraka from Paupaise is not seen as 'conversion' while becoming Christian from Heraka or Paupaise is 'conversion'. One can draw parallels with a general Christian model of conversion. A change within the faith, if not Roman Catholic, is not seen as 'conversion', just as Paupaise to Heraka is not. From Protestantism to Roman Catholicism is seen as 'conversion' because the Roman Catholics demand exclusivism. With regard to the process enacted between Paupaise and Heraka, a strict 'conversion' model is difficult to follow because the Heraka do not demand exclusivism. But equally, in the Zeme context, becoming a Baptist from a Presbyterian is seen as 'conversion' due to the Baptists' exclusivism. The way this interaction is fashioned in the Zeme context could make important contributions to the study of 'conversions' generally, and in relation to 'religious pluralism' and 'exclusivism'.

Situating the rhetoric of conversion between the Christian church and various 'Hindu' organizations, notions of ethnic allegiance, nationalist perceptions and locally constructed boundaries shape the ongoing debate regarding identity and boundaries. To safeguard the functioning of the community as both 'indigenous', and preserving the *vanvasi* (jungle dweller) population from Christian and Western influence, the use of Hindutva (Hinduness) as encompassing 'indigenous' populations highlights an important point. Primordial ethnic notions are also used effectively by the Zeme Heraka in determining group membership against Christians who are viewed as 'foreign' and hence *perua* (empty), not Zeme. The book, therefore, not only points out the important issues raised in these chapters with regard to Heraka identity and its fluid constructions according to contexts, but it also aims at remedying shortcomings in Heraka scholarship and indeed the position of marginalized religious traditions caught in the whirlwind of the dominant Christian and 'Hindu' discourse with regard to South and Southeast Asia.

Just how difficult and constraining such a view can be is illustrated by providing two vignettes related to the larger question of ethnicity and religious affiliation and the larger project of nationalism they encompass in India. An ethnic group is one which identifies itself through shared history, common cultural forms and overwhelming solidarity, and is identified by others as such (Barth 1969: 10–11). On the other hand, nationalism simply means that humanity can be divided into units – nations – based on shared culture and language, sometimes a common religion and occasionally a shared history, ruled through self-determination (Spencer 2006: 391).

To illustrate this point I wish to recall two episodes. The first one is my conversation with an RSS worker in Dimapur, Nagaland. During our brief meeting he said, 'we will help the Heraka and the Nagas like our own brothers and sisters, both financially and spiritually, but once the Nagas ask for independence from India, we will withdraw all support.' This comment links the idea of Heraka identity, and its ability to maintain itself, with the wider question of Naga identity and nationalism.

There is a perception, held primarily by Naga Christians, that the Heraka are 'Hindu'. They say that the Heraka must be 'Hindu' since they are associated with 'Hindu' organizations. But what is 'Hindu'? In this case, the Christians are the dominant 'other' who question Heraka identity. As a form of resisting, the Heraka adopt so-called Hindu symbols (the *om* and *swastika* are quite common in homes, and publications). Therefore, there are layers of identification going on that are both religious and ethnically based.

The second instance is an article in the local newspapers of a speech of N. C. Zeliang, the past-President of the Heraka Association. In this he attacked Christian proselytizing. In what were many responses to the article, the President of the Sumi (also Sema) Baptist Churches Convention perhaps gave the most accurate description when he said: 'Lastly, it appears that you [referring to the Heraka] are very closely associated with the people from Kalyan Ashram, Dimapur and Vidya Bharti from Gujarat. For the sake of intellectual appetite, kindly clarify the difference between your Heraka religion and Hinduism. I hope your feathers are still true with the Nagas and not coloured with Hinduism.'[1]

There is therefore a perception that all Nagas must be Christian, and there is also the perception that since the dominant 'other' in relation to the Nagas is 'India', then Christianity is not only a tool for difference but a form of resistance.

'Naga' nationalism and forming a separate nation from India has been envisaged for almost 50 years. 'Nagas' have tried to forge a distinct ethnic 'Naga' identity that is supposedly based on shared history, culture and common religion. But, as I have shown, the term 'Naga' itself is an evolving concept that is difficult to pin down as it can be worn and shed according to circumstances. The 'political identity' or 'ethnic mobilization' that is mushrooming in the minds of 'Nagas' must allow its boundaries to be more flexible. The strong forms of overt zealousness on the part of some Naga Christians in proclaiming 'Nagaland (or Nagalim (that includes all Naga inhabited areas)) for Christ' has alienated the Zeme Heraka as they see their aims as a threat to the Zeme Heraka religious practice. Hence, they drift away from the Naga Christians and instead rely on 'Hindu' groups for financial and organizational support. Due to this the 'Hindu' groups extend their ideology and include the Zeme Heraka in the project of 'Hinduness', while keeping Christian proselytization under scrutiny. For the Heraka, it is more a question of survival and day-to-day resistance, than the overt pandering to the idea of nationhood. This is not to say that the Zeme Heraka feel less 'Naga' due to their affiliations with 'Hindu' groups, but it shows how the Zeme Heraka can accommodate different identities without fixing themselves to any one and how in the process they are able to be so many things at once.

A marginalized group such as the Heraka can illuminate notions of identity based on religious reform. By situating the Heraka within the dialogue of ethnicity and nationalism, which is a vital topic in Northeast India, this book throws light on the future of the Heraka vis-à-vis notions of 'Naga nationalism' and pan-Hindu projects of 'Hinduness' with regard to 'tribal' populations in Northeast India specifically, and India generally. This could also lead to further study on religious modernization, ethnic mobilization, conversion and nationalism with regard to India and the neighbouring Southeast regions such as Bangladesh and Myanmar, examining how the 'tribal' populations are perceived in relation to the 'State' and the dominant 'other(s)'. The realities of power are exercised in how these representations are formed, and the views of dominant groups, such as Christians and Hindus, tend to override those of subalterns such as the Heraka, not to speak of the Paupaise. It is here that a subaltern consciousness constantly challenges and relocates the strength for resistance against those that undermine them. In a way, this represents the destiny of those who hope in the present and in the future.

Notes

Chapter 1: Introduction

1 The Paupaise population in North Cachar Hills is now negligible. For example, they comprise only about 12 households (60 people) in Lozeihe village.

2 Known primarily in Nagaland as those who have missed the mark, referring to their false message.

3 The name was coined in a conference held at Beisumpui (Ntangkam), Nagaland. There is scarce information as to what actually transpired during the conference, as the minutes of the meeting are not available or were not kept in the first place.

4 Recent literature on this movement is recounted in Namthiubuiyang Pamei's book *The Trail from Makuilongdi* (2001) that attempts to present the Zeliangrong people as a coherent whole from past narratives to present situations.

5 'Haomei' is supposedly an ancient name which also means 'people of . . . God as well as cultured people' (Mukherjee et al. 1982: 72).

6 In a somewhat confusing passage, according to a different source, William Shaw, an administrator working in the Tamenglong area in 1927, suggested,

> 'Haomai' is merely an attempt to separate by those who have intermarried with Kacha Nagas [Zeme and Liangmai] and come under Kuki or Angami influences. It is only those on the fringe claim 'Haomai' as their own name for themselves (Haamai). 'Hao' is the Manipuri name for Nagas. (J. C. Higgins, MS 95022 (Box 1: files 1–10). SOAS)

7 On the notion of 'Naga' identity and its recent (re)interpretations see Joshi (2001) who bases her study on the Angami, another 'Naga' tribe in Nagaland. She draws on historical material from the beginning of colonialism and the subsequent influence of Christianity which had major ramifications on the political, cultural and religious identities of the 'Nagas' and the Angami in particular.

8 These views were confirmed when I conducted an interview in April 2005 with him as well as his wife, who is the General Secretary of the Zeliangrong Heraka Mahila (women's) Samiti (ZHMS). The time frame of the stages is unclear in the text. It must also be emphasized that Pautanzen's summation regarding sacrifices is contested. The first phase, as I gathered in my own fieldwork, seems to have been the one having the most impact. Sacrifices were greatly reduced in the first phase, though some were still permitted. The next three phases were more gradual.

9 The Naga club, supported by the British administrators, was subsequently formed in 1919, after the return of several Nagas who served in the labour corps in France during the First World War. This was the first sign of pan-Naga nationalism as different Naga 'tribes' came together abroad thus reifying their common solidarity in the midst of such strangeness (see Jacobs et al. 1998: 151–64).

Chapter 2: Circling the Altar Stone: Bhuban Cave and the Symbolism of Religious Traditions

1 A rare footnote in administrative archives recounts a form of pilgrimage to the cave in 1931. It says, 'at Bhuban they offered the god a *dao* [a hacking knife], for prosperity, which was presented to the god by Jadonang' (Proceedings/11892: 23, British Library, India Office Records; henceforth referred as P/11892). Jadonang is revered by the Heraka for being the first reformer. He was executed in 1931 by the British authorities for allegedly murdering two traders and sacrificing them to his God.

2 Similarly, on how Vaisnava traditions mediates between 'Hindu civilization' and 'tribal culture' through a process of 'acculturation' see Surajit Sinha (1966: 64–89); on how 'Sankritization' of Manipur became a tool whereby the process of 'Hinduization' was not only about upward mobility of caste, but was also about adopting 'Hindu' religious symbols and adapting local deities to those of the high Hindu deities (Kamei 2002a: 41–4).

3 An ethnic group found predominantly in the Indian state of Meghalaya and parts of Bangladesh.

4 Mela, from the Sanskrit, means an assembly. It is used largely in connection with 'Hindu' pilgrimages.

5 There are only two temples in the area and the Heraka do not go to the temple; their only interest is in the Bhuban cave.

6 The plantain leaf represents purity for the pilgrims. In fact, it is adapted by the Heraka as part of their official emblem.

7 My gratitude to Abuan Kamei who translated from Rongmei the 'Latling (Mansei Leh Raa Kak Khou)' and 'Chapriak Kaba' texts. Gangmumei Kamei also discusses the importance of Tingkao Ragwang Chapriak (which is similar to Poupei Chapriak) (2004: 278–9), which he somewhat confusingly classifies as 'Zeliangrong indigenous religion'.

8 MS 95022 Higgins Collection (SOAS): 11–18.

9 P/11892: 33. Kangrellung could be a local god. Kamei (2002b: 18–19) says that 'Khangrillung [*sic*] is the son of God Bishnu of Bhuban Hills.' Parratt (2005: 46) suggests that 'the coincidence of the names, Bhishnu with Vishnu – is so close that we can scarcely avoid the conclusion that by the 1920s the god Khangrillung had become hinduised and identified with Vishnu'.

10 P/11892: 22.

11 Gangmumei Kamei strongly asserts this when he says 'God Bisnu is *not* the Hindu God Vishnu. Bisnu is the god of the Zeliangrong pantheon. He is known by different names, *Munchanu*, *Bonchanu*, *Buisnu* and *Bisnu* [*sic*]' (2004: 148; see also Arambam and John Parratt 1995: 289).

[12] It is believed that the open one was used by Rani Gaidinliu while the other one was used by Jadonang until it was closed by Tingwang out of anger towards Jadonang for not obeying certain instructions.

[13] The meaning of the title is unclear. It loosely refers to Rani (as in Rani Gaidinliu) and is believed to be first sung by Gaidinliu in her first visit to Bhuban cave. The theme of the song is about freedom from oppression. Most of the Heraka songs were written by Ranima using many languages: Rongmei, Zeme, Liangmei, Bengali, Hindi, Nepali, Mizo, Khasi, Assamese, Nagamese, Meitei. Therefore, the songs are difficult to translate and hence impenetrable to most people. The Heraka hold the view that these songs are written in God language and therefore to translate them into Zeme would lose their meaning.

[14] Again, the title is unclear. Usually sung before entering the cave. It praises Bhuban God and asks for victory.

[15] The idea that holy water is collected and then taken back to the four corners is also common among 'Hindus' and some Christian groups. The water possesses a symbolic sacredness that can be accessed anytime to bestow blessings and as a cure for illness and ailments.

[16] P/11892: 50.

[17] The Heraka more generally refer to ancestral traditions or 'Paupaise'. The only reason they are treated synonymously is because Poupei Chapriak is largely accepted as that which preceded the Heraka, so, hence 'ancestral' and by association 'Paupaise'.

[18] This roughly translates as 'God's Creatures'. It is a prayer song sung on every occasion, which celebrates the relationship between Ragwang (God) and humans.

[19] Ndibangtu translates as 'under the earth'. This is an interesting song, as it pits Herawang (King of gods), known to the Heraka as Tingwang, against the evil spirits, who might cause havoc. So with Tingwang's power, the evil spirits will be 'cut'. It also has interesting connotations regarding rebirth: the song says: 'we don't want to live underground, Banglawang, please send us back on the earth.'

Chapter 3: Millenarianism and Refashioning the Social Fabric

[1] The Kuki are a nomadic people who belong to the same ethnic group as the Chins of Myanmar and the Lushai of Mizoram (Grierson 1904). Specifically, the word 'Kuki' could also apply to those who were driven from the Lushai and Chin Hills to the north and west (Singh 2002: 44).

[2] The Kabui consider themselves as 'Naga' who live predominantly in the present state of Manipur, North Cachar Hills and Cachar district of Assam. They have adopted the name Rongmei in recent years. For the sake of simplicity, I retain the word 'Kabui' because of its use in Administrative Reports.

[3] P/11892 and Political and Secret Department/13/1002, British Library, India Office Records; henceforth referred as L/PS/13/1002.

[4] *Pothang* literally means *pot* (baggage) and *thang* (to carry). Under Manipuri law, every village had to cater to the visiting king, members of his family and state

officials when they toured the village or the region. This was abolished in 1913 with the help of the British, but the practice continued illegally in some regions.

5 P/11892: 64.

6 The geography of the Jadonang movement stretched to Manipur, North Cachar Hills and the Naga Hills. However, the Gaidinliu movement retained much of its popular support only in North Cachar Hills and the Naga Hills.

7 The source of this statement could not be found; the former Personal Assistant to Rani Gaidinliu, Abuan Kamei, kindly lent me his copy. However, for a similar account, told from the perspective of the second person (the Political Agent in Manipur), see L/PS/13/1002: Folio 665–7. In a later description, Jadonang is said to have been in a procession with a Manipuri Brahmin returning from Bhuban cave with an old Kabui who was called their 'lai' (God). This description could correspond with Meitei religious practice (Ursula Graham Bower's private collection: http://bamdemo.lemurconsulting.com/bamdemo/db/naga/doc/1119226690_00011?hit=3&q_=lai. Accessed 30 Nov. 2006). This is a database that stores a lot of 'Naga material' based on the 'Naga Videodisc' project of 1987 undertaken by the University of Cambridge. For more information on this project and other links see: www.alanmacfarlane.com.

8 Meiteis have largely moved from 'traditional Meitei religion to the Vaishnavite form of Hinduism', as Vaishnavite Hinduism became the main religious practice in Manipur by a royal edict in 1705 (Dena 1988: 31). While this transition was accepted to a large extent by the Meitei kings, they had to accommodate the *maibas* and *maibis* within the functioning of the state, in order to slowly legitimize Hinduism as a state religion. Hence, traditional Meitei religion was allowed to exist alongside Hinduism (Brara 1998: 16–17).

9 L/PS/13/1002: Folios 437–9 and 441–6.

10 Jadonang's movement is often seen as medico-religious by some administrative accounts that reduce his activities to that merely of healer and magician. However, it is worth noting that wandering healers or dream interpreters are generally given a gift (money or rice beer) as a token of appreciation; they seldom exact an amount that is fixed or required for the examination and cure to take place.

11 Higgins, while interviewing the Kambiron villagers, was informed that Jadonang was a *maiba* for four years and a god for two years (P/11892: 64).

12 L/PS/13/1002: Folios 668–9. Some like Parratt (2005: 50) regard him as *mhu* (shaman) and Kamei (2002a: 14–29) as the 'seer of Kambiron'. My speculations are primarily based on administrative reports.

13 For a general survey of messianic movements in India see Stephen Fuchs (1965); for a more general review on millenarian movements across the globe see Carole A. Myscofski (1988); Sylvia L. Thrupp (1962); Bryan R. Wilson (1973).

14 K. S. Singh draws upon the definition of 'revitalization movements' to include other tribal protests in the late nineteenth century to the early part of the twentieth century in India. He includes the Kharwar movement among the Santals (1871–80), the Munda-Oraon Sardar movement (1869–95), Birsa Munda among the Mundas (1895–1921) to name a few, which attempted to restore their rights, expressed through the popular borrowed idiom of Christianity and Hinduism. See K. S. Singh (1983b: 21). For detailed studies of similar protests, see Tanika Sarkar (1985: 136–64); K. S. Singh (1983b; 1988: 36–50); Michael Adas (1987).

15 Hutton Ms. Box 2, Pitt Rivers Museum Archive, Oxford.

[16] L/PS/13/1002: Folio 14.

[17] L/PS/13/1002: Folios 441–6.

[18] L/PS/13/1002: Folios 636–9. This view is reiterated by Bower (1952).

[19] Schools were started primarily by the Christian churches (Catholics and the Presbyterians) and by the British government in the townships of Haflong, Mahur, Maibong, Asalu.

[20] U. V. G. Betts' Manuscripts (Pitt Rivers Museum): 7.23 (J. P. Mills' Tour Diary for March, 1927).

[21] These were associated with feasts of merits. Large houses of great magnificence in both artistry and size were constructed primarily for display in association with the feast. Most of the wealthy could perform only one feast, the *kumarumki*, because the next one, involving the building of *kapeoki*, would have required double the wealth. As for the final feast, Bower remarks, 'no specimen of hekwi-ki [*hekuiki*] existed, and it was doubtful whether the ritual formulae of this feast survived in the Central Nzemi [Zeme] area' (Betts 1950: 70). The last *kumarumki* was performed in 1941 as recorded by Betts (1950: 83). Post 1941 no one living has ever seen any of these feasts – only stories and songs of these remain.

[22] The feast giver could become a *hangseoki kazeipeo* (warden of the young men's house) or he could be chosen as *kedeipeu* (landowner) (Betts 1950: 71).

[23] The feast giver can adorn their body cloths with decorations signifying their merit status, which are often passed down to their progeny as well.

[24] In some feasts of merit, where there was a strong structure of hierarchy, the individuals managing power would manipulate the system to enhance their own social status. For example, among the Thendu Konyak, the feasts of merit were monopolized by the Great Ang clans, or chiefs, using it to enhance their own powers (Jacobs et al. 1998: 78–80; Stirn and Ham 2003: 102).

[25] The current Paupaise are aware of this argument and have told me on several occasions that they realize these prohibitions create many restrictions, but that it is a way of life for them.

[26] The Heraka realized that sacrifices could not be banned outright but only incrementally. Big sacrifices like the killing of buffalo and *mithun* were banned, while smaller animals like hen and fowls were tolerated until 1974, when a total ban was put in place.

[27] There is a story about the Nriame and Newme clans. According to this, Nriame cousins bore an illegitimate child. To avoid expulsion from the village, they placed some eggs near the house and put a fence around these. They told their parents that the eggs were from heaven and had to be protected. They then placed the child near the eggs and explained that it had been hatched. This child was called Newme (taken from *neube*), meaning taboo.

[28] While touring the North Cachar Hills in 1921, J. H. Hutton also makes the similar point, that a disastrous harvest had reduced the villages in North Cachar Hills to abject poverty and that application for loans were on the rise (Hutton Ms. Box 2, Pitt Rivers Museum Archive, Oxford).

[29] Bower notes that the meticulous referencing of village objects are memorized with the help of markers or sometimes committed to memory: migration history is remembered in detail back a few generations, as to the exact location of the

village sites and the transition to another one. The *hezoa*, in particular is marked with a monolith (Betts 1950: 122).

30 L/PS/13/1002: Folio 649. In my fieldwork, I did not see any enmity towards the Kuki in any way. Part of the mobilization against the Kukis by Jadonang and Gaidinliu could have been related to unresolved grievances during the Kuki rebellion (1917–19). With the publication of Bower's central thesis (1946) that the Kuki immigration led to the collapse of the Zeme cycle migration, the Kuki National Assembly (KNA) in 1947 questions the validity of her claim. In the KNA's comment, it states that the British should be the ones to blame since they controlled Kuki movement. It further states that the Kukis and Nagas have always lived amicably (Betts Papers, Folder 7: Centre for South Asian Studies, Cambridge: http://bamdemo.lemurconsulting.com/bamdemo/db/naga/doc/1119226705_00000?hit=0&q_=Kuki+National+Assembly. Accessed 10 Oct. 2007).

31 Jacobs et al. point out that not only does wet terrace cultivation require extensive labour, but related to extensive labour, it also encourages 'egalitarian principles of social organisation' that nurture fair competition to produce surplus and hence gain higher status (1998: 35).

32 L/PS/13/1002: Folios 636–9.

33 Hutton Ms. Box 2, Pitt Rivers Museum Archive, Oxford.

34 This question concerning how peasant societies deal with the rapid changes brought about by modernity is not new. For a detailed study on this process see Todd A. Diacon (2002); also Michael Taussig (1977: 130–55).

35 Bower's private collection (1937–46): http://bamdemo.lemurconsulting.com/bamdemo/db/naga/doc/1119226693_00004?hit=1&q_=bower+1945. Accessed 12 June 07.

36 In rural life, Scott says, communities avoid 'outright confrontation with the authorities over taxes, cropping patterns, development policies or onerous new laws' (1985: xvi). For the Zeme denial and deception became a way of resisting. When the administrators toured the affected regions, almost all villages denied any involvement with the Gaidinliu movement. This baffled the administration.

37 Weber's notion of 'rationalization' has been criticized by some scholars as being too narrowly formulated to deal with 'traditional societies'. Peter Worsley in fact argues that 'traditional action' is not 'irrational'; it is moreover rational if 'one examines its application in a particular situation' (1970: 268). In this sense, I am not suggesting a complete shift from 'magical' to 'rational' thinking within the Heraka, but Weber's model does allow us to understand why the religious and economic change was effective.

38 For this section, I am relying on contemporary oral sources collected from my fieldwork (from Jan.–July 2005), to help me understand how village organization changed. The link between landowners, priests and the redefinition of their roles in Heraka society became clearer.

39 During this time, Christian missions were also gaining a foothold in the Zeme villages and conversions were going on among the Zeme. For some, Christianity was the answer to the burden of Paupaise and for others it was Heraka. Obviously, Christians were also adapting to this change in their own way. But the Heraka was

a more popular movement among the Zeme during that time, in part because of Gaidinliu's involvement.

40 For a helpful introduction to the subject on oral history and written history see Ajay Skaria (1999). Skaria argues that one must take oral tradition seriously rather than dismissing it as myth or superstition. He achieves this through his concept of 'hybrid history', which is critical of hyperreal Europe with its metanarrative of defining the norm in history. He suggests placing subaltern oral traditions based on 'memory' on serious footing to challenge the hyperreal Europe by 'going beyond it but marked by it' (13).

41 These meetings are mostly attended by the woman folk held after every *Jalua* (full moon day); they talk about household issues like childcare, education and certain problems like the abuse of *zao* by the men.

42 This is a contested area: in the western region blood sacrifices are still performed, and in parts of Nagaland, the Heraka perform sacrifices as an important part of their practice.

43 Perhaps this implies the idea that Zeliangrong is big enough, like the lake, for everybody to be included in the category.

44 This is my translation with the help of Tahulung and Adeule.

45 PPMS 58/16, p. 9. School of Oriental and African Studies, London.

Chapter 4: Changing Cosmology and the Process of Reform

1 The one Paupaise village left in North Cachar Hills, Lozeihe, also refer to themselves as Paupaise, 'the first given practice of the Zeme people'. Their view on Christianity and Heraka are that both are 'foreign religious traditions'. Lately, the Paupaise are also engaged in actively structuring their tradition by printing songbooks, and maintaining a uniform religious tradition with those in Nagaland under the auspices of the Pau Pai Chen (ancestral practice) Association.

2 Hingde, as already mentioned, is 'rules governing everyday life'. In this chapter, sometimes I have shortened it to 'rules'; therefore, I am using the two synonymously. *Mitulung,* which literally means 'my-nature', is often connected with 'action' which over time becomes 'habit' and hence 'natural'. Therefore, I often distinguish between the various processes and how 'action' eventually becomes 'my-nature'.

3 MS 95022 Higgins Collection (SOAS): 15: 11–18.

4 MS 95022 Higgins Collection (SOAS): 15: 11–18. Victor and Edith Turner (1978) contend that pilgrimages are primarily 'world religion' phenomena.

5 He criticizes Mbiti's book *African Religions and Philosophy* for taking the position that African traditional religions are not universal but tribal, in the sense that they do not interact in any way, but are locally bounded within their group (Ranger 1993: 71). A similar criticism of the study of Nagas was made by Leach (1977: 291) in relation to the misleading categorization of Nagas as bounded groups, who have no interaction with each other in any 'institutionalized sense'.

6 MS 95022 Higgins Collection (1–10), No. 6, Nagas of Manipur (SOAS library).

[7] Bower's private collection (1937–46): http://bamdemo.lemurconsulting.com/bamdemo/db/naga/doc/1119226691_00007?hit=1&q_=creation+story+of+the+Zeme. Accessed 8 Apr. 07.

[8] Christoph von Fürer Haimendorf's private collection (1970): http://bamdemo.lemurconsulting.com/bamdemo/db/naga/doc/1119225686_00022?hit=0&q_=tingwang. Accessed 8 May 07. The Zeme had a female deity Heratinrangpui, the creator, which has largely been replaced by Banglawang, male deity, as the creator.

[9] I have heard the creation story in the field which is also in the 'Hingde Book'. The oral versions are more extensive at certain points in contrast to the 'Hingde Book'. This particular creation story is a combination of the above, corroborated with other written sources.

[10] The names may vary according to region: for example, Mishnu (in Zeme) is referred to as Munchanu in Liangmei, Bonchanu in upper Rongmei and Buisnu or Bisnu in lower Rongmei (Kamei 2004: 27).

[11] The Zeme believe that the Barail (comes from the Assamese Bura, meaning old) Range is the abode of Gechingpeu (also known as Mahadeo), which is called Gechingpeuki in Zeme. Chuprai is known to have his abode in the Naga Hills, Japfu peak, on the southern side of Kohima, while Mishnu moved to the Bhuban Hills in Cachar District. Among the Zeme Paupaise, it is believed that all of these gods became evil and bloodthirsty; only Chuprai was viewed as kind and modest as he was the god of rain and crops: he is also known as Herawang (the king of the gods).

[12] This is also connected with Tingwang's earlier prophecy in the creation narrative: that if Banglawang touched the water (which he does upon climbing down the iron ladder) then he cannot be king.

[13] This confusion could be between the text and oral traditions: thus dual narratives are accommodated without contradiction. The point of the written form is to emphasize Tingwang's status over Banglawang's. It also makes the high god higher and more remote perhaps.

[14] The Heraka sing a song called *Ndibangthu* (under the earth). In this song they request Banglawang to send the Heraka back to earth, as this is where they are supposed to live, on earth.

[15] These reforms have not been uniform; some proponents of the Heraka, known as *Perie se* (old practice) still pray and sacrifice to Chuprai.

[16] Weber observes that a sharp differentiation was made between early Christianity and Judaism by adopting the day of the sun god as the day of rest, as opposed to the Sabbath practised by the Jews (1965: 71).

[17] Unlike the abundance of mission records in Nagaland and Manipur, in the North Cachar Hills, mission records are scarce. Therefore, I rely mostly on oral accounts.

[18] N. C. Zeliang is hugely controversial among the Zeliangrong people. He was a Christian who studied theology and later converted to Heraka. The reason for his conversion, he told me, was to protect indigenous culture, which was being uprooted by Christian missionaries and by modernity. Due to his awareness of these issues, he joined the Heraka at the request of Rani Gaidinliu. Other people are more suspicious of his intentions. Christians have told me that he became Heraka because he divorced his wife and was barred from the church.

[19] The Heraka often use Hingde (capitalized) as opposed to the common *hingde*. I have maintained this distinction throughout the chapter.

[20] It is ironic that in the Paupaise narrative, Herakandingpeu is also viewed with respect and awe – they often call him the superman: a man capable of doing anything. But the Heraka made him the enemy of the Paupaise.

[21] Kamei (2004: 21–2) notes that 'traditional periodization' of Zeliangrong history called *zuks* has been adapted from the Hindu notion of jug [*yug*]. It is quite vague as to what he means by this, but there are some similarities with the Yuga Purana (Story of the Ages), an ancient Indian text. According to the Yuga Purana, there are four ages (*yugas*). Each age represents a different time: Krta or Satya, Treta, Dvapara and Kali. Each of these *yugas* consists of a certain dharma that is replenished at the end of the Kali *yuga*. The entire cycle – consisting of the four *yuga* – is called Mahayuga. At the beginning of every Mahayuga, it is the task of Manu (law giver) and the Seven Rsis (ascetics and mystics) to instruct humans in the Vedas and to renew dharma (Mitchiner 1982: 48).

[22] In Rongmei narrative *Mun-shoi* is a ritual associated with a powerful regulator, Tingpu Rengsonnang, between the gods and humans; he was also known as the divine patriarch (Kamei 2004: 25).

[23] In fact the Heraka have two versions of generation narrative. The other is the official one written in the Hingde Book (Newme 1991). For this chapter and for my present argument, the present narrative will suffice because it deals specifically with the question of Heraka Hingde.

[24] The notebooks are housed in Pitt Rivers Museum, Oxford (1928.69.1570.14). Writings of similar kind were also exhibited by Pau Hau Chin during his movement in the Chin Hills during the 1930s (Bennison 1933).

[25] I am not arguing for a strict dichotomy between the two. In some cases, even the Heraka who can read choose to ignore the Hingde Book. For example, in a funeral I attended in Hsongle village, the entire scene was consciously infused with Paupaise elements, due to the social susceptibility that the older members of the community had towards what they saw as 'old custom' (Paupaise custom). They chose to ignore the funeral procedures outlined in the Hingde Book.

[26] This story was collected from Haimiabuing Nriame, a Heraka from Hsongle village. Parts of it have been incorporated from Ursula Graham Bower's collection from the Centre of South Asian Studies, Cambridge (Box II file 2), Accessed: 14 Sept. 2007: http://bamdemo.lemurconsulting.com/bamdemo/db/naga/doc/1119226709_00000?hit=3&q_=ginger+spittle

[27] This story is common with both the Heraka and Paupaise. What the Heraka have done with it is to make Chuprai the conspirator and blame him for their troubles.

[28] From Tingwang Hingde (Newme 1991: 10–11). Tahulung Nriame aided in the translation of the text from Zeme.

[29] These are girls especially chosen to serve the Heraka community. They must be young virgins and model citizens in the village. They usually serve the *zao* (rice beer) after the *Kelumki* service, help in the Paiki (house of the leader of a Heraka village) when there are guests, and are also designated to pray when someone is sick, for instance.

30 This dualism of the sacred/profane associated with the right/left hand is the central thesis of Robert Hertz (1960). The Durkheimian understanding of the sacred/profane is underpinned by Hertz' study of this dualism as 'religious polarity'. He says that with 'the right hand go honours, flattering designations, prerogatives: it acts, orders, and *takes*. The left hand, on the contrary, is despised and reduced to the role of a humble auxiliary: but itself it can do nothing; it helps, it supports, it *holds*' (1960: 89). For other works on the right/left hand see Beidelman (1973), Needham (1973), and the use of right and left in 'Hindu' rituals see Das (1977).

31 On one level, the view is that the Kelumki is a miniscule representation of the social structure of Zeme society. The placing of the sexes in dualist perspective, female on the left and male on the right, re-enacts a social construct. However, in the ritual context, there seems to be an intermingling of categories, whereby both male and female have access to the altar space, but privileging the right over the left. It is not that Tingwang can reward only males, because both male and female, at a general level, undergo life-death-life which is accorded importance to all Zeme Heraka. These categories themselves, though highly representational on the social level, remain fluid in a ritual context.

32 The *hezoa* is a mound of earth necessary to every Paupaise village. It was considered 'sacred' only during ritual. It was being used as a jumping pit, in everyday life, whenever a ritual was not taking place, therefore emphasizing the 'sacred' as all encompassing yet fluctuating, rather than permanent and 'fixed' in a particular place as in the Heraka Kelumki.

33 Asad's discussion on the *shari'a* and its embodiment by the subject as habitus, is an interesting way of locating the discussion of 'law' and 'action'; both interrelated in the context of the community (2003: 205–56). A similar point can be drawn for the Heraka.

34 During Paupaise, premarital sex was accepted and even to some extent glorified. But at the same time, marriage was monogamous and taken with outmost seriousness.

35 The word 'secular' and its association with modernity is a difficult word to translate in Zeme society because of the relative isolation of most Zeme villages. Electricity, for example, has not yet arrived in most villages; nor are there roads. Only recently have gas cylinders penetrated the Zeme household; albeit affordable only by a few. With the advent of electricity and with it television, the landscape will definitely alter. This is yet to be assessed.

Chapter 5: Negotiating Boundaries

1 The headquarters later shifted to Gunjung and then to Haflong (Kamei 2004: 73).

2 L/P&S/13/1004. Usually in local customs, all have to contribute, and to opt out as the Christians did would have caused problems (see Chapter 4).

3 L/P&S/13/1004.

4 Baite people are of the same ethnic group as the Lushai of Mizoram in the state of India.

[5] The Welsh Presbyterians were primarily operating from the Lushai Hills (present Mizoram) in 1891 (Dena 1988: 41–6).

[6] According to Rabi Pame (1996: 219), the Heraka population is almost 70 per cent in North Cachar Hills making it one of the largest non-Christian areas in the Naga Hills. The focus of Zeme Christian missionaries is to evangelize and help convert the Zeme Heraka and bring them back into the 'Naga fold'. There is scarce information regarding the spread of Christian missions among the Zeme Nagas of North Cachar Hills. For accounts of Christianity in Zeme villages, I have relied on Rabi Pame's thesis (1996).

[7] Zeme Baptists on several occasions said that being 'Naga' was being 'Baptist'. The conflict between the Presbyterians and the Baptists reared its ugly head in May 2005 when the Presbyterians and Heraka refused to allow the Baptists to build a church in Lodiram, a Zeme village outside Haflong. The reason (although not the only one) was that traditionally Lodiram had only two worship places: the Presbyterian Church and the Heraka Kelumki (prayer house). The Baptists were also accused of using 'underground factions' to enforce their agenda. This upset many villagers.

[8] Headhunting was a central part of Naga culture. The capture of a head, it was believed, was essential for maintaining the fertility of the crops and social order. The ban on headhunting by Christian missionaries was also important for attracting Nagas. Some Nagas joined Christian villages for protection as a way of escaping punishment or attack from a larger and more powerful village (see also Jacobs et al. 1998: 171–6).

[9] On one occasion, a Heraka family converted to the Presbyterian Church. But the husband's father-in-law wanted them to become Baptists. An internal problem thus ensued between the two families. To avoid further grievances, the family reconverted to Heraka.

[10] Durkheim makes an interesting point regarding the use of intoxicants as stimulants for religious inspiration for prophets, founders of religions, great saints (1995: 228).

[11] P/11892: 64.

[12] Here primarily referring to the Presbyterians and the Baptists, as the Roman Catholics are still a small community and sometimes their excessive use of *zao* is compared to that of the Heraka, with the same issues arising. The issue of public control of *zao* is also vital in this regard, and it is this which differentiates the Christians from the Heraka. The notion the preacher is emphasizing here is that the public drinking of *zao* can be very expensive; the buying and making of it is also very time consuming. To engage with development and education, these activities, according to the preacher, must be curtailed and controlled. Since the Christians are less engaged in the production of *zao* for public occasions, they incur less expense.

[13] The first documented European contact with the Nagas was not until 1832 when Captains Jenkins and Pemberton crossed with the Manipuri Durbar from Manipur to the Assam Valley via Angami Naga territory. Lieutenant Gordon conducted the next expedition in 1833 into the Angami hills. While these expeditions were going on, the British had annexed the Cachar region in August 1832. This provided a proper base from which to enter into the Angami Naga regions (Moffatt Mills 1969: 114–15; Mackenzie 1969: 147–9).

14 Another observer, H. B. Rowney, in 'The Wild Tribes of India' uses this description for the Nagas: 'The word "Naga" means a serpent, but it is not pretended that the Nagas are of serpent or Scythic descent. The name was more probably given to them originally as being best expressive of their character, for of all wild tribes they are held to be the most subtle and treacherous' (1969: 98). Most of the names for the Nagas are not indigenous but derived from how their neighbours addressed them. For instance, Konyak is derived from the neighbouring Chang word for man, likewise Ao, was referred to the people that went ahead.

15 This is obscured by the use of language: it could also indicate an unoccupied place, not inhabited by anybody (Hutton 1965: 17). McCrindle (2000: 223) in his collection of essays by Ptolemy, similarly links the present Nagas as the 'Nangas' recorded by Ptolemy.

16 The classification of people into bounded subjects has been criticized by Edmund Leach as well. He questions the role of ethnographers/administrators (such as Hutton, Mills and Parry) who separated groups due to the different language they spoke, although they were geographically adjacent. Leach says such differentiations based on languages isolated the Nagas into bounded groups and portrayed them as not 'interacting in any institutional sense', in a misleading way (Leach 1977: 291).

17 Hindutva is used not in the sense of 'Hinduism' but as a contemporary construction of 'communal forces', such as the RSS and VHP, that use this banner (Basu et al. 1993: 1).

18 www.rss.org: http://www.rss.org/New_RSS/History/Evolution.jsp. Accessed 26 Apr. 2007.

19 Also known as the World Hindu Council. Its aim is to strengthen 'Hindu' society by uniting 'Hindu' groups around the world.

20 The use of Ram/Sita is a major RSS and VHP project. The RSS and VHP see Ram as the hero and epitome of Hinduness. Dr Hedgewar (the founder of the RSS) deliberately chose Vijaya Dashami for its inauguration. It is believed that on this day Ram defeated Ravana in the epic battle between good and evil as found in the epic Ramayana. The symbol of Ram, for the RSS and VHP, has itself taken epic proportions. It is carefully manufactured to depict a certain message and variously depicts Ram as the warrior, Ram as the king, and so on (see Basu et al. 1993: 12, 62–4). These posters of Ram are commonly found in many Heraka homes as well. For a detailed analysis of the debate on Ayodhya as the supposed birthplace of Ram (known as Ramjanmabhumi) and the Babri Masjid, see Thapar (1993), Ludden (2006: 1–23).

21 This is an *emic* (insider) view of Hinduism; according to this view Hinduism is synonymous with 'sanatan (eternal) dharma'.

22 This term was translated locally to me by an RSS worker as follows: sanatan (eternal) and dharma (natural law). He implied that this is something universal and all embracing.

23 Janjati is a problematic term: it was translated to me by an RSS worker, as meaning jungle dweller, same as *vanvasi.* However, *jana* (people or tribe) and *jati* (caste) have meanings of their own (and could have no relation with janjati in the sense of jungle dweller). For a treatise on this subject see K. S. Singh's chapter Varna, Jati and Jana (1985: 70–86) and also Hardiman (1987: 16).

24 Literally meaning 'All India Tribal Development Society'. They are a part of the RSS organization. Their aim is to help 'tribals' with development, while at the same time helping them understand the notion of Bharat.

25 This is an interesting translation. Usually, the word 'Bharat Mata' means 'Mother India', but in this case it was translated to me as 'mother land' probably to give some sense of ownership to the *vanvasi,* as in one's own 'mother land'. This could also be a deliberate translation, in this context an attempt to avoid the 'India' concept altogether with 'tribes' in the northeast. The latter often have a negative view of 'India' as a state, in relation to the 'tribal' areas.

26 Ramaswamy (2001: 98) has shown how maps of India, especially those that depict 'Mother India' (Bharat Mata) attempt to reconceive a nation that is 'gendered'. This brings about a nationalistic and patriotic urge centred on the 'Goddess' (Bharat Mata). He calls this a 'strategy of spatializing'.

27 www.stephen-knapp.com/my_northeast_india_mission_.htm. Accessed 17 May 2006. Kamei refutes this association by saying that it could be a case of mistaken identity. He says that 'The Naga of the Sanskrit literature may be identified with the Nagas, who in their climax of glory came to rule in Northern India after the fall of the great Kushanas before the rise of the imperial Guptas in Northern India' (2002b: 11). Of course, people like Koenraad Elst and David Frawley, who similarly espouse a revisionist reading of Hinduism and Hindu identity, reiterate the view of Stephen Knapp. See also Elst's book, *Who is a Hindu?* (http://koenraadelst.voiceofdharma.com/books/wiah/index.htm). Accessed 17 May 2006.

28 The Heraka believe that this script is written in God language and is highly coded. Some fragments of the script are in circulation and the original notebook written in the script, is housed in Pitt Rivers Museum. J. P. Mills confiscated the notebook in 1932 after Gaidinliu was captured.

29 He said it is a form of ancient Hinduism, probably meaning 'tradition'. My understanding is that *parampara* usually refers to a long chain of *Gurus* (teachers) and *shishyas* (disciples) through which knowledge is passed down over generations. In this context, Rani Gaidinliu is seen as the Guru and her *shishyas* as those who pass on that knowledge to the general populace and so on until it becomes routine.

30 This ambiguity is interesting, though it is difficult to tell what he means by it.

31 This is an observation by Stephen Knapp of a Christmas party in Nagaland: www.stephen-knapp.com/my_northeast_india_mission_.htm. Accessed 17 May 2006.

32 Asad defines agency as that which 'operates through a particular network of concepts within which the historical possibilities and limits of responsibility are defined' (1996: 271).

33 I was told, on one occasion, the NSCN-IM commander of a region convened a meeting in one of the villages and ordered the village elders not to interfere with the missionizing of Heraka children.

34 The five-decade Naga war could be one of the longest running wars in the world (see Baruah 2003: 321 note 1).

35 Under the 1997 ceasefire with the NSCN-IM, the territory of the ceasefire was deliberately made vague by the GOI due to the sensitivities of other states with which the Naga inhabited areas overlap. On 14 June 2001, a clarification was sought by the NSCN-IM and a joint statement was issued that said the ceasefire

was between the GOI and the NSCN-IM 'without territorial limits'. This immediately caused an uproar in the neighbouring states, but was felt particularly strongly in Manipur where agitations and civil unrest resulted in the GOI revising their previous statement and dropping 'without territorial limits' altogether on 27 July 2001 (see also Baruah 2003: 323, 334).

36 My aim is to briefly recount the events and not go into too much detail. For detailed accounts of the Naga movements see Maxwell 1973, Chasie 1999; Nibedon 2000; Steyn 2002; Parratt 2005.

37 For detailed accounts on the meetings see Maxwell (1973: 8); Steyn (2002: 71). Nehru's idea of a strong nation state can be found in *The Discovery of India* (1947: 453).

38 Under the 9 Point Agreement it was agreed that the Governor of Assam would act as a special agent between the GOI and the 'Nagas' for a period of ten years, after which the NNC would take a decision regarding the future of the Nagas. The 16 Point Agreement basically centres around the formation of the Nagaland state in two areas. The 'Naga Tribal Area' (known as Tuensang area) which was under NEFA merged with the Naga Hills District to form the Naga Hills Tuensang Area (NHTA) in 1957. The NHTA was renamed Nagaland in 1961 before being inaugurated into statehood. Though rejected at that time, this agreement has been heralded recently as an achievement for 'Naga identity' and the recognition of the Nagas in the state of Nagaland. This is based on a very controversial report titled the 'Bed Rock of Naga Society' by the Nagaland Pradesh Congress Committee (I) in 2002.

39 www.nscnonline.org. Accessed Jan. 2007.

40 Isak Swu, the Chairman of the NSCN-IM, in a recent statement to the press, highlighted the various supporting organizations such as Unrepresented Nations and People's Organization (UNPO), International Peace Council for States, Peoples and Minorities (Kreddha) and the Naga International Support Centre (NISC) in the Netherlands, Parliamentarians for National Self Determination (PNSD) in the United Kingdom, Support Group of Indigenous Peoples (KWIA) in Belgium, International Work Group on Indigenous Affairs (IWGIA) in Denmark, Forum Asia in Thailand, Society for Threatened People in Germany, Naga American Council (NAC) in the United States, Naga People's Friendship Network for Korea (NPFNK) in South Korea (*The Morung Express*, Dimapur, 14 August 2006). In fact the Naga American Council (NAC) has a *Goodwill Mission Team Report: Unofficial White Paper Report of the Fact Finding Mission to Nagalim (16–25 May 2005)*. It can be accessed through their website: www.freenagalim.org (or http://freenagalim.org/index.php?option=com_content&task=view&id=85&Itemid=41). They sanction the NSCN-IM as the legitimate voice of the Naga people (Goodwill Mission 2006: 1–4). Accessed 24 Sept. 2007.

41 These estimates vary. Some sources say that 95 per cent of the Nagas are Christian (Nuh 2006: 224).

42 Many portrayals of Ranima are as a freedom fighter for India: in fact, she is glorified and used by the Heraka, the Zeliangrong people and also the Nagas to legitimize their cause. She even agreed to have her image used to represent the Nagaland state at the national level (Kamei 2004: 228). In a recent article by Nakaulang Nriame, her exploits for the nation are summed up with the

title: 'Rani Gaidinliu: A unique freedom fighter of India' (*The Sentinel*, Guwahati, 30 May 2004).

43 *Prospectus*, Saraswati Vidya Mandir, Laisong (2004).

44 When the speech of the President of the Heraka Organisation at the annual Heraka gathering in Peren, Nagaland, February 2005 was quoted by the press, there was a huge response condemning the remark N. C. Zeliang made concerning Christian conversion. He criticized Christian missionaries for undermining tribal culture to 'save' and 'civilize' them from 'satanic' clutches. While some of this diatribe could be accurate, the President of the Sumi Baptist Churches Convention's response was far-fetched, and clearly made with the intention to incite nationalistic sentiment. He said: 'Lastly, it appears that you are very closely associated with the people from Kalyan Ashram, Dimapur and Vidya Bharti from Gujarat. For the sake of intellectual appetite, kindly clarify the difference between your Heraka religion and Hinduism. I hope your feathers are still true with the Nagas and not coloured with Hinduism' (Post Mortem section, *Nagaland Post*, 14 February 2005).

45 The association of VHP and Kalyan Ashram with literacy and education is reflected in a vast network of schools and colleges. Annually, many Heraka students are sent to these schools on scholarships. Schools and colleges based in Chhattisgarh, Uttaranchal, Haryana and Maharastra are common destinations for these students, who, along with their studies are also fed right-wing Hindu ideology. But overall, the education has been beneficial for students except when it comes to religious education; they are told to follow the system of religion (Hinduism) practised in the schools. For insight on how such schools are run by the RSS, see also Hansen (1999: 104–7). For a helpful picture on the role of literacy and conversion, see Viswanathan (2002: 190–208). She primarily examines the role of Christian missions in development.

46 J. P. Rajkhowa, 'Protect and Project Indigenous Culture', *The Sentinel*, Guwahati, 21 Jan. 07.

47 See for example, the RSS and VHP websites, *The Voice of Dharma*, the RSS magazine Organizer, and Stephen Knapp's web (www.stephen-knapp.com); an RSS worker in Dimapur encouraged me to seek out his website and any literature by him, as his articulate vision might appeal to me. Another high profile visit made to the Northeast India and Nagaland during my fieldwork in February of 2005 was Fred Stella, an American scholar. He severely criticized conversion to Christianity as the most dangerous element that threatens 'indigenous culture'.

48 The use of generations explaining a particular practice, which is similar to the Yuga (ages), is explained in Chapter 4. The Heraka view themselves as the fourth generation in this cycle.

Chapter 6: Community Imaginings and the Ideal of Heguangram

1 The notion of kingship, with regard to millennial movements, is evident in Southeast Asia (Scott 1985: 333). Such instances are recorded in Java, for example, where we have the image of the king (*ratu adil*) who will restore justice

(Kartodirdjo 1978) or the image of a just king (*Setkya min*) in Burma who coexists with the Buddha-Deliverer (*Buddha yaza*) (Sarkisyanz 1965).

2 L/PS/13/1002: Folios 641–3.

3 MS 95022 Higgins Collection (SOAS), 15: 11–18.

4 L/PS/13/1002: Folios 534–44.

5 L/PS/13/1002: Folios 534–44.

6 For Nehru's full article see L/PS/13/1002: Folios 483–4.

7 See Jan Vansina (1985) work on oral tradition as history and Elizabeth Tonkin (1995) on the social construction of oral history for alternative ways to situate this dialogue.

8 The author who interviewed an elderly Gaidinliu for a period of time before writing her biography told me that the typed text was his own copy and the only other copy he possesses is a handwritten one. Therefore, it is highly unlikely that the Heraka public would possess the text in Zeme.

9 For similar correlatives, see Dube (1999: 121–58); Juan M. Ossio (1977), regarding the use of text and myth.

10 Here, I am reminded of Rosaldo's argument that the denial of the line of succession for males is much more difficult than it is for females. For women 'the threat of formal exclusion probably appears more like another dose of everyday life than a form of intimidation.' For men, however, disinheritance from the line of succession is akin to banishment, wandering 'forever in the wilderness'. This notion, for Rosaldo, is the productive entry point for a critique of patriarchy from a male position (1993).

11 I would like to thank Adeule Nriame and P. C. Modi for help in the Zeme original and Hindi translation respectively. I have used no pagination in the body of the chapter when referring to the text. For academic purposes, I have included the Hindi version in the Bibliography.

12 Kamei is vague about what he means by this. He translates *Gwangdi* as kingdom and *Makam* as Zeliangrong or Nagas (2004: 150).

13 For further details on the importance of the python see Bower (1952: 127–30). There is another story of Benperiuria (magic rope) that will aid the Heraka in crisis and tie their enemies down. It is said that some people are entrusted with this secret and kept in Hangrum camp.

14 'Heguang' in quotes is different from the ideal (italicized) *heguang*. The 'heguang' referred to here is self-proclaimed, but his status is contested to say the least. This is discussed in detail when I talk about the king's court.

15 Here I refer to socially defined positions of gender (see also Rosaldo 1993: 81).

16 There is a level of give and take in this exchange: for Ranima, a woman, to be seen as a leader, there must be a level of adherence to social conventions and roles. Abu-Lughod (1990) makes a similar argument regarding creative resistance among Bedouin women.

17 The symbol of eight is popular in the story of Asa and Munserung. Asa and Munserung fall out and to escape from his friend, Asa hides in the Barak River by making eight different lines of current in the river for his protection (Miri 1991: 61–3). It is, however, difficult to say why the world has eight corners.

18 Lila Abu-Lughod similarly questions the use of the word resistance as it fails to examine power. She takes Foucault's argument 'where there is power, there is resistance' and looks for a way to understand resistance as a 'diagnostic of power'

or forms of power one is up against. Instead, what is important is the creative manifestations of resistance in everyday life that do not necessarily reject but support the existing system of power (1990: 42, 47). One could draw parallels with Ranima and the Heraka from the latter point.

19 The link between Ranima and Mother Goddess (instead of just Goddess in the Zeme version) predominates in the Hindi version. This, one can suggest, is due to the strong RSS and VHP base it is writing for.

20 I am aware of Hocart's evolutionary bias, but I have stuck with this definition because, as I will show, this is the intended goal of the Heraka. Their rituals are preserved in Hangrum to represent a kingdom characterized by such processes as life giving rather than life denying. For a different view on this see Maurice Bloch who says that 'rituals vary but the basic point is the same: the cultivation of the hatred of life for the sake of authority' (quoted in Kelly and Kaplan 1990: 125; Bloch 1986: 175).

21 Taken from E. E. Evans-Pritchard's introduction to *Kings and Councillors* (1970: x).

22 Unless I have done so, the songs and their titles are untranslatable. The songs themselves are written in several languages such as Zeme, English, Hindi, Bengali; it signifies the worlds they are trying to encompass.

23 The use of the word 'prophet' here is important because that's what I heard people refer to him as, prior to my coming to Hangrum. That was also one of the reasons why he was a little edgy with me: that I called him a prophet and not a 'heguang' as he wanted to be called.

24 These change according to the generation. See Chapter 4 for a thorough discussion.

25 Hemui is translated as sin in the Christian context.

Chapter 7: Conclusion

1 Post Mortem section, *Nagaland Post*, 14 February 2005.

Glossary

Unless stated, all the words are from Zeme. It must also be noted that most of the words are Sanskrit derived and common to Hindi, Assamese and Bengali among other languages. Therefore, the classification 'Sanskrit' can also be read as 'Sanskrit derived'.

Aarti (Sanskrit): Prayer.

Abori (Assamese): Untamed. Used initially by the British as a classification of 'naked Nagas' in the early nineteenth century.

Acharya (Sanskrit): A prominent guru or great teacher.

Adivasi (Sanskrit): Original inhabitant. A term used commonly for central Indian tribes and not in usage with the Northeastern tribes of India.

Almirah: Wardrobe.

Banglawang (Rongmei): Underground god. He is also viewed as the creator before voluntary exile underground. He is becoming more popular for the Zeme Heraka.

Bharat (Hindi): India.

Bhuban (also Bhuvan in Sanskrit): World, universe or seven heavens and seven hells.

Bori (Assamese): Tame. Used initially by the British as a classification of 'clothed Nagas', due to the kilt they wore.

Buibak riata: A brass braclet worn by men and women.

Chillums (Hindi): Smoking pipes.

Chuprai: God of grain. He is considered a very important god along with Tingwang for some Zeme Heraka especially in the western parts of North Cachar Hills.

Dao (Chinese): A sharp blade with a wooden handle, also known as a hacking knife.

Dharma (Sanskrit): Used as an equivalent for religion; it is often used in conjunction with Sanatan Dharma, translated as 'eternal religion' or 'eternal faith and culture'.

Duizao: Rice beer that uses the bark of a tree as external fermenting agent.

Ganja (Hindi): Cannabis.

Gennas: Usually a rite carrying certain prohibitions. From the Angami *kenna.*

Guru (Sanskrit): Teacher.

Hangrum: A sacred place for the Heraka. Known for the Hangrum war of 1932 as the starting-place of Heraka *heguangram* (free community). It is believed that the next *heguang* (agent of the free community) will come from Hangrum. Currently, there is a self-proclaimed 'heguang' taking care of the Rani Gaidinliu Inspiration Home, where Rani Gaidinliu lived in for many years.

Hangseoki: Male dormitory; also 'young men's house'. In Paupaise the Hangseoki was a centre of village organization, structure and protection. Now, it is used primarily as a meeting centre and used in special occasions.

Hangseoki kazeipeu: Warden of the young men's house (Hangseoki).

Haomei: It means 'ourselves', which was apparently preferred over the category Zeliangrong (see below) by Rani Gaidinliu to refer to the Zeme, Liangmai and the Rongmei and other 'Naga' communities such as the Maram, Mpumei, Kourang, Wainem and Toite.

Hechaiki: Market-place/town.

Hechit Siabe: Unlucky or impure death.

Hedachakpe: Communicating through God.

Heduara: A feast usually given by the one who receives the largest grain in that yearly cycle.

Hegangi: End-of-year festival.

Hegi: Curry.

Hegia kanchibe: Holy marriage.

Heguang: Freedom or king. Often the two are used for the same effect.

Heguangram: Free community or kingdom.

Helauraube: Act of selflessness.

Heleomi gi kalang: Skeins of cotton thread given by the girl to the man when he becomes a *katsingmi* (elder) to prove his sexual liaisons.

Heliengi: Harvest festival.

Heling: Three pieces of wood tied together for animal sacrifices. The image is used by the Christians as well to signify Jesus' sacrifice on the cross.

Hepumra: New year festival.

Herakandingpeu: Ancestral folk hero and a renown healer who cured without any sacrifices. He was killed by Chuprai and other smaller gods so that humans had to sacrifice again to these bloodthirsty gods.

Herakapeu: Male shaman (Paupaise rather than Heraka).

Herakapui: Female shaman (Paupaise rather than Heraka).

Heramrai: Physical boundaries, used in demarcating the boundaries between paddy fields or between villages. Nowadays, the meaning has been extended to mean symbolic boundaries as well, between, say, Christians and Heraka.

Heramui: God month.

Herateube: Divination.

Heruimeram: Soul village.

Hezoa: A pit in the centre of the village, usually called the heart of the village.

Hiangbutchi: A sour fruit.

Hingde: Rules governing everyday life. Also used as Law/commandment. According to the context, these meanings can vary.

Ishvar (Sanskrit): Lord.

Jalua: Full moon day.

Jana (Sanskrit): Tribe.

Jati (Sanskrit): Caste.

Jemena (also Zemena): People.

Jhum (Assamese?): Cutting, burning and planting of seeds for agriculture. This is also referred to as slash and burn or swidden cultivation.

Kabui Naga (unknown): Usually referred to the Rongmei in the state of Manipur.

Kacha Naga (unknown): Usually referred to the Zeme; it was also used collectively to indicate the Zeme, Liangmai and the Rongmei. This is a term no longer in use as it is viewed pejoratively.

Kakejakpe: Striking the air horizontally with a *dao.* This expression is used primarily during the funeral.

Kalyan Ashram (Hindi): Welfare organization. They are a support unit of the RSS and work with the Zeme Heraka and other tribals in the state. They have similar RSS ideologies.

Kambiron: Kambiron is the birthplace of Rani Gaidinliu and Jadonang. It is situated in the present state of Manipur, in Tamenglong district.

Kancha be: Light.

Kangsipeu: Chaperone.

Kantiabe: Reform.

Karchi be: New.

Katsingmi: Male elder.

Kedeipeu (also kadepeo): Landowner.

Kelua: Village.

Kelumki: Prayer house.

Kelumse: The name of one of the stages of Heraka reform, referring to the way they prayed with folded hands.

Kemeume: Prophecy.

Keringbe-kechaibe-keringbe: Used together to mean life-death-life.

Kha: A basket for men which sits at the back with a belt diagonally attached; usually a dao and tobacco are carried in this kha.

Khampai: Another name for the Heraka primarily in Nagaland as those who have missed the mark, referring to their false message.

Ki: House.

Kienga: Peers who lived together in the Hangseoki or people of the same age group.

Kuak: Book.

Leseoki: Female dormitory.

Makuilongdi: The supposed ancestral home for the Zeme, Liangmai and Rongmei, who are together known as Zeliangrong (see below).

Mandir (Sanskrit): Temple.

Meitei: Referring primarily to the valley population of Manipur in contrast to the hill population of the Nagas and Kukis.

Mela: From the Sanskrit, an assembly.

Mikise: Mi (my), ki (house), se (practice/rules).

Mirase: Mi (my), ra (god), se (practice/rules).

Mithun (Assamese): Semi-wild bison, Bos Frontalis.

Mitulung: Mi (my), tulung (nature). Also used as action.

Naimik kakelum: Sunrise prayer.

Naka (Burmese): Pierced ear.

Nchichiak: Pure.

Neube: forbidden; used interchangeably with genna.

Nkiadang: A special stick used to kill smaller animals.

Nkita: A brass braclet worn by men and women.
Noka (Assamese): Hillman.
Nrei: Observance, the period of ritual where neube is observed.
Nruipiateime: Elders of the kienga.
Nsung: Laundry basket.
Paiki: The house of the Paipeu.
Paileu Baudi: Women's organization.
Paimang: Black body cloth.
Paingum: White body cloth.
Paipeu: The head of a Heraka village. He is usually the wealthiest in the village. The origin of the Paipeu came about when Rani Gaidinliu used cloths (*pai*) to make a prayer tent when communicating with Tingwang; *peu* is used for someone who is an elder.
Paithik: A dark blue cloth worn by old men.
Parampara: Referred to a lineage of teachers and disciples.
Pau Pai Chen (Liangmai): Traditional practice, similar to Paupaise in practice.
Paupaise: Pau (grandfather), pai (grandmother), se (practice). Here used as traditional practice and ancestral practice interchangeably.
Pedui: A small group.
Perie be: Old.
Poupei Chapriak (Rongmei): A form of Rongmei neo-traditional practice. Poupei meaning ancestral while Chap means godly nature and riak means existence of the soul and mind. They hold Jadonang to be their first reformer and revere him as such. In some sense, for the Heraka they fall under the category Paupaise due to its semantic similarities. In Liangmai they are known as Paupai Chen, denoting a similar meaning.
Puja (Sanskrit): A form of reverence or worship.
Pujari (Sanskrit): One who officiates in pujas, here it is also used as priest.
Pukpet: Sowing festival.
Purnima (Sanskrit): Full moon.
Ranise: Referring to the first stage of the Heraka reform. Still practised by some Zeme in west North Cachar Hills.
Rashtriya Swayamsevak Sangh (RSS) (Hindi): Known by its abbreviation RSS, they are the 'National Volunteer's Association' whose ideology is that of cultural nationalism in espousing for the preservation of the spiritual and moral traditions of India. Closely aligned with VHP, Kalyan Ashram in working with the Zeme Heraka.
Rehoi: A chant used in special ritual occasions.
Rit pe: Heavy.
Sadhu (Sanskrit): Holy man.
Sanatan (Sanskrit): Eternal.
Sanatan dharma (Sanskrit): Here used as 'eternal culture' or 'eternal faith and culture'.
Shishya (also sisya) (Sanskrit): Usually meaning student or disciple, used in connection with guru (teacher).
Talau ndui: Holy water, water collected from Bhuban cave.
Tela tau: An important necklace made with conch shells worn by married women.
Telung ndui: Cultural meeting.

Tesata: A brass bracelet.
Tesuangkanpetbe: Giving to god.
Tingchura: God of stone.
Tingkao Ragwang (Rongmei): Supreme God.
Tingkopau: Priest.
Tingna: Period of ritual.
Tingwang: God of the sky.
Trishul (Sanskrit): Trident. Literally meaning 'three-spear' and usually associated with the Lord Shiva.
Tsami: Extended patrilineal family.
Vanvasi (Sanskrit): Jungle dweller. A common term used by the RSS and VHP when referring to the Zeme.
Vishva Hindu Parishad (VHP) (Hindi): Translated as World Hindu Council. They operate under the slogan 'Dharma protects those who protect Dharma'. Their attempts to integrate the Zeme Heraka with the larger 'Hindu' nation is done by providing them with organizational support primarily in education. Works closely with the RSS and Kalyan Ashram.
Yatra: Pilgrimage.
Zailad: A lake in the state of Manipur. It is known for its mysterious qualities and it is also a pilgrimage site for some Heraka people. It is believed that Hechawang (python god) resides in Zailad and keeps the magical weapons for the *heguangram*.
Zao (also Jau): Rice beer.
Zeliangrong: Zeliangrong was coined in 1947, and that it is a combination of the three prefixes of these 'tribes': Zeme, Liangme and Rongme (Ze-liang-rong). Gangmumei Kamei, the Rongmei historian, says,

> Though chronologically the name was coined in 1947, a faint notion of their common ancestry was contained in their legends and the idea of inter-tribal solidarity and unity was implanted by Jadonang and Gaidinliu during their uprisings (1930–32). (1982: 53)

Zeme: Also spelt Jeme, Nzemi, Zemi, Zemei comes from the word *zemena* (human).
Zemena: To be Zemena is to be human, the Paupaise say.
Zemese: Zeme practice.

Bibliography

Archive

British Library, London

Political and Secret Department: L/PS/13/1002. British Library, Asia, Pacific and Africa Collections, India Office Records.
Proceedings Series: P/11892. British Library, Asia, Pacific and Africa Collections, India Office Records.

Pitt Rivers Museum Archive, Oxford

Betts, Ursula Graham. Mrs U. V. G. Betts' Manuscripts: 7.23 (Mr J. P. Mills' Tour Diary for March, 1927).
Hutton, J. H. Hutton Ms. Box 2.
Mills, J. P. Gaidiliu Notebooks. 1928.69.1570.14.

School of Oriental and African Studies, London

Higgins, J. C. MS 95022 Higgins Manuscript Collection on the Manipur State, India, Library, School of Oriental and African Studies (SOAS), London.
Mills, J. P. PP MS 58/16, Library, School of Oriental and African Studies (SOAS), London.

Primary Sources (Pamphlets and Books)

Dharmaraj. 2004. *A Rousing Call from the Northeast.* Guwahati: Heritage Foundation.
Makuga, G. 1994. *Introduction to the Rongmei Nagas.* Imphal.
Newme, Pautanzan. 2002. 'The Origin and Reformation of Heraka Religion' in *Regional Zeliangrong Heraka Association, Assam: Silver Jubilee Celebrations 1977–2002 Souvenir.* Haflong: Regional Zeliangrong Heraka Association.
Newme, Ramkui. 1990. *Rani Maa Gaidinliu.* New Delhi: Suruchi Prakashan.
—. 1991. *Tingwang Hingde* (in Zeme). Haflong: Regional Zeliangrong Heraka Association.
Saraswati Vidya Mandir. 2004. *Prospectus.* Laisong, North Cachar Hills.

Souvenir. 1999. *Silver Jubilee: Zeliangrong Heraka Association North-East India 1974–1999.* Publisher unknown.
—. 2003. *Naga Dawn: Silver Jubilee 1978–2003.* Dimapur: Zeliangrong Heraka Youth Organisation.
Zeliang, N. C. 1980. *The Word of God (Tingwang Hingde).* Dimapur.
—. 1998. *The Zeliangrong Heraka Preacher Handbook.* Nagaland: Zeliangrong Heraka Council.
Zeliang, Thunbui. 2005. *Haipou Jadonang (1905–1931).* Guwahati: Heritage Foundation.

General Bibliography

Abu-Lughod, Lila. 1990. 'The Romance of Resistance: Tracing Transformations of Power through Bedouin Women'. *American Ethnologist,* Vol. 17: 41–55.
Adas, Michael. 1974. *The Burma Delta: Economic Development and Social Change on an Asian Rice Frontier, 1852–1941.* Madison: University of Wisconsin Press.
—. [1979] 1987. *Prophets of Rebellion: Millenarian Protest Movements against the European Colonial Order.* Cambridge: Cambridge University Press.
Anderson, Benedict. 1991. *Imagined Communities: Reflections on the Origin and Spread of Nationalism.* London: Verso.
Andersson, Efraim. 1958. *Messianic Popular Movements in the Lower Congo.* Uppsala: Studia Ethnographica Upsaliensia XIV.
Andreski, Stanislav (ed.). 1983. *Max Weber on Capitalism, Bureaucracy and Religion: A Selection of Texts.* London: George Allen & Unwin.
Anttonen, Veikko. 2000. 'Sacred', in McCutcheon, Russell T. and Willi Braun (eds). *Guide to the Study of Religion.* New York: Cassell.
Asad, Talal. 1993. *Genealogies of Religion: Discipline and Reasons of Power in Christianity and Islam.* Baltimore: Johns Hopkins University Press.
—. 1996. 'Comments on Conversion', in Peter van der Veer (ed.). *Conversion to Modernities: The Globalization of Christianity.* New York: Routledge.
—. 2003. *Formations of the Secular: Christianity, Islam, Modernity.* Stanford: Stanford University Press.
Balwally, Darshan. 2003. *Growth of Totalitarianism in Arunachal Pradesh, Mizoram and Nagaland.* Guwahati: Spectrum Publications.
Barker, John. 1993. '"We are Ekelesia": Conversion in Uiaku, Papua New Guinea', in Robert W. Hefner (ed.). *Conversion to Christianity: Historical and Anthropological Perspectives on a Great Transformation.* Berkeley: University of California Press.
Barth, Fredrik (ed.). 1969. *Ethnic Groups and Boundaries: The Social Organization of Culture Difference.* Bergen: Univertsitetsforlaget.
—. 2000. 'Boundaries and Connections', in Anthony P. Cohen (ed.). *Signifying Identities.* London: Routledge.
Barthes, Roland. 1977. *Image-Music-Text.* Essays selected and translated by Stephen Heath. Glasgow: Fontana/Collins.
—. 1993. *Mythologies.* Selected and translated from the French by Annette Lavers. London: Vintage.

Baruah, Sanjib. 2002. 'Gulliver's Troubles: State and Militants in North-East India'. *Economic and Political Weekly*. October 12.

—. 2003. 'Confronting Constructionism: Ending India's Naga War'. *Journal of Peace Research*, Vol. 40, No. 3 (May): 321–38.

Basu, Tapan, Pradip Datta, Sumit Sarkar, Tanika Sarkar and Sambuddha Sen. 1993. *Khaki Shorts, Saffron Flags: A Critique of the Hindu Right*. New Delhi: Orient Longman.

Beidelman, T. O. 1973. 'Kaguru Symbolic Classification', in R. Needham (ed.). *Right and Left: Essays in Dual Symbolic Classification*. Chicago: University of Chicago Press.

Benjamin, Walter. 1999. *Illuminations*. Edited and with an Introduction by Hannah Arendt, trans. Harry Zorn. London: Pimlico.

Bennison, J. J. 1933. 'Pau Chin Hau Script', in *Census of India 1931*. Part I, Chapter 10, 194–5. Delhi: Manager of Publications.

Beteille, Andre. 1998. 'The Idea of Indigenous People'. *Current Anthropology*, Vol. 39, No. 2: 187–91.

Bhadra, Gautam. 1975. 'The Kuki Uprising (1917–1919): Its Causes and Nature'. *Man in India*, Vol. 55, No. 1 (January–March): 10–56.

Bhuyan, A. C. 1978. *Political History of Assam Vol. 2*. Gauhati: Department for the Preparation of Political History of Assam, Government of Assam.

Blau, Joseph L. 1987. 'Reform', in Mircea Eliade (ed.). *The Encyclopedia of Religion: Volume 12*. New York: Macmillan, pp. 238–44.

Bloch, Maurice. 1986. *From Blessing to Violence: History and Ideology in the Circumcision Ritual of the Merina of Madagascar*. Cambridge, Cambridge University Press.

Boal, Barbara M. 1982. *The Konds Human Sacrifice and Religious Change*. Warminster: Aris & Phillips.

Bower, Ursula Graham. 1946. 'Cycle-Migration of the Zemi Nagas, North Cachar Hills, Assam'. *Man in India*, pp. 52.

—. 1952. *Naga Path*. London: Readers Union/John Murray.

Brara, Vijaylakshmi N. 1998. *Politics, Society, and Cosmology in India's North East*. New Delhi: Oxford University Press.

Brown, Judith. 2002. 'Introduction' in Judith M. Brown and Robert Eric Frykenberg (eds). *Christians, Cultural Interactions, and India's Religious Traditions*. Michigan/London: William B. Eerdmans and Routledge Curzon.

Brown, Judith M. and Robert Eric Frykenberg (eds). 2002. *Christians, Cultural Interactions, and India's Religious Traditions*. Michigan/London: William B. Eerdmans and Routledge Curzon.

Brown, Michael F. 1991. 'Beyond Resistance: A Comparative Study of Utopian Renewal in Amazonia'. *Ethnohistory*, Vol. 38, No. 4 (Autumn): 388–413.

Burlings, Robbins. 1963. *Rengsanggri: Family and Kinship in a Garo Village*. Philadelphia: University of Philadelphia.

Burridge, Kenelm. 1969. *New Heaven, New Earth: A Study of Millenarian Activities*. New York: Schocken Books.

—. 1985. 'Millennialims and the Recreation of History', in Bruce Lincoln (ed.). *Religion, Rebellion, Revolution: An Interdisciplinary and Cross-Cultural Collection of Essays*. Hamshire: Macmillan.

Census of India, 1931. 1933. Part I, Chapter 10, Para 120 and Chapter 11, Para 135, pp. 194–5, 217–18. Delhi: Manager of Publications.

Chasie, Charles. 1999. *The Naga Imbroglio: A Personal Perspective.* Kohima: Standard Printers & Publishers.

Chaube, S. K. 1999. *Hill Politics in Northeast India.* New Delhi: Orient Longman.

Chidester, David. 1996. *Savage Systems: Colonialism and Comparative Religion in Southern Africa.* Charlottesville: University Press of Virginia.

Clifford, James and George E. Marcus (eds). 1986. *Writing Culture: The Poetics and Politics of Ethnography.* Berkeley: University of California Press.

Cohen, Anthony P. 2003. *The Symbolic Construction of Community.* London: Routledge.

Cohen, Ronald. 1977. 'Oedipus Rex and Regina: The Queen Mother in Africa'. *Journal of the International African Institute,* Vol. 47, No. 1: 14–30.

Cohn, Norman. 1957. *The Pursuit of the Millennium: A History of Popular Religious and Social Movements in Europe from the Eleventh to the Sixteenth entury.* London: Secker & Warburg.

—. 1997. 'Medieval Millenarianism: Its Bearing on the Comparative Study of Millenarian Movements', in Charles B. Strozier and Michael Flynn (eds). *The Year 2000: Essays on the End.* New York: New York University Press.

—. 2001. *Cosmos, Chaos and the World to Come: The Ancient Roots of Apocalyptic Faith.* Second edition. New Haven: Yale University Press.

Collins English Dictionary. 2003. Sixth edition. Glasgow: Harper Collins.

Comaroff, Jean. 1985. *Body of Power, Spirit of Resistance: The Culture and History of a South African People.* Chicago: University of Chicago Press.

Comaroff, Jean and John. 1986. 'Christianity and Colonialism in South Africa'. *American Ethnologist,* Vol. 13, No. 1 (February): 1–22.

—. 1991. *Of Revelation and Revolution: Christianity, Colonialism, and Consciousness in South Africa, Volume 1.* Chicago: University of Chicago Press.

Cornille, Catherine (ed.). 2002. *Many Mansions?: Multiple Religious Belonging and Christian Identity.* New York: Orbis Books.

Daniel, Valentine E. 1984. *Fluid Signs: Being a Person the Tamil Way.* Berkeley: University of California Press.

Das, Veena. 1977. 'On the Categorization of Space in Hindu Ritual', in Ravindra K. Jain (ed.). *Text and Context: The Social Anthropology of Tradition.* Philadelphia: Institute for the Study of Human Issues.

De Certeau, Michel. 1984. *The Practice of Everyday Life.* Berkeley: University of California Press.

Dena, Lal. 1988. *Christian Missions and Colonialism: A Study of Missionary Movement in Northeast India with Particular Reference to Manipur and Lushai Hills 1894–1947.* Shillong: Vendrame Institute.

Derrida, Jacques. 1982. *Margins of Philosophy.* Translated with additional notes by Alan Bass. Brighton: Harvester Press.

Dev, S. C. 1988. *Nagaland: The Untold Story.* Calcutta: Mrs Gouri Dev, Regent Estate.

Diacon, Todd A. 2002. *Millenarian Vision, Capitalist Reality: Brazil's Contestado Rebellion, 1912–1916.* Durham: Duke University Press.

Douglas, Mary. 2003. *Purity and Danger: An Analysis of Concepts of Pollution and Taboo.* London: Routledge.

Downs, F. S. 1983. *Christianity in North East India: Historical Perspectives.* Delhi: ISPCK.

Dube, Saurabh. 1999. 'Myths, Symbols and Community: Satnampanth of Chhattisgarh', in Partha Chatterjee and Gyanendra Pandey (eds). *Subaltern Studies VII: Writings on South Asian History and Society.* New Delhi: Oxford University Press.

Dumont, Louis. 1971. 'Religion, Politics, and Society in the Individualistic Universe'. *Proceedings of the Royal Anthropological Institute for 1970.*

Durkheim, Émile. 1984 [1893]. *The Division of Labour in Society.* Translated by W. D. Hall. London: Macmillan.

—. 1995. *The Elementary Forms of Religious Life.* Translated and with an introduction by Karen E. Fields. New York: Free Press.

Eade, John and Michael J. Sallnow (eds). 2000. *Contesting the Sacred: The Anthropology of Christian Pilgrimage.* Chicago: University of Illinois Press.

Eaton, Richard M. 1984. 'Conversion to Christianity among the Nagas, 1876–1971'. *Indian Economic and Social History Review 11,* No. 1: 1–43.

—. 2000. *Essays on Islam and Indian History.* New Delhi: Oxford University Press.

Eliade, Mircea. 1958. *Patterns in Comparative Religion.* London: Sheed & Ward.

Elwin, Verrier. 1959. *A Philosophy of NEFA.* Shillong: NEFA Administration.

Fitzgerald, Timothy. 2000. *The Ideology of Religious Studies.* New York: Oxford University Press.

Freud, Sigmund. 1983. *Totem and Taboo.* London: Ark Paperbacks.

Friedman, Norman L. 1967. 'Nativism'. *Phylon,* Vol. 28, No. 4: 408–15.

Friedman, Susan Stanford. 1989. 'The Return of the Repressed in Women's Narrative'. *The Journal of Narrative Technique,* Vol. 19, No. 1: 141–56.

Fuchs, Stephen. 1965. *Rebellious Prophets: A Study of Messianic Movements in Indian Religions.* London: Asia Publishing House.

Fuller, C. J. 1992. *The Camphor Flame: Popular Hinduism and Society in India.* Princeton: Princeton University Press.

Ganguli, Milada. 1984. *A Pilgrimage to the Nagas.* New Delhi: Oxford and IBH Publishing.

Geertz, Clifford. 1973. *The Interpretations of Cultures.* New York: Basic Books.

—. 1979. 'From the Native's Point of View: On the Nature of Anthropological Understanding', in Paul Rabinow and William M. Sullivan (eds). *Interpretive Social Science: A Reader.* Berkeley: University of California Press.

—. 1980. *Negara: The Theatre State in Nineteenth-Century Bali.* Princeton: Princeton University Press.

Goffman, Erving. 1959. *The Presentation of Self in Everyday Life.* Garden City, NY: Doubleday.

Goody, Jack. 1996. *The Logic of Writing and the Organisation of Society.* Cambridge: Cambridge University Press.

Gorst, John E. 1959. *The Maori King.* Edited with an introduction by Keith Sinclair. Hamilton and Auckland: Paul's Book Arcade; London: Oxford University Press.

Grierson, G. A. (ed.). 1904. *Linguistic Survey of India. Vol. 3, Tibeto-Burman Family. Pt.3, Specimens of the Kuki-Chin and Burma Groups.* Calcutta: Superintendent of Government Printing.

Guha, Ranajit. 1983. *Elementary Aspects of Peasant Insurgency in Colonial India.* Delhi: Oxford University Press.

Hall, Stuart. 1997. 'The Local and the Global: Globalization and Ethnicity' and 'Old and New Identities, Old and New Ethnicities', in A. D. King (ed.). *Culture, Globalization and the World-system.* Hampshire and London: Macmillan.

Hall, Stuart and Paul Du Gay (eds). 1996. *Questions of Cultural Identity.* London: Sage.

Hall, Stuart and Sarat Maharaj. 2001. *Modernity and Difference.* London: Institute of International Visual Arts.

Hansen, Thomas Blom. 1999. *The Saffron Wave: Democracy and Hindu Nationalism in Modern India.* Princeton, NJ: Princeton University Press.

Hardiman, David. 1987. *The Coming of the Devi: Adivasi Assertion in Western India.* Delhi: Oxford University Press.

Harle, James C. 1963. 'Durga, Goddess of Victory'. *Artibus Asiae,* Vol. 26, No. 3/4: 237–46.

Hart, Janet. 1992. 'Cracking the Code: Narrative and Political Mobilization in the Greek Resistance'. *Social Science History,* Vol. 16, No. 4: 631–68.

Hefner, Robert W. 1993. 'World Building and the Rationality of Conversion', in Robert W. Hefner (ed.). *Conversion to Christianity: Historical and Anthropological Perspectives on a Great Transformation.* Berkeley: University of California Press.

Hertz, Robert. 1960. *Death, and, the Right Hand.* Translated by Rodney and Claudia Needham. London.

Hervieu-Léger, Daniéle. 2000. *Religion as a Chain of Memory.* Cambridge: Polity Press.

Hobsbawm, Eric J. [1959] 1965. *Primitive Rebels: Studies in Archaic Forms of Social Movement I the 19th and 20th Centuries.* New York: W. W. Norton.

Hocart, A. M. 1970. *Kings and Councillors: An Essay in the Comparative Anatomy of Human Society.* Chicago: University of Chicago Press.

Hodson, T. C. 1911. *The Naga Tribes of Manipur.* London: Macmillan.

Horton, Robin. 1975. 'On the Rationality of Conversion Part I'. *Journal of the International African Institute,* Vol. 45, No. 3: 219–35.

Hutton, J. H. 1965. 'The Mixed Culture of the Naga Tribes'. *The Journal of the Royal Anthropological Institute of Great Britain and Ireland,* Vol. 95, No. 1 (January–June): 16–43.

—. 1969. *The Angami Nagas with Some Notes on Neighbouring Tribes.* London: Oxford University Press.

Ingold, Tim and Jo Lee Vergunst (eds). 2008. *Ways of Walking: Ethnography and Practice on Foot.* London: Ashgate.

Jacobs, Julian, Alan Macfarlane, Sarah Harrison and Anita Herle. 1998. *The Nagas: Society, Culture and the Colonial Encounter.* London: Thames and Hudson.

Johnstone, James Sir. 1896. *My Experiences in Manipur and the Naga Hills.* London: Sampson Low, Marston and Co.

Jordan, David K. 1993. 'The Glyphomancy Factor: Observations on Chinese Conversion', in Robert W. Hefner (ed.). *Conversion to Christianity: Historical and Anthropological Perspective on a Great Transformation.* Berkeley: University of California Press.

Kabui, Gangmumei. 1982. 'The Zeliangrong Movement: An Historical Study', in K. S. Singh (ed.). *Tribal Movements in India Vol. 1.* Delhi: Manohar.

Kamei, Gangmumei. 2002a. *Jadonang: A Mystic Naga Rebel.* Imphal: Lamyanba Printers.

—. 2002b. *Ethnicity and Social Change: An Anthology of Essays.* Imphal, Manipur: Smt. Pouganglu Gangmei.

—. 2004. *A History of the Zeliangrong Nagas: From Makhel to Rani Gaidinliu.* New Delhi: Spectrum.

Kammerer, C. A. 1990. 'Custom and Christian Conversion among Akha Highlanders of Burma and Thailand'. *American Ethnology,* Vol. 17, No. 2: 277–91.

Karlsson, Bengt G. 2000. *Contested Belonging: Indigenous People's Struggle for Forest and Identity in Sub-Himalayan Bengal.* London: Routledge Curzon.

—. 2002. 'Entering into the Christian Dharma: Contemporary "Tribal" Conversions in India', in Judith M. Brown and Robert Eric Frykenberg (eds). *Christians, Cultural Interactions, and India's Religious Traditions.* Michigan/London: William B. Eerdmans and Routledge Curzon.

Kartodirdjo, Sartono. 1978. *Protest Movements in Rural Java: A Study of Agrarian Unrest in the 19th and Early 20th Centuries.* Singapore: Oxford University Press.

Kelly, John D. and Martha Kaplan. 1990. 'History, Structure, and Ritual'. *Annual Review of Anthropology,* Vol. 19: 119–50.

Kinsley, David. 1978. 'The Portrait of the Goddess in the Devi-Mahatmya'. *Journal of the American Academy of Religion,* Vol. 46, No. 4: 489–506.

Kirschner, Suzanne R. 1987. '"Then What Have I to do with Thee?": On Identity, Fieldwork, and Ethnographic Knowledge'. *Cultural Anthropology,* Vol. 2, No. 2: 211–34.

Knott, Kim. 2005. *The Location of Religion: A Spatial Analysis.* London: Equinox.

Korieh, 2003. 'Alcohol and Empire: "Illicit" Gin Prohibition and Control in Colonial Eastern Nigeria'. *African Economic History,* No. 31: 111–34.

Kristeva, Julia. 1982. *Powers of Horror: An Essay on Abjection.* Translated by Len S. Roudiez. New York: Columbia University Press.

Lanternari, Vittorio. 1962. 'Messianism: Its Historical Origin and Morphology'. *History of Religions,* Vol. 2, No. 1 (Summer): 52–72.

—. 1963. *The Religions of the Oppressed: A Study of Modern Messianic Cults.* Translated from the Italian by Lisa Sergio. London: Macgibbon & Kee.

Leach, Edmund. 1977. *Political Systems of Highland Burma: A Study of Kachin Social Structure.* London: Athlone Press.

Lee, Sang Taek. 1996. *Religion and Social Formation in Korea: Minjung and Millenarianism.* Berlin: Mouton de Gruyter.

Lévi-Strauss, Claude. 1974. *The Savage Mind.* London: Weidenfeld and Nicholson.

Lévi-Strauss, Claude and F. C. T. Moore. 1974. 'How Myths Die'. *New Literary History,* Vol. 5, No. 2, Changing Views of Character: 269–81.

Linton, Ralph and Irving A. Hallowell. 1943. 'Nativistic Movements'. *American Anthropologist.* New Series, Vol. 45, No. 2. Centenary of the American Ethnological Society: 230–40.

Longkumer, Arkotong. 2007. 'Religious and Economic Reform: The Gaidinliu Movement and the Heraka in North Cachar Hills'. *Journal of South Asian Studies,* Vol. 30, No. 3 (December): 499–515.

—. 2008. 'Circling the Altar Stone: Bhuban Cave and the Symbolism of Religious Traditions', in Michael Oppitz, Thomas Kaiser, Alban von Stockhausen and Marion Wettstein (eds.). *Changing Local Cultures in the Northeast of India.* Gent: Snoeck Publishers, pp. 403–17.

—. Forthcoming. 'Exploring the Diversity of Religion: The Geo-Political Dimensions of Fieldwork and Identity in the North East of India'. *Fieldwork in Religion*. London: Equinox Publishers.

Ludden, David. 2006. 'Introduction. Ayodhya: A Window on the World', in David Ludden (ed.). *Making India Hindu: Religion, Community, and the Politics of Democracy in India*. New Delhi: Oxford University Press.

Luker, Victoria. 1998. 'Millenarianism in India: The Movement of Birsa Munda', in Geoffrey A. Oddie (ed.). *Religious Traditions in South Asia: Interaction and Change*. Surrey: Curzon Press.

McCrindle, John W. [1927] 2000. *Ancient India as Described by Ptolemy*. New Delhi: Munshiram Manoharlal Publishers.

Mckean, Lise. 1996. 'Bharat Mata: Mother India and Her Militant, Matriots', in John Stratton Hawley and Donna Marie Wulff (eds). *Devi: Goddesses of India*. Berkeley: University of California Press.

Mackenzie, Alexander. 1884. *History of the Relations of the Government with the Hill Tribes of the North-East Frontier of Bengal*. Calcutta: Home Department Press.

—. [1884] 1969. 'Mackenzie's History', in Elwin Verrier (ed.). *The Nagas in the Nineteenth Century*. London: Oxford University Press.

—. 1979. *The North-East Frontier of India*. Delhi: Mittal Publications.

Mahadevan, Raman. 1974. 'Zeliangrong Naga Uprising of 1930–32: A Brief Summary', in *Indian History Congress: Proceedings of the Thirty-fifth session Jadavpur (Calcutta)*. New Delhi: B. R. Grover.

Marriott, Mckim (ed.). 1972. *Village India: Studies in the Little Community*. Chicago: University of Chicago Press.

Maxwell, Neville. 1973. *Indian and the Nagas*. London 36 Craven St.:WC2N 5NG Minority Rights Group.

Mills, J. P. 1926. *The Ao Nagas*. Bombay: Oxford University Press.

Mills, Moffatt A. J. [1854] 1969. 'Military Expeditions to the Angami Naga Hills' in Elwin Verrier, (ed.) *The Nagas in the Nineteenth Century*. London: Oxford University Press.

Miri, Sujata. 1991. *Liangmai Nagas: Legends and Stories*. New Delhi: Vikas.

Mitchiner, John E. 1982. *Traditions of the Seven Rishis*. Delhi: Motilal Banarsidass.

Mukherjee, D. P., P. Gupta and N. K. Das. 1982. 'The Zeliangrong or Haomei Movement: An Historical Study', in K. S. Singh (ed.). *Tribal Movements in India Vol. 1*. Delhi: Manohar.

Myscofski, Carole A. 1988. *When Men Walk Dry: Portuguese Messianism in Brazil*. Atlanta, GA: Scholars Press.

Needham, R (ed.). 1973. *Right and Left: Essays on Dual Symbolic Classification*. Chicago: University of Chicago Press.

Nehru, Jawaharlal. 1947. *The Discovery of India*. London: Meridian Books.

Nibedon, Nirmal. 2000. *Nagaland: The Night of the Guerrillas*. New Delhi: Lancer; South Godstone: Spantech & Lancer.

Nuh, V. K. 2006. *165 Years History of Naga Baptist Churches*. Kohima: Council of Naga Baptist Churches.

Oberoi, Harjot. 1997. *The Construction of Religious Boundaries: Culture, Identity and Diversity in the Sikh Tradition*. Delhi: Oxford University Press.

Ossio, Juan M. 1977. 'Myth and History: The Seventeenth-Century Chronicle of Guaman Poma de Ayala', in Ravindra K. Jain (ed.). *Text and Context: The Social Anthropology of Tradition.* Philadelphia: Institute for the Study of Human Issues.

Pamei, Namthiubuiyang. 2001. *The Trail from Makuilongdi: The Continuing Saga of the Zeliangrong People.* Tamenglong, Manipur: Gironta Charitable Foundation.

Parratt, John. 2005. *Wounded Land: Politics and Identity in Modern Manipur.* New Delhi: Mittal.

Parratt, Saroj N. Arambam and Parratt, John. 1995. 'Kabui Messiah': The Jadonong Movement in Manipur'. *Internationales Asienforum,* Vol. 26, No. 3–4: 285–302.

—. 1997. *The Pleasing of the Gods: Meitei Lai Haraoba.* New Delhi: Vikas.

Pintchman, Tracy. 1994. *The Rise of the Goddess in the Hindu Tradition.* Albany: State University of the New York Press.

Ramaswamy, Sumathi. 2001. 'Maps and Mother Goddesses in Modern India'. *Imago Mundi,* Vol. 53: 97–114.

Ranger, Terence. 1993. 'The Local and Global in Southern African Religious History', in Robert W. Hefner (ed.). *Conversion to Christianity: Historical and Anthropological Perspectives on a Great Transformation.* Berkeley: University of California Press.

Regunathan, Sudhamahi. 2000. *Siku: Faith and Conversion: Donyipolo Movement in Arunachal Pradesh.* New Delhi: HarAnand.

Reid, Robert. [1942] 1997. *History of the Frontier Areas Bordering on Assam from 1883–1941.* Guwahati: Spectrum.

Rosaldo, Renato. 1993. 'Notes toward a Critique of Patriarchy from a Male Position'. *Anthropological Quarterly,* Vol. 66, No. 2: 81–6.

Rowney, H. B. [1882] 1969. 'The Wild Tribes of India', in Elwin Verrier (ed.). *The Nagas in the Nineteenth Century.* London: Oxford University Press.

Russell, Claire. 1981. 'The Life Tree and the Death Tree'. *Folklore,* Vol. 92, No. 1: 56–66.

Sallnow, Michael. 1981. 'Communitas Reconsidered: The Sociology of Andean Pilgrimage'. *Man,* Vol. 16: 163–82.

Santiko, Hariani. 1997. 'The Goddess Durga in the East-Javanese Period'. *Asian Folklore Studies,* Vol. 56, No. 2: 209–26.

Sarkar, Sumit. 2002. *Beyond Nationalist Frames: Relocating Postmodernism, Hindutva, History.* Delhi: Permanent Black.

—. 2006. 'Indian Nationalism and the Politics of Hindutva', in David Ludden (ed.). *Making India Hindu: Religion, Community, and the Politics of Democracy in India.* New Delhi: Oxford University Press.

Sarkar, Tanika. 1985. 'Jitu Santal's Movement in Malda, 1924–1932: A Study in Tribal Protest', in Ranajit Guha (ed.). *Subaltern Studies IV, Writings on South Asian History and Society.* New Delhi: Oxford University Press.

—. 2001. *Hindu Wife, Hindu Nation: Community, Religion, and Cultural Nationalism.* London: Hurst & Company.

Sarkisyanz, E. 1965. *Buddhist Backgrounds of the Burmese Revolution.* The Hague: Martinus Nijhoff.

Saul, Jamie. 2005. *The Naga of Burma: Their Festivals, Customs, and Way of Life.* Bangkok: Orchid Press.

Savarkar, Veer Vinayak Damodar. [1923] 1969. *Hindutva: Who is Hindu?* Bombay: Veer Savarkar Prakashan.

Schnepel, Burkhard. 1995. 'Durga and the King: Ethnohistorical Aspects of Politico-Ritual Life in a South Orissan Jungle Kingdom'. *The Journal of the Royal Anthropological Institute*, Vol. 1, No. 1 (March): 145–66.

Scott, James C. 1976. *The Moral Economy of the Peasant: Rebellion and Subsistence in Southeast Asia.* New Haven and London: Yale University Press.

—. 1985. *Weapons of the Weak: Everyday Reforms of Peasant Resistance.* New Haven and London: Yale University Press.

Sen, Amiya P (ed.). 2003. *Social and Religious Reform.* New Delhi: Oxford University Press.

Singh, Joykumar N. 1992. *Social Movements in Manipur (1917–1951).* New Delhi: Mittal.

—. 2002. *Colonialism to Democracy: A History of Manipur 1819–1972.* Guwahati: Spectrum.

Singh, K. S. 1983a. *Tribal Movements in India.* New Delhi: Manohar.

—. 1983b. *Birsa Munda and His Movement 1897–1901: A Study of a Millenarian Movement in Chotanagpur.* Calcutta; London: Oxford University Press.

—. 1985. 'Varna, Jati and Jana', in K. S. Singh (ed.). *Tribal Society in India: An Anthropo-historical Perspective.* New Delhi: Manohar.

—. 1988. 'Tribal Peasantry, Millenarianism, Anarchism and Nationalism: A Case Study of the Tanabhagats in Chotanagpur, 1914–25'. *Social Scientist*, Vol. 16, No. 11: 36–50.

Sinha, Surajit. 1966. 'Vaisnava Influence on a Tribal Culture', in Milton Singer (ed.). *Krishna: Myths, Rites, and Attitudes.* Honolulu: East-West Center Press.

Skaria, Ajay. 1999. *Hybrid Histories: Forests, Frontiers and Wildness in Western India.* New Delhi: Oxford University Press.

Soppitt, C. A. [1885] 1969. 'A Short Account of the Kachcha Naga (Empeo) Tribe in the North Cachar Hills', in Verrier Elwin (ed.). *The Nagas in the Nineteenth Century.* London: Oxford University Press.

Spencer, Jonathan. 2006. 'Nationalism', in Alan Barnard and Jonathan Spencer (ed.). *Encyclopedia of Social and Cultural Anthropology.* London: Routledge.

Stern, Theodore. 1968. 'Ariya and the Golden Book: A Millenarian Buddhist Sect among the Karen'. *The Journal of Asian Studies*, Vol. 27, No. 2: 297–328.

Steyn, Pieter. 2002. *Zapuphizo: Voice of the Nagas.* London: Kegan Paul.

Stirn, Aglaja and Peter van Ham. 2003. *The Hidden World of the Naga: Living Traditions in Northeast India and Burma.* Munich: Prestel.

Stokes, Eric. 1978. *The Peasant and the Raj: Studies in Agrarian Society and Peasant Rebellion in Colonial India.* Cambridge University Press, Cambridge.

Sundar, Nandini. 2006. 'Village Histories: Coalescing the Past and Present', in Partha Chatterjee and Anjan Ghosh (eds). *History and the Present.* Delhi: Permanent Black.

Tambiah, Stanley J. 1976. *World Conqueror and World Renouncer: A Study of Buddhism and Polity in Thailand against a Historical Background.* Cambridge: Cambridge University Press.

—. 1990. *Magic, Science, Religion, and the Scope of Rationality.* Cambridge: Cambridge University Press.

Taussig, Michael. 1977. 'The Genesis of Capitalism amongst a South American Peasantry: Devil's Labor and the Baptism of Money'. *Comparative Studies in Society and History*, Vol. 19, No. 2: 130–55.

Tcherkézoff, Serge. 1987. *Dual Classification Reconsidered: Nyamwezi Sacred Kingship and other Examples.* Translated by Martin Thom. Cambridge: Cambridge University Press.

Thapar, Romila. 1989. 'Imagined Religious Communities? Ancient History and the Modern Search for a Hindu Identity'. *Modern Asian Studies*, Vol. 23, No. 2: 209–31.

—. 1993. 'A Historical Perspective on the Story of Rama', in Gopal Sarvepalli (ed.). *Anatomy of a Confrontation: Ayodhya and the Rise of Communal Politics in India.* London: Zed Books.

Thomson, Alistair and Robert Perks. 1998. *The Oral History Reader.* London: Routledge.

Thrupp, Sylvia L (ed.). 1962. *Millennial Dreams in Action.* The Hague: Mouton.

Tonkin, Elizabeth. 1995. *Narrating Our Pasts: The Social Construction of Oral History.* Cambridge: University of Cambridge Press.

Tsing, Anna L. 1993. *In the Realm of the Diamond Queen: Marginality in an Out-of-the-Way Place.* Princeton: Princeton University Press.

Turner, Victor. 1969. *The Ritual Process: Structure and Anti-Structure.* London: Routledge & Kegan.

Turner, Victor and Edith Turner. 1978. *Image and Pilgrimage in Christian Culture: Anthropological Perspective.* New York: Columbia University Press.

Vansina, Jan. 1985. *Oral Tradition as History.* Wisconsin: University of Wisconsin Press.

Veer, Peter van der (ed.). 1996. *Conversion to Modernities: The Globalization of Christianity.* New York: Routledge.

Viswanathan, Gauri. 1996. 'Religious Conversion and the Politics of Dissent' in Peter van der Veer (ed.). *Conversion to Modernities: The Globalization of Christianity.* New York: Routledge.

—. 1998. *Outside the Fold: Conversion, Modernity, and Belief.* Princeton: Princeton University Press.

—. 2002. 'Literacy in the Eye of the Conversion Storm', in Derek Peterson and Darren Walhof (eds). *The Invention of Religion: Rethinking Belief in Politics and History.* New Brunswick: Rutgers University Press.

von Fürer-Haimendorf, Christoph. 1946. *The Naked Nagas: Head-hunters of Assam in Peace and War.* Calcutta: Thacker, Spink & Co.

—. 1976. *Return to the Naked Nagas: An Anthropologist's View of Nagaland 1936–1970.* Delhi: Vikas.

Wallace, Anthony F. 1956. 'Revitalization Movements'. *American Anthropologist*, Vol. 58: 264–81.

Weber, Max. 1965. *The Sociology of Religion.* Translated by Ephraim Fischoff. London: Methuen.

—. 2003. *The Protestant Ethic and the Spirit of Capitalism.* Translated by Talcott Parsons. New York: Dover.

Wessinger, Catherine. 1997. 'Millennialism with and without the Mayhem', in Thomas Robbins and Susan J. Palmer (eds). *Millennium, Messiahs, and Mayhem: Contemporary Apocalyptic Movements.* New York: Routledge.

—. 2000. 'The Interacting Dynamics of Millennial Beliefs, Persecution, and Violence' in Catherine Wessinger (ed.). *Millennialism, Persecution, and Violence: Historical Cases.* Syracuse: Syracuse University Press.

Wilson, Bryan R. 1973. *Magic and the Millennium: A Sociological Study of Religious Movements of Protest among Tribal and Third-World Peoples.* London: Heinemann Educational Books.

Woodthorpe, R. G. [1881] 1969. 'Notes on the Wild Tribes Inhabiting the So-Called Naga Hills, on our North-East Frontier of India', in Elwin Verrier (ed.). *The Nagas in the Nineteenth Century.* London: Oxford University Press.

Worsley, Peter. 1970. *The Trumpet Shall Sound: A Study of 'Cargo' Cults in Melanesia.* London: Paladin.

Yamaguchi, Masao. 1977. 'Kingship, Theatricality, and Marginal Reality in Japan' in Ravindra K. Jain (ed.). *Text and Context: The Social Anthropology of Tradition.* Philadelphia: Institute for the Study of Human Issues.

Yonuo, Asoso. 1982. *Nagas Struggle against the British Rule under Jadonang and Rani Gaidinliu 1925–1947.* Kohima, Nagaland: Leno Printing Press.

Theses

Betts, U. V. G. 1950. 'Village Organisation among the Central Nzemi Nagas', Diploma in Anthropology Thesis. London: University College London.

Joshi, Vibha. 2001. 'Christian and non-Christian Angami Nagas with special reference to Traditional Healing Practices', Doctor of Philosophy Thesis. Oxford University: Institute of Social and Cultural Anthropology, School of Anthropology and Museum Ethnography.

Pame, Rabi. 1996. 'The Zeme Naga Baptist Church, North Cachar Hills, Assam: A Study of culture and the Church', Doctor of Missiology Thesis. Bangalore: South Asia Institute of Advanced Christian Studies.

Newspapers

Nriame, Nakaulang. 2004 'Rani Gaidinliu: A unique freedom fighter of India', *The Sentinel,* Guwahati, 30 May.

Post Mortem Section. 2005. *Nagaland Post,* 14 February.

'No solution within Indian Union or its Constitution'. 2006. *The Morung Express,* Dimapur, 14 August.

Rajkhowa, J. P. 2007. 'Protect and project indigenous culture', *The Sentinel,* Guwahati, 21 January.

Internet

Betts [also Bower], Ursula G. 2007. 'Collection from the Centre of South Asian Studies, Cambridge (Betts Papers Folder 7)'. *Rivers Video Project, Department of*

Social Anthropology, Free School Lane, Cambridge. <http://bamdemo.lemurconsulting.com/bamdemo/db/naga/doc/1119226705_00000?hit=0&q_=Kuki+National+Assembly>.

Bower, Ursula G. 2006. 'Private Collection 1937–1946'. *Rivers Video Project, Department of Social Anthropology, Free School Lane, Cambridge*. <http://bamdemo.lemurconsulting.com/bamdemo/db/naga/doc/1119226690_00011?hit=3&q_=lai>.

—. 2007. 'Collection from the Centre of South Asian Studies, Cambridge (Box II file 2)'. *Rivers Video Project, Department of Social Anthropology, Free School Lane, Cambridge*. <http://bamdemo.lemurconsulting.com/bamdemo/db/naga/doc/1119226709_00000?hit=3&q_=ginger+spittle>.

Elst, Koenraad. 2006. *Who is a Hindu?* www.voiceofdharma.com, or <http://koenraadelst.voiceofdharma.com/books/wiah/index.htm>.

Goodwill Mission Team Report. 2006. *Unofficial White Paper Report of the Fact Finding Mission to Nagalim (16–25*th *May 2005*), www.freenagalim.org, or <http://freenagalim.org/index.php?option=com_content&task=view&id=85&Itemid=41>.

Knapp, Stephen. 2006. 'My Northeast India Mission of 2003–4': <www.stephen-knapp.com/my_northeast_india_mission_.htm>.

Nationalist Socialist Council of Nagalim (Isak-Muivah). 2007. <www.nscnonline.org>.

Rashtriya Swayamsevak Sangh. 2007. 'Sangh: Unique and Evergreen': <www.rss.org: http://www.rss.org/New_RSS/History/Evolution.jsp>.

von Fürer Haimendorf, Christoph. 2007. 'Private collection 1970'. *Rivers Video Project, Department of Social Anthropology, Free School Lane, Cambridge*. <http://bamdemo.lemurconsulting.com/bamdemo/db/naga/doc/1119225686_00022?hit=0&q_=tingwang>.

Index

Note: The **bold** numbers denote that the subject is covered in the whole chapter.